Start & Run Your Own Record Label, was one of the first books I bought when I wanted to start my label. Three years later I still refer to it for a refresher course. It's a solid foundation for any indie label.

— RaQuel V. Sanders, CEO, Kuji Music Group/ KMG Records, Columbia, SC

I started my own label after reading this book. It gave me a sense of "this can be done" rather than "Oh my God, what am I doing."

— Nathan Temby, Merica Records, San Francisco, CA

I found everything I needed to know, from A–Z, in *Start & Run Your Own Record Label.* When people ask how I did what regarding my label, I simply refer them to the book.

— DJ Minx, Women On Wax Recordings, Detroit, MI

Daylle's book has been a guidebook to success for me and my small label. With my zeal for success and her ideas and testimony I've been able to turn my dreams into a living reality!

— Matt Allison, Recording Artist and Indie Label Owner, Capetown, South Africa

Start & Run Your Own Record Label is a great reference for anyone in the music business to keep on hand. Even if you think you know it all, this book quickly clarifies any foggy moments. As a former label GM (Popular Records/ BMG, West End Records), now publicity/ marketing company owner, I find it a perfect compliment to *This Business of Music.*

— Andy Reynolds, President, Penetration, Inc., New York, NY

Not only does Daylle Deanna Schwartz demystify the complicated music business by cutting through all the BS to give you a real look at the world of music, but she also provides you with the tools and the juice to get your venture off the ground. This book is not only a must-have for anyone wanting to start their own label; it is a great motivator for living! Jam-packed with a positive vibe.

— Patrick J. Fernandez, Producer, MilleniaChild Records, Aliso Viejo, CA

P9-DNV-200

Daylle brings the reality of the music industry to the table, and leaves out the hype. *Start & Run Your Own Record Label* helped me walk a path I may never have attempted. It's an incredible resource. Though I originally bought the book simply to gain insight into the industry, I'm now on my way to building my own label as I follow her advice.

— Candice Jackson, CJR Entertainment, New York, NY

Daylle has a straightforward way of explaining the business. However, while making clear all the work and effort entailed in making things happen, she also inspires and instills the belief that it is indeed all possible. This is an informative and motivational book that everyone serious about putting their music out into the world should read, and then keep re-reading.

— Michael Gilboe, Copperheadz Productions, New York, NY

A road map full of step-by-step instructions which lead to accomplishing goals in the music industry; a good reference book to help make sound business decisions; and most of all, encouragement and inspiration to keep pressing on.

— MJ Brown, Emjay Sound Manufacturing, LLC, Jonesboro, GA

I want to create my own label in Europe and this book is a "bible" for those who want to start their own record company and develop it to the max.

— Vincent Habryn, Gravelines, France

Start & Run Your Own Record Label is my bible. Daylle's friendly writing style simplifies the process of marketing and promoting my CDs as it educates, step by step.

— Garvin Lloyd, GL Records, Los Angeles, CA

The music industry feels like a safer place when I'm armed with [Daylle's] wisdom and positive attitude.

— Claude Mosler, Gemstone Productions, Minneapolis, MN

START & RUN YOUR OWN RECORD LABEL

UPDATED & EXPANDED EDITION

DAYLLE DEANNA SCHWARTZ

START & RUN YOUR OWN RECORD LABEL

UPDATED & EXPANDED EDITION
DAYLLE DEANNA SCHWARTZ

BILLBOARD BOOKS
an imprint of watson-guptill publications/new york

Executive Editor: Bob Nirkind
Editor: Elizabeth Wright
Front and back cover design: Cooley Design Lab
Interior design: Sivan Earnest
Production manager: Ellen Greene

First published in 1998 by Billboard Books,
revised edition first published in 2003 by Billboard Books,
an imprint of Watson-Guptill Publications,
a division of VNU Business Media, Inc.,
770 Broadway, New York, NY 10003
www.watsonguptill.com

Library of Congress Cataloging-in-Publication data for this title may be
obtained from the Library of Congress.
Library of Congress Control Number:

ISBN: 0-8230-8433-7

Manufactured in the United States of America

First printing, 2003

3 4 5 6 7 8 9 / 08 07 06 05 04

THIS BOOK IS DEDICATED WITH LOVE TO MY SISTER, CARLA HERMAN, FOR HER CONSISTENT SUPPORT AND ENCOURAGEMENT, AND FOR SHOWING BY EXAMPLE THAT WOMEN CAN BE VERY SUCCESSFUL IN THE BUSINESS WORLD, AND TO MY WONDERFUL BROTHER-IN-LAW, DOUG LANDY, FOR BEING A SUPPORTIVE MEMBER OF MY FAMILY.

CONTENTS

FINANCING YOUR BUSINESS 60

THE NUTS & BOLTS OF KEEPING YOUR LABEL SOLVENT 67

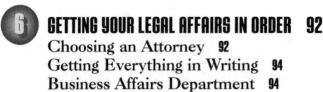

19 USING THE INTERNET TO PROMOTE AND MARKET YOUR PRODUCT   251

20 SOME ADVICE FROM THE PROS   271

INDEX 279

ACKNOWLEDGMENTS

First, I want to thank God and the Universe for all of my blessings. I wouldn't be where I am today without my faith. This book wouldn't have reached its fruition without the support of many people. I'd like to acknowledge everyone who helped me. I consider all the following folks part of my blessings!

Thank you Bob Nirkind, Executive Editor at Billboard Books, for your sustained faith in me and your consistent support. It continues to be a great pleasure to work with you! Thank you to my editor, Elizabeth Wright, for working with me to make the book as good as possible and for your positive attitude during trying times. It's always fantastic for a writer to have editors on her side!

I've said it before and I'll say it again. The music industry is known for its cutthroat reputation, yet the folks who took time to share their experience and knowledge prove how many wonderful people are in this business. You're all terrific! Thank you to the people I interviewed for sharing your knowledge and experience with me. You were all such a pleasure to talk to and are definitely an inspiration for others who want to start and run a record label.

Thank you a million times to (in alphabetical order): Lee Abrams (XM Satellite Radio), Andy Allen (Alternative Distribution Alliance), Christopher Applegren (Lookout! Records), Patrick Arn (Gotham Records), David M. Bailey, K. Banger (The Dirt Department), Alan Becker (RED Distribution), Nicole Blackman, Jonatha Brooke (Bad Dog Records), Dave Brown (Muddle Fanzine), Tony Brummel (Victory Records), Michael Bull (Caroline Distribution), Aaron Burgess (Alternative Press Magazine), Mark Carpentieri (MC Records), Rudy Chavarria (Rude College Promotions), Cliff Chenfeld (Razor & Tie Music), Edward Chmelewski (Blind Pig Records), Jason Consoli (TVT Records), Jay Cooper, Esq., Bill Craig (MIDEM),

Damon Dash (Roc-A-Fella Records), Ramona De'Breaux (Hot 1079), Darren Doane, Michael Ellis (Billboard), Richard Ellis (Aron's Records), Ritch Esra, Jesse Ferguson (Definitive Jux Records), Tom Ferguson (Billboard), Bobbito Garcia (Fondle'em Records), Suzanne Glass (Indie-Music.com), Keith Grimwood (Trout Fishing in America), Ellyn Harris (Buzz Publicity), Paul Hartman (Dirty Linen), Michael Hausman (United Musicians), Rita Houston (FUV), Lydia Hutchinson (Performing Songwriter), Ezra Idlet (Trout Fishing in America), Florence Isaacs, Michael Jonathon (Poetman Records), Philippe Kern (IMPALA), Michael Koch (Koch International Corp.), Beth Krakower (CineMedia Promotions), John T. Kunz (Waterloo Records), Onno Lakeman (Red to Violet), Lorenzo LaRoc, Trudy Lartz (Nielsen SoundScan), Gregg Latterman (Aware Records), Karen Leipziger (KL Productions), Jonathon Levy (Moonshine Music), Mike Levine (Onstage), John Luneau (Palm Pictures), Geoff Mayfield (Billboard), Michael Mollura (Music Connection), Brian Muni (13 Stories Records), Robb Nansel (Saddle Creek Records), Anthony Orlando, CPA, Angela Piva (INFX), Steve Pritchitt (Navarre Entertainment Media), Dick Renko (Trout Records), Mitchell Rowen (CVC Report), Larry Rudolph, Esq, Susan Rush (Pinnacle Records), Reiner Schloemer (Popkomm), Sean Seymour (Cropduster Records), Jane Siberry (Sheeba Records), Derek Sivers (CDBaby), Arty Skye (SkyeLab Sound Studio), Brian Stillman (Revolver Magazine), Jeff Stone (Pollstar), Brian Surgitz (Elementree Records), John Szuch (Deep Elm Records), Dedra Tate (Flavor Unit Entertainment), Jim Testa (Jersey Beat), Peter Thompson (Vital Distribution), Tony van Veen (Disc Makers), Israel Vasquetelle (Insomniac Magazine), Valerie Vigoda (GrooveLily), Susan Walker (Tried & True Music), Jay Woods (New West Records), Lisa Worden (KROQ), Dan Zanes (Festival 5 Records), Walter Zelnick (City Hall Records), Jay Ziskrout (CMJ). Thanks to Mike G. at SkyeLab Sound Studio for your support. Thanks Jackie Jones for doing some research.

I could write a long paragraph about each of the people above but my space is limited. I do want to say a special thanks to people who went above and beyond to support my efforts as an educator. Thank you Danny Goldberg (Artemis Records) for allowing me to come to your office so that you could share wisdom gleaned from your vast experience with record labels. Thank you EL-P (Definitive Jux Records), for making time while you were on the road to contribute your inspirational view of the music industry and many accomplishments. Thank you Dave Roberge (Everfine Records) for all the great info you shared about your tremendous accomplishments and for giving me the honor of knowing that my books have helped you get there!

The music industry has shown me lots of friendship. Thank you Wallace Collins, Esq, for many years of friendship and support, and for allowing me to share your legal knowledge. Thank you David Wimble *The Indie Bible* for your friendship and for being my angel whenever I need help. Thank you Jeff Epstein (Cropduster Records and Disc Makers) for your continued friendship and support, and for enlightening me about your success. Thank you Charlie Cheney for creating the Indie Band Manager and for coming to my rescue when my computer drives me nuts! Thank you Ron Stone (Gold Mountain Management) for continuing to be my mentor. Thank you Rich Hardesty for coming to New York to do an interview about your amazing accomplishments and for becoming a friend in the process. And last, but absolutely not least, thank you Ryan Kuper (Redemption Records), for sharing your knowledge, for being my mentor and taking the time to read each chapter as I wrote it, and for becoming a friend. A special thank you to my friends and family who put up with me and gave me support when I was buried in writing this book. Thanks also to all the guys at the Silver Spoon on First Avenue (the BEST diner in New York City!), for pampering me with delicious food and caring, attentive service when I come in with my laptop and stay for hours.

I feel very blessed to have had the privilege of getting to know so many supportive industry people! Thank you all once again!

INTRODUCTION

The music industry changed since I wrote the first edition of *Start & Run Your Own Record Label.* More people than ever before are taking the independent route, at least to start. And there are more opportunities for making money once you have a finished product.

I've completely re-written this edition to reflect the current climate of the music industry in relation to independent labels. It includes almost all new interviews with many fantastic people to provide fresh ideas for successfully starting and running a record label. I've expanded on and included more details about the business end of a label and ways to make money with it. I've also added a chapter called "Road Warriors," which profiles indie labels and indie artists with CDs that have been successful. Their stories are presented as good examples to follow and to motivate you to do it yourself.

I don't want to delude you. Opening a record label isn't easy. There are no miracle formulas for creating good music and marketing it successfully. Competition is getting stiffer as more people than ever market their own product. Technology makes it cheaper and easier to create music in a computer and burn it onto a CD-R. The reality is that anyone can start a record label, i.e., call themselves one. But running one successfully is what strikes most people out of the ballgame. It takes work and perseverance, *great material,* and money. And, it takes patience to stay in a race that feels like a battle that can't be won. Have I hammered in the impression that it's not easy? You'll have to work your butt off to succeed. But when all the pieces are in place, opening your own record label can be a very satisfying endeavor.

This book was hard to write. My readers have a variety of needs. Many of you are new to the industry while some are pros. Many of you have teeny budgets while others have extensive financing. You're producing music in a variety of musical genres, requiring different strategies to market and promote. Many of you are pressing a CD as a vehicle for attracting a deal with a larger label. You may also use it to book gigs, develop your press kit, and make money on the road to a record deal. Some of you are starting a label as a long-term business, to give unsigned talent an opportunity. I hope that as you read *Start & Run Your Own Record Label,* you'll take from it what serves you and understand I've included as much information in the pages available to cover a variety of needs.

In order to maximize your chances for success, immerse yourself in your music as much as possible. I provide knowledge and tools to get an indie label started and running. You have to plug in the specifics about the music you're marketing. Do your homework and learn as much about your music as you can. Start compiling a list of all publications that might review your record or profile your artist. Become aware of stores that might sell your products. Read trades to learn what's going on in the industry. The more knowledge you gather, the more prepared you'll be. If you learn everything you can about your genre, you can apply what's in this book to your music and have the best chance of success.

Starting and running a record label is do-able, if you want it enough. I know, because if I did it, anyone can! I was a schoolteacher when I entered the music industry. No experience. No contacts. I knew nothing about music except how to put on the radio. While teaching in the public schools of New York City, my students laughed when I said I could make a rap record. Why not? Because I was a white woman. These young people said I wasn't the right color or sex to rap. I knew I had to prove that limitations can be overcome or they'd grow up allowing stereotypes to block their ambitions. Determined to prove they can be broken, I learned how to rap and eventually was labeled "the rappin' teach."

When I recorded "Girl's Can Do," the kids loved it, but no label would sign a white female rapper. People promised me the world but didn't follow through. I paid folks to shop tapes and hired supposed consultants who gave crumbs instead of an education. My students got angry and advised revenge on those who were jerking me around. They offered to slash tires, spray–paint houses, etc., of those who didn't play fair with me. I decided to prove that it's better to use the energy behind anger to do something positive for yourself. If I wanted to succeed, I had to educate myself, and stop depending on others. In my quest for a positive revenge, I opened Revenge Productions, then Revenge Records. It was the beginning of a fruitful career in the music industry — very sweet revenge.

Starting Revenge Records wasn't easy. Without a clue, I worked very hard and endured costly mistakes along the way. Eventually I learned enough to get a reasonable picture of what needed to be done, and finally established my label. My first record was "Girls Can Do." I talked a local distributor into getting my records into stores. I did a second rap called "Wrap It Up," and it sold more than the first. I learned from every mistake. Sales enabled me to pay label expenses from label income. My third record established my label. I wrote "Never Again," a Latin free-style dance record, and signed my first artist. It took off quickly in DJ circles. Distributors called me! Large labels offered to pick it up. I took a deal that gave credibility to my label and to me as a songwriter.

I continued signing artists, selling lots of records, and learning about the music business. Since I'm a teacher, people came to me for accurate information on breaking into the music industry. In 1990 I put together music biz seminars and have been teaching them ever since. I get people attending from all over the country, and from other countries as well. I also speak in colleges and at music conferences. My first book published by Billboard Books, *The Real Deal: How to Get Signed to a Record Label,* is in its second edition.

If you get discouraged, remind yourself that if a teacher with no knowledge or contacts could start and run a record label, you can too! The "secret" is signing/having marketable music, learning the biz, and working your butt off applying it. People whine that they have day jobs and time is limited. Hello! This is a business. You won't get more out of it than you put in. When I began, I was teaching and running a summer recreational program. I didn't sleep much but did what I had to. No one gives extras because you have a day job. There are no shortcuts or special programs for the working class. This is a commitment. Start VERY slowly and be realistic. If you want it, be prepared to work hard. Keep in mind that you must begin with great music, or you'll never get out of the box.

From the get-go, network as much as possible. Get to industry seminars. Talk with industry people and everyone attending. Go to clubs and make friends with the DJs, performers, and those around you. Learn from everyone you meet. Go to record stores that sell your genre and get friendly with the folks who work there. They were my best friends when I opened Revenge Records. Who knows more about music retail than those selling it? My friends in stores listened to my demos and advised me on what to release. They pushed my records and hooked me up with industry contacts. I wouldn't have successfully operated Revenge Records without their friendship and support!

Educate yourself as much as possible. If you haven't read my other book, *The Real Deal: How to Get Signed to a Record Label*, I recommend that you do. Most of the basic info included is helpful in starting a record label. *The Real Deal* focuses on artist development, which all of you will need. The chapters on networking are much more detailed and the resource list at the back of the book is useful in getting your label off the ground. Be forewarned: I don't plan on reinventing the wheel here by repeating what's in my other book.

When I was writing the first edition of this book, long time industry pros threw negative pictures at me. The record industry has been in a slump. I became very confused by the picture that was painted. On the one hand, I was told, "Forget opening an independent label. Business is bad." On the other hand, indie labels were being heralded as the best way to break new music, or to get attention for talented artists who couldn't get a deal with an established label. Yet I consistently hear that major labels have flooded the market with product, as stores go out of business. More product with fewer outlets doesn't leave as much room for indies. It got depressing!

So why bother reading this book? Because opening your own record label gives you a shot at breaking music that may not have any other outlet. Because folks are still succeeding at breaking indie music every day. Because it's as good a shot as trying to shop a tape to a larger label, if not better. I've talked to dozens of heads of indie labels of all sizes who shared their knowledge and experience in this book. I do believe that an indie label is still be the best way to break new artists. To do this, you must be prepared to bite the bullet, work extremely hard, have money in the bank or a day job, and be totally passionate about the music. Opening your own label is a chance to control the destiny of music you love.

As far as I'm concerned, today's market offers more opportunity than ever before to make money as an indie. *Much more than ever!* As most music is edged out of commercial radio and major markets, consumers are hungering for music they love, not what they're told they have to love because it's all they'll get. One major advantage that indie labels have over the majors is that they don't have to sell nearly as many records to turn a profit. While a major might drop an artist who "only" sells 30,000 records, or even 130,000, an indie can make a decent profit with those numbers. The overhead at a major is substantially greater: All the promotional fuel needed to drive the big machine costs stupidly spent mega-dollars. Indies can keep costs to a minimum. Therefore, we can sell a much smaller number of records and consider ourselves happily solvent.

I've noticed that the folks who are most negative about opening a label have been in the record biz for a long time. They remember how the industry used to be and want to market records as they once did. In contrast, those starting labels today are finding their way in today's market. Rather than fighting to fit into the old system, they're creating their own ways to market music. Many people running more recent indie labels say they enjoy what they do. They've managed to find alternative marketing strategies and loyal fans for their acts.

The key to being successful with an indie label lies in finding your niche market and working it in every way you can. Indie music is selling very well. *Very!* I'm not asking you to take my word. That's why I interviewed the heads of dozens of labels that are solvent. Some might sell better in bookstores than in a chain of record stores. Some might sell mainly by touring. The college market has been kind to indie music. Commercial radio hasn't. If you can accept the music industry as it is, and learn to work around the big major machines, you can find a comfortable home for the music you want to market. It IS possible to break through the bullshit of the system. If you're prepared to work hard to develop or work with your artists to develop a fan base, and do as much as possible to promote and market them, you have a chance of joining the ranks of those who are happily running successful indie labels. The tools to achieve those goals are on the following pages.

DECISIONS FOR STARTING A RECORD LABEL

Do you have a great act that you believe in? Are you frustrated by the lack of response from record labels to whom you pitch? Or, have you been offered a crappy deal? More and more artists are getting tired of the way large record labels treat them. The allure of signing to a big label gets overshadowed by the reality of what such deals are like: Few artists make much money on major labels; most get low priority with the company; many albums never reach stores; promotional support can be scarce; and the practice of *artist development is history.* Signed artists can die before they're born. So what can you do? Take charge by starting a record label and putting your material out yourself!

People are starting their own record labels for various reasons. Some of the most common are:

- *Wanting to press up something to sell at gigs and use to promote one's music in order to attract a record deal.*
- *Wanting to stay independent and have a product to sell at gigs, to pitch for use in films and television, and to use to make more money on one's own.*
- *Wanting to use one's own label as a vehicle for discovering and developing new talent and artists and as a way of getting hooked up with a larger label.*
- *Being a music lover who wants to market the wealth of unsigned talent out there.*
- *After having worked in the industry for years, wanting to use one's hard work and contacts to establish one's own business.*

WHY START YOUR OWN LABEL?

Because you can! Jeff Epstein, co-founder of Cropduster Records and sales and marketing manager at Disc Makers, works with indie labels every day and insists, "It's proven that you can sell records and make a living by putting out your own release." More than ever, independent record labels are experiencing success on many levels. There are many thousands of small labels; collectively, they comprise an impressive presence in the music industry. Michael Ellis, managing editor for *Billboard* magazine, the authority for music industry information, explains:

> When you look at market share, collectively, the independently distributed labels are a huge segment of the business. After Universal, they're the second biggest segment. They're bigger in the U.S. than the next four majors, collectively. The independent sector is . . . composed of thousands of labels, not one. People tend to forget that. But when you add up all those thousands of little labels, they add up to one very, very big segment of the business.

The best talent often comes from innovative folks who put music out themselves. Major labels don't tap into the cutting edge or have the patience to nurture an act with tremendous potential. Artist development ranges from slight to non-existent at majors. Indies provide it. An A&R person I talked to compared indie labels to farm clubs that develop baseball players. Majors watch them and pick up acts once they're developed. There's always an opportunity to get to the big leagues if the development is successful. Michael Ellis says that indie labels are the most innovative segment of the industry:

> [Independents are] often the first to start a trend. They are able to react very quickly to changes in music consumers' taste. They're extremely important to the record industry because not every artist is going to sell a half million albums. But there are hundreds and hundreds of recording artists that can make a perfectly good living by selling modest numbers of records. This is what independent labels do. They can make a profit on 5,000 albums, 10,000 albums, 50,000 albums. A major loses money on those types of sales. Lots and lots of artists may never be a gold or platinum artist. But they can do very well between touring and selling modest numbers of records.

Many folks start a label when they can't get signed. Since I couldn't get a deal, I chose to put out my own music. A finished product is a better vehicle for getting the attention of a record label. If you get radio play, sell CDs, and get good reviews, you can attract a better deal. Since large labels watch indies, releasing your own recording can help you get your foot through a door that was previously locked. Others start a record label to establish a solid business in the music industry. And some artists start labels because they want to control their careers. Hip-hop artist EL-P co-founded Definitive Jux Records (see profile in Chapter 3) in 1996. His success as an independent is inspirational. He says:

> We don't want to be on a major label. We are proud of this independent route. This is a long-term plan. We're addicted to the creativity, control and the hands-on experience of learning how to become an adult as opposed to becoming someone with a patriarch, which is how I look at a lot of artists who are involved with major labels. Once I realized the margins between what you have to sell on a major label and what you have to sell on an independent label to make the same amount of money—once I really broke them down mathematically—I realized I never wanted to be signed as an artist on a major label. For years, no one was saying or even thinking about this. We were the first group to come out and put a voice to that logic and make it a movement. It's not an anti-major-label thing. It's self-empowerment. My goal is to get where I wanted to go on my terms, the right way. And to reap the benefits of my hard work as I go along, and also to make the mistakes.

Record labels are notorious for pissing off artists. While a record deal is still considered a brass ring, it tarnishes quickly in the reality of the music biz. Few artists are happy with how they're treated, and fewer make money. Since I wrote the first edition of this book, more signed recording artists are leaving their labels and taking control of their musical destiny. Some have been dropped. Some break their contract because they're unhappy. Some just don't sign again when they fulfill the terms of their agreement. Singer/songwriter Aimee Mann chose the independent route. Her manager Michael Hausman calls it an "artist's decision":

Aimee finally realized that it was one of these kind of bad relationships where they were always looking for something from her that she wasn't able to deliver. That was getting in the way of creating music. Creatively she came to a point where she wanted to be free. She actually had pretty low expectations at that point as far as sales. I did a rough budget. We figured we'd start small but ended up doing much better than we thought we would. Not only has it been incredibly successful for her artistically—she can basically do what she wants—but financially it's been more successful as well.

When Hausman realized how difficult it was for individual artists to have their own record companies, he created United Musicians, a distribution, marketing, and promotion co-op for artist-owned labels (see Chapter 5 for more details). When I spoke to Hausman, Aimee Mann, Michael Penn, Pete Droge, and Bob Mould were in it. Other artists were being considered. Once you've been on the inside, the outside offers more potential. I must repeat a story from my book *The Real Deal*. Country legend Jerry Jeff Walker had a gold album in 1973 when he signed with MCA. In the '80s, he and his wife Susan, who works with him, went to Nashville with his new CD to speak with MCA about a new contract. Susan Walker says:

I told the head we had a CD completed and wanted to see if he'd like to release it. He said, as he sat pompously with his feet up, "I'll take it home, smoke a joint and see if I can figure out a formula." I was furious. It was so insulting to Jerry's artistic integrity. He'd already been in the business for 25 years. But that's the way labels are. I told Jerry Jeff. "That's it. We're starting our own label." I want to thank every one of them for not signing Jerry Jeff because it's been very lucrative for us.

It's easy to get disillusioned with being signed to a major label. Most artists are at least somewhat disappointed. Jonatha Brooke (see profile in Chapter 3) began Bad Dog Records when MCA Records dropped her in the middle of a tour. I asked her how she felt about being signed to a major. She says:

I have no beef with the majors and like to make that clear. For the brief moments I had, with the kind of exposure that deep pocket can give you, I had a nice little run, with tour support. I got to make beautiful records with a nice budget, so I can't complain about the initial support. It's just that it's very hard for majors to stick with artists who aren't immediately selling gazillions of records. They're not great at creative alternative marketing. They can't switch gears that quickly. The problem was getting dropped in the middle of a national tour, which wasn't convenient for me [she said laughingly]. It was a roller coaster for my ego, but I was able to parlay it into something else, which was my own label.

Independent labels can be flexible and get creative with their marketing. Recording artist Jane Siberry left Warner Bros. to start Sheeba Records:

I left Warner Bros. because I could. I was becoming quite frustrated with not being able to do a certain kind of work. I'm the kind of person who thinks sideways and has a lot of spin-off projects . . . Warner Bros. didn't know what to do with what I was presenting so I felt quite limited . . . I knew the ropes and the structure of sending work out into the world. I had the advantage of having a lot of people expecting my new release . . . I didn't think it would be that hard so I just did it.

Other labels were founded for different reasons.
Damon Dash, *Founder, Roc-A-Fella Records, New York City*

I was a manager first . . . on Atlantic. They didn't know how to market music to the street—they didn't know how to paint that picture or promote it to the people who were painting the picture, so I had to learn it myself. In learning that, I thought I might as well do it myself. When learning the money and point structure I felt, why should I get 20 percent of 12 points instead of giving out 20 percent and having 80 percent? I was doing all the work for a little bit of money. I was shopping Jay-Z and wasn't getting the response I wanted. People weren't reacting as fast as I thought they should. We pressed up our own white label, which means it's not available commercially. We gave it to DJs and the underground radio stations. They started playing it.

Being that we got a response, we put up some money and did a video. Then we got more response and build-up so we did another white label. Eventually we got one of our records added to radio in full rotation.

Edward Chmelewski, *President, Blind Pig Records, Chicago and San Francisco*

I started my label for love of the music. The people that I have dealt with over the years don't get into this with the idea of getting rich or figure, "I'm going to make a lot of money at this and that's why I want to do it." Most of the people who get into the independent label business do it because they have a love for the music. My partner Jerry Giudice and I both have a love for this blues and R&B music we produce. We also thought it would be a good creative vehicle for both of us to work in—a way to do something interesting and creative. The label got started out of a little bar in Ann Arbor, Michigan, called the Blind Pig Cafe. It ran a little blues club in the basement and we got to know a lot of the musicians. The label grew out of that.

THE UPSIDE OF OPENING YOUR OWN LABEL

If I had to sum up the advantages of starting your own record label in one word, I would choose "control." With your own label, decisions and choices are in your hands. You may not have the resources that the majors do, but the freedom of choice and action can give you the edge that indies are known for. Larger labels get bogged down in red tape. Indies can act quickly. Majors have a lot more money but often don't have the feel for the street or the drive that indies do. Today, there are more alternative opportunities than ever to break a record. Valerie Vigoda of Groovelily (see profile in Chapter 3) explains:

It's exhilarating, and also overwhelming. There are *so* many (non-musical) things to do—I find myself working longer hours than anyone I know—but I love it. This is a wonderful time to be independent in music. Consolidation in the industry has put a chokehold on commercial radio, concert venues and record stores, so the independent music scene is growing incredibly fast in reaction. People are seeking alternatives to the shrinking song lists on their radio dials. New nontraditional music venues, such as house concerts, are popping up everywhere. There are twice as many music festivals in the U.S. as there were only ten years ago! Independent, grassroots promotion is working for more and more artists and bands, many of whom have been dropped by record labels in the past few years. The upshot is, there is a middle ground which did not use to exist! There is a third option, between blockbuster chart hits and penury-independent success.

Independent success. When you achieve that, little else tastes as sweet! Why? Success on a large label may be disappointing. You can sell a half million CDs and not make money. If you don't sell huge numbers, label support dries up. You can sell 100,000 copies and be treated as a failure. Sell that on your own and you'll be thrilled if you've been careful about spending, which you control. Danny Goldberg, CEO of Artemis Records (see profile in Chapter 3), *Billboard's* choice as #1 indie label in the last few years, says:

> The good news is that we can be successful at a lower level of sales. We can get excited about a focus of getting to 200-300,000 albums instead of 1,000,000. It gives you a certain kind of artist you can really work on passionately, whereas in the context of a major, some of them would not be important. For example, Steve Earle was selling 125,000 at Warner. We got him to 200,000. That difference wouldn't make a difference to Warner or Columbia. Whereas at Artemis, it does make a difference—to us and to Steve.

When you're signed to a label, the label can spend what they like and bill a lot of it to you. You have no say, yet you pay! Many expenses are recouped out of the artist's royalties. When you're the boss, you can be more practical about how money is used for promotion. Jonatha Brooke loves having the "freedom and power to make decisions quickly, on your own terms, and to implement them, rather than going through a chain of command and hearing 'no' all the time." Singer/songwriter Rich Hardesty (see profile in Chapter 3) adds, "Being independent, I do what I want whenever I want. It seems like others are trapped in a mold." Jay Woods, senior vice president and general manager of New West Records (see profile in Chapter 3) likes being able to do artist development:

An advantage is our ability to stay focused on projects for longer periods of time and being more personally involved in all aspects of the business. We get really close to the projects and stay with them for a long time. We don't have the luxury to throw something against the wall to see if it sticks, so to speak. We need everything to have a certain amount of success or it doesn't make sense for us to do it. Essentially we're spending our money.

Having your own label means you're not at someone else's mercy. Michael Hausman likes "having that freedom to follow your instincts musically and creatively. Artists waste a lot of energy convincing people how it should be done. We decide what to do and just do it." You can get a record out quickly instead of waiting for another label to diddle around with it. Majors are notorious for producing albums that never see the light of a record store. Releases get stalled. Master tapes are put on a shelf indefinitely. Plus, many artists on major labels get little or no promotion. If you put it out yourself, you're in control! EL-P likes being able to take chances, rather than getting stuck using recycled ideas as many labels do:

At the very least what I come out with is trial and error—learning something. It doesn't appeal to my personality to be involved in a situation where you're an artist and the label is literally like a giant robot with 30 levels of technology and one human somewhere, if you can find them. Taking care of your own destiny is a powerful thing. I believe an independent label has to have a spirit behind it—a philosophy and an idea. [If it's] "I want to make money," that means that you are simply a chip off of daddy's block, but without the resources and daddy doesn't want to talk to you. I look at it a different way. I believe in the consistent release of quality, creative, artistic, beautiful music—that's my only philosophy.

Ryan Kuper, President, Redemption Records (see Chapter 3) likes:

Having complete control of everything . . . what band I sign, what kind of contract we'll have, what the artwork will look like, to how it's going to be marketed. All the while I know that if it fails it's my fault, but if it does well it's also, in part, because of the decisions I made. Another advantage is not having to work for someone who's incompetent or who isn't as passionate about the bands as I am.

Jay Woods adds:

We won a Grammy for our label in 2001. We were thrilled to be nominated. That was enough. Delbert McClinton won for best contemporary blues, but we were part of it in some way. You walk in people's offices and there's a zillion Grammys and gold records. Well, we've got one! That's a thrill.

A big advantage for artists who put out their own music is that they get to retain ownership of their copyright. Many artists hate losing control of when and how their songs are used by the label they're signed to. Michael Hausman believes that not giving away the copyright gives you power:

The root of most of the artist's problems can be traced back to the artist signing away their copyright in an artist contract. In a traditional record contract you sign away your copyright and then try to get back certain controls over how the copyright is going to be used, release commitments, certain approvals you have to give if the song will be used in a commercial, etc. My philosophy is you're in a much better position if you never give away that copyright and just license your records/songs for whatever specific situation you want to license them for.

Ezra Idlet of the popular group Trout Fishing in America says that people wanted to hear their songs, so they recorded them and made them available on Trout Records (see profile in Chapter 3): "We thought we might be able to pick up a little extra change if we did it." Now it's a thriving label and he's happy:

You see more money on each record sold than you would on a big label. You're closer to the accounting process. My wife is doing the accounting. That's more secure than somebody that's just pushing numbers. When it comes to recording our record, we have more say in what goes on it.

Having your own record label allows you control over your product, from producing to marketing. You can control your budget wisely, instead of creating the sort of exorbitant budgets that larger labels are known for. The control factor is what drives a lot of people to start their own label. Dave Roberge, president of Everfine Records (see profile in Chapter 3) says:

> The biggest advantage of having an independent label is to be able to think creatively, freely, and outside the box. For us, there's less financial expectation because we're not owned by a parent company or investor group where we have quarterly expectations. We aren't looking for that next hit single, or big hit with an artist that doesn't necessarily fit into what some would consider a commercial format. It allows us to work with artists that are just starting out and want to develop something. As an independent, we want to be a niche sort of a label—a little different and off the cuff—and provide opportunities for artists that might not have an opportunity immediately from a major label. We don't feel entitled to success. We have to work for it. We want to position the label as one that doesn't fall under your typical mentality of trying to find hits, but finds unique cool artists that have an audience and need to spread that audience. We can help deliver that artist to a bigger and wider audience. That's where I think as an indie we separate ourselves. I give my employees the freedom to think outside of the box. They can bring things to the table that [aren't] going to get them fired.

THE DOWNSIDE OF STARTING YOUR OWN LABEL

I could leave you reveling in the optimism of the last pages, but I must present both sides. It's easy to start your own label. It's much harder to make it succeed. No matter how great your record, if you can't get it on radio, if you don't have a budget for promoting it, if you can't afford a good video, if you have no way to get exposure for it, no one will know it exists. If you can't get it into stores or get the act touring, how will you sell it? You'll need all the determination, marketing savvy, and cash you can muster to compete with the majors. Jay Woods agrees:

> You don't have the leverage that a lot of major companies have. That comes into play in all sorts of promotional arenas, such as

radio. It's a give and take sort of game. We're gaining leverage, but on a very small scale compared to these other companies. We try to make up for it with integrity and trying to do consistently good quality music that represents who and what we are.

When it comes to starting your own label, I've found that the flipside of having control is having a lot of frustration. It's frustrating when you don't have a large enough budget to do what you know needs to be done. Often, independent labels are funded by the founder's personal bank accounts. A low budget—or no budget—can make you feel like the brass ring is just out of your grasp. Jonatha Brooke says having to pay for everything yourself is the biggest disadvantage:

> People get this idea that when you're independent, you're making so much more money out of the pot. You're getting everything, instead of just your percent of an artist deal. But you have all the expenses. It's naïve to think that all of a sudden you're going to be raking it in—it just ain't true.

It's frustrating when you find it hard to get good distribution and sometimes it's even harder waiting to get paid. It's especially frustrating when you have a record that you know absolutely belongs on the radio, and you can't get airplay. If you're also the artist, the frustration of the business side of running a record label interferes with your creativity. However, Mark Carpentieri, president and owner of MC Records, says the disadvantage has a bright side, too:

> You don't have the paternal person writing the check for you or providing a more established background. It's nice to get that kind of extra help or push if you have something that's really cooking. But with money comes demand. Perhaps, in the overall picture, it's best not to have that if you need to adjust quickly or sign who you think is the right artist.

One thing that I found frustrating at first was the lack of respect paid to me. Stores, distributors, publications, clubs, etc., will lump you among the many thousands of other people pressing up their own records. Many won't acknowledge you until your accomplishments give them no choice but to do so. When I went to my first big music seminar, people read my name tag and moved on, which made me feel like a nonentity. It was an awful feeling, but it also motivated me to succeed. I swore I'd return the following year as a somebody. And I did, as a panelist! Just don't expect to get respect until you've seriously earned it. Danny Goldberg says:

> The bad thing is we have less power. When you believe in an artist, you want to be able to get 100 radio stations and spend millions of dollars. We have to be much more cautious about spending money, and we don't have the clout. We don't have a catalogue to help buffer the ups and downs of the business.

The dues in this industry can be very high. With so many indie labels popping up daily, how can you expect people to pay you any serious mind until you've proven yourself? Industry people know that anyone can open a label, so they wait to see what you do with it before giving you any attention. But your anonymity can change very quickly after breaking your first act.

Singer/songwriter David M. Bailey (see profile in Chapter 3) says his biggest disadvantage is "being completely overwhelmed. Blessings create work. I don't think people realize how much time goes into it." Many of you will start out like I did, as a jack of all trades at the label if you can't afford to pay a staff. I was "the staff" for Revenge Records, from president to stock girl. Sometimes I'd haul boxes of records from the pressing plant, or cut boxes at 2:00 A.M. to prepare them for shipping. I'd keep reminding myself that this was what I wanted. While friends tried to support me, they had no idea what it was like to have that kind of responsibility for such a tenuous business. Ezra Idlet says, "It's a lot of work. We had to learn the business, more than I would want. My interest is the music. We see more money out of each individual unit that we sell, but don't sell as many units. But, we make a living at it. That's good." Ryan Kuper adds:

> I work my ass off. I go to bed thinking about my bands and wake up thinking about them as well. I honestly have dreams about things I need to take care of. Your work's never done, and at times it limits your social life. It's tough not having the resources major labels have, but they waste money in ridiculous amounts and at ridiculous rates. It's frustrating seeing that, knowing that you could achieve more, with longer lasting results, on a fraction of what they spend.

Now that I've given you a taste of the reality of starting and running a record label, you have two choices: squash any thoughts of opening yours, or accept what I've talked about and find ways to compensate or get around the road blocks. You can. I did. If you want to do it yourself, find ways to do it yourself! They exist. Look at all the indie labels that are surviving. As Valerie Vigoda said, you can find ways to be independent and not be poor. There's never been a better time to take control of your music, or music that you believe in, and create a business around it. Accepting the reality helps you to conquer the pitfalls!

SETTING GOALS AND STRATEGIES

Before jumping into any business, there's lots to think about. Many variables come into play in running a record label, such as whether or not the artist has a fan base or reasonable potential for media coverage. Buyers don't magically appear because you've pressed something. If you want to sell product, you have to identify how you'll sell it before starting the label. You'll have the best shot at succeeding if you first figure out what you're getting yourself into—without the blinders of what fun it will be or a belief that a good product guarantees sales. The only sure thing is that you need to work your ass off. Taking care of business now puts you in a better position to have a record label with longevity. So get the stars out of your eyes and put on your business cap!

PREPLANNING

Preplanning increases your chances of ending up with a viable record label. Before starting a record label, create long- and short-term goals. Too many folks press CDs without thinking about what they need to do once it's ready. They manufacture product without looking beyond the present. All they know is that they have good material they want to get out. So they press it up without a clue about what to do with it once it's manufactured. By the time they figure out their next step, they may find themselves without enough money or time to do what's necessary to market it. A record can die before it reaches the starting line. Prepare in advance! Opening your own record label, even if it's only to put out your own material, means starting a business and should be approached as such.

Put together a game plan ahead of time. Writing a business plan (see Chapter 2) helps you set goals and define what you expect to get out of your label. It's critical to think ahead. If you're a creative person, it can be painful to force yourself to do business stuff. Biz on the brain definitely makes it hard for me to be creative. I'd much rather someone else handled mine. But life doesn't allow us to skip the business part if we want to make money from our creativity. Dealing with the business matters now will open doors for your music later. In the long run, success can free you from a lot of such work. Once you're making money, hire people to handle some of it.

Force yourself to sit down and really think through your goals. Where would you like to be a year after pressing your first record? Where do you plan to sell your records? Who's going to buy them? Will your label be an ongoing business or will it exist only until you get an artist deal? Do you want to be affiliated with a larger label or stay independent? Do you have access to more financing if you need it? Get these answers before you invest even one dime.

Since I wrote the first edition of this book, making a CD has become much cheaper. CD-Rs can be burned off a computer. Because of this, there's more potential to use CDs for a variety of goals. Marketing your own music can be profitable, as long as you take it seriously as a business.

IDENTIFYING YOUR MARKET

The key to a successful record label, in my eyes, is to find your market and figure out how to reach it. Before investing in creating CDs, decide who's going to buy them. Too many folks record an album they love and run to manufacture copies to sell without giving thought to who the target audience is. The first step in starting a record label is to identify the group most likely to buy your product, such as college students, adults over forty, etc., and the avenue for promoting and marketing your product so that the audience knows about it. Gregg Latterman, president of Aware Records, advises, "Understand who your audience is. Intelligently target that audience." This record label game isn't just about good music. It's about finding a market for it and creating a plan to reach those potential buyers. Music lovers won't buy your records if they don't know your artist exists. It's up to you to let them know.

How will people become familiar with your artist? Is the artist playing in live clubs regularly where his or her product can be sold?

Will it work on college radio? Find out what outlets there are for your genre, and gather resources from the onset of the project. There are many alternative markets for music. Can you fit into outside traditional markets? Do you have a good Internet presence or plan to get one? Are you hiring promoters or publicists to let people know about the product? Until you can identify a specific group who might buy your product and figure out how to reach the people in it, you're better off waiting to put product out. If you can't identify the target audience, there may not be one, no matter how great the music is.

A HIT RECORD CAN BE YOUR DOWNFALL

The first time I heard that a hit record could be a liability, I was discouraged. After all, wasn't having a hit record my goal? But after running a label for five years, I understand how this can happen.

Let's say you release a record and work it hard. Stores push it. It gets radio play and local distributors are behind it. Sounds great so far? People take serious notice of your record and large orders come in. They're selling out. Terrific! Before you know it you've gotten orders for 10,000 pieces. Hurray? No. Not if you don't have the finances to press them. If you haven't looked beyond the first pressing, you can sink your label if you can't meet orders quickly. According to Richard Ellis, manager of Aron's Records, a record store in L.A.:

> Don't promise something you can't fulfill—a killer for labels. Don't take orders for stuff you can't send. That's the first thing that will set a store off on the wrong foot with you. I've seen it happen dozens of times when they can't get the records pressed. Momentum on a record will die in thirty seconds.

Running out of money is common for indies. Manufacturers won't give credit just because you have orders. There are no guarantees that you'll ever get paid. Thus a huge order can actually put you out of business if you can't deliver it. The reality of a large demand is discouraging: Keep stores and distributors waiting indefinitely after they've pushed your record hard and they probably won't help again. Many labels are competing for market share. Why should anyone work with one that can't fulfill orders? Your advance planning must take into account that you always need inventory available. Orders must be filled promptly.

The best insurance against getting caught short is to identify your options in advance. For example, I knew that one record would be a big seller and called everyone I was close to and asked how much each could loan me if necessary. Fortunately, I got paid fast enough to meet the demand on my own. Otherwise, there were sources to borrow from. If you have no access to money, another option is to get affiliated with a larger label or distributor. Larger distributors will do Pressing & Distribution (P&D) deals (see Chapter 13) with labels that have a big demand for product. Research now to target appropriate ones. Then contact them if your record takes off fast.

BRIGHTER INDIE FUTURE

The future of independents has brightened substantially since I wrote the first edition of this book. I asked a few successful indies for their thoughts on being an independent label. Danny Goldberg sees a future for indie labels:

> I think that indies are a permanent part of the music business . . . The cost of making a recording is a tiny fraction of the cost of other media [where] the ability to expose somebody and find a following doesn't exist. The scarcity that exists on TV channels or the amount of movie screens is not analogous to the way you can get records into stores. Therefore indies can compete and develop artists. It's about 15-20 percent indie today, and I think that will continue. It's one of the few or maybe only entertainment media that's very accessible to some indie companies . . . There are a lot a successful indie labels now, there were a lot 20 years ago, and there will be a lot 20 years from now.

EL-P is certain that independence is the way to go:

> This is the industry that's based on cult fan base, that's based on grassroots promotion. There is no event marketing. We don't have to come up with splashy, explosive ways to sell a

new artist, because we know what we're going to do with one. We're going to tour him for a straight year. I'm a businessman. I wouldn't be doing it if it were ethereal—all about heart, struggle and power. It's more that I believe in my heart of hearts that *this is* the industry that will be surviving when everything collapses.

And Tony Brummel, president of Victory Records, loves the free spiritedness of the business:

I love putting out independent music. I feel like our founding fathers when I wake up every day, as ridiculous as it sounds, because we really are fighting against a system. We're renegades, rebels, in the trenches, and they're not. It's a fight every day. But we're conditioned to that. It's not something that grinds us down.

SETTING UP YOUR RECORD LABEL

Whether your intention for starting a record label is to attract a label deal or to sign and market other artists, you'll have a better shot at success if you approach your endeavor as a real business. Even if you don't formally set up a business, operate in a business mode. This may sound intimidating to many of you; it did to me. I've included an assortment of resources in this chapter that can make the business of running a label easier. Keep in mind that marketing music, even if it's your own, is a business, unless you don't want to make money. A business mind-set instills the right attitude. I've emphasized this already and will continue to. Developing business sense can mean the difference between making money and running your label as a hobby.

REGISTERING YOUR COMPANY

The first step toward starting your own business is to decide how you want it registered. Should you incorporate, or just file a business certificate with your local county (see below)? Are you working with someone? You better have a written agreement! It can be as simple as a letter stating the terms of everything decided between the two of you, or you can create a formal partnership.

A corporation keeps your company separate from your personal business. Many labels incorporate immediately to protect personal assets from lawsuits. A limited liability company, commonly known as an LLC, offers an alternative to creating a partnership or a corporation. It provides the corporate advantages of limited liability but has better tax options and more flexible partnership arrangements. More people than ever are choosing this option. Determine your needs and possible liability based on your circumstances. If you choose to incorporate or create an LLC, register through the state in which you operate your business.

It's possible to file on your own, but most people use an attorney. Get specific information from your state.

If you choose not to incorporate, you can register your business with the appropriate office in your local county. Counties vary in their procedures as well as their fees. Check your local phone book under the listing for your county government offices. Often a business certificate is issued through the county clerk's office. Get an application for a business license, follow the instructions on the form, pay the fee, and you'll be issued a certificate that's considered a "doing business as" (DBA) license. Some call it a fictitious name certificate. Once you have this, you can open a bank account in your business's name.

When I started Revenge Records, I spoke with both my lawyer and accountant. After assessing my situation, we decided I didn't need to incorporate right away. For this book, I asked both a lawyer and an accountant to give their points of view on incorporating and to provide more specifics. According to Wallace Collins, Esq., an entertainment/intellectual property lawyer in private practice in New York City:

> As a practical matter, sooner or later you may want to incorporate in order to limit your personal liability. If properly employed, a corporate entity can be used as a shield to protect you and can have certain tax advantages. In most cases, however, it is not really necessary to incorporate at the start of your career. The law of most states does require that, if you use a name professionally other than your personal name, then you should file a business certificate (DBA) in the county in which you reside or do business under that name. Also, as a business matter, the individual members of a group or company may want to enter into a partnership agreement between and among themselves in order to spell out the particulars with respect to certain rights such as songwriting and ownership of the trademark rights in the name. Otherwise, any group of two or more persons operating a business for profit is considered a partnership for the purposes of applying the laws of partnership under the laws of most states. These laws generally employ a rule of sharing evenly in profits and losses, including all assets of the business. As a corporation, you create a separate legal entity that you own as a shareholder but for which you work as

an officer and/or director and draw a salary or dividends. In the event that the corporation, despite being properly documented and operated, encounters financial problems, the claim would be against the corporation and its assets and not your personal assets (e.g., the house, car, and boat that you purchased with your salary for the five years that the corporation operated successfully).

Anthony Orlando, a certified public accountant practicing in New York, adds:

The decision to incorporate most of the time depends on the net worth of the person who is starting the label. If that person has substantial assets, which may need to be protected, they probably want to incorporate. Incorporating adds a level of both accounting and tax complexity that a small label grossing under $100,000 doesn't really need. Not that it won't do them good, but there are costs and taxes associated with a corporation that they may not need to incur. Operating as a sole-proprietorship is really for accounting simplicity. When it appears a business will gross over $100,000 a year on a consistent basis, you definitely want to start thinking about incorporating. Again, there may not be significant tax advantages, but you do want the personal protection a corporation offers. Another form of business entity that gives you personal liability protection from your business creditors is an (LLC) limited liability company. This is a hybrid between a partnership and a corporation. It shields the owners from liability and the income or loss is actually taxed to the owners, so there is no separate corporate level tax. Also, it is much more flexible as far as how profits, losses, and ownership percentages can be split. You can basically come up with any formula you want as long as you put it into your partnership agreement.

Everyone's circumstances are different. Before deciding how to set up your business, I highly recommend consulting with both a lawyer and an accountant. Talk over your options with professionals and make a decision based on what seems to suit your needs best. Every state varies in its laws and policies, which is why legal advice is a good idea.

I called the IRS and was told that anyone other than a sole proprietor (someone running an unincorporated business with no partners) with no employees needs to fill out form SS-4, an application for an employer identification number (EIN). If tax stuff intimidates you, as it does me, you can get help by calling the IRS at 800-829-3676. They'll send you a free business tax kit, which explains all forms that may need to be filed. You can also call the appropriate number in your state to get a resale number. That means you won't pay taxes on supplies that will eventually be resold as part of your product.

Don't make a decision to go one way instead of another because you're lazy or uncomfortable about a direction you don't know enough about. When you take business one step at a time and learn as you go, it eventually starts to make sense!

DEVELOPING YOUR BUSINESS

You've made the decision to start a record label and chosen a direction to take in terms of structuring your business. Now what do you do? Your mind-set should be the same as that of someone starting any business. Read books covering business in general. Locate free resources in your area.

BUSINESS RESOURCES

Many organizations offer support for start-up businesses. Search on-line. With research, you'll find an amazing number of free or inexpensive resources for the general task of setting up a business. The Small Business Administration (SBA) offers quality information about starting a small business. In many large cities, they have a program called Service Corps of Retired Executives (SCORE), a nonprofit organization for which retired businesspeople volunteer time to give advice on starting up businesses. This program also sponsors low-cost or free business seminars on a variety of topics. For information on the program located nearest to where you live, call 800-634-0245 or look on-line at www.score.org. You can e-mail a counselor with business questions and get an electronic reply.

As discussed in the next section, starting up a new business requires a business plan, and there are also resources for writing such a plan. Check out adult education programs and libraries for free or inexpensive classes. Call the nearest SBA to see if people there can refer you to a program, such as a Small Business Development Center (SBDC) in your area that provides free or low-cost support in writing such a plan. The SBA itself has a kit on small businesses containing valuable information on various topics, including how to write a business plan. Call 800-8-ASK-SBA to locate the SBA office nearest you.

WRITING A BUSINESS PLAN

From a business standpoint, a business plan is essential. It's an outline of what you need to do. You'll almost definitely need one if you're trying to get financing for your label. Few people or financial institutions will loan you money without having seen one. If you're working with a partner, it's good to have all your intentions on paper.

Even if no one else sees it, a business plan helps you develop steps for getting your label up and running. Formally organizing goals helps you stay focused. Following typical patterns laid down in business highlights things that you may need to do, or should keep in mind. Otherwise, they may not come up until it's too late. A business plan can be used as a checklist for starting your label. It shows people, including yourself, that you're serious about what you're doing.

How do you begin to write a business plan for a record label? Aside from organizations that can help you, go to a bookstore and browse through books on business plans. Buy the one you like the most. Use what works for you. There's no right or wrong way to write a business plan. Key elements that are essential to cover include the following:

- *Start with a summary of your project. This should include who you are (e.g., a producer who's worked in the industry for ten years; a musician with a fan base; a studio owner with lots of talent coming through). It should also include short- and long-range goals (e.g., to record, manufacture, and market a record independently; to eventually get picked up for distribution by a larger label). Describe your strongest assets for accomplishing each goal. What do you have going for you that will enhance your chances for success? How do you plan to finance your business?*

- *Provide a brief history of your project. How did you get to the point of starting a label? Specify how your label will be managed. Will you do it all or will there be* a staff? Are you planning to hire independent promoters? Be very specific about how the record label will be run. How will it be structured? Will it be a corporation or DBA? A sole proprietorship, a partnership, or an LLC? Be very clear about the path your business will take.

- In addition, describe the music industry as a larger picture and how you plan to fit into it. What type of music will you put out and who will be your audience? Be specific in targeting your niche. Why will they buy your records? How will your product hold up against competition? How are labels that are marketing similar music doing it? Are you offering something unique? How will you get distribution? What radio stations will you go to? How will you price your products? Will you have a budget for advertising or publicity? Answer these questions for your own reference. Just believing in your product isn't enough to market it properly. There are thousands of others with the same belief in their music. What can set you apart from them is a specific idea of how and where you market your product.

- Include a description of all facilities you may use, and what equipment you'll need. Will you operate out of your home or from a separate office? Where will you record your material? Where will your product be stored? Will you buy supplies to get the business going? What's your growth potential? Do you plan to expand in the future or just use your label to market yourself? What's your project time line? Guesstimate how long you'll need for each step of the process, from the studio to profit. Include any critical risks or problems that may arise.

- Include a detailed financial summary. If you're looking for financial backing, this section is especially important. Estimate the amount of money you expect to need over the next three years, and how much you *expect to take in. Create a very specific budget, taking time to list every expense you can think of. Don't forget phone bills, shipping, and transportation to get your artist to promotional gigs. Allow for printing, press kits, and postage. Don't forget promotional copies to give away. Will you have bank, lawyer, or accounting fees? Order catalogues from pressing plants to estimate costs. Providing financial info will probably be the hardest part of preparing your business plan. Be realistic. Estimate higher than you think you'll need to allow for unexpected expenses. Be conservative about what you expect to sell and what your cash flow will be. There's no sense in playing games on paper. Don't be too optimistic in your assessment.*

Finally, get help with the actual writing of your business plan. As already noted, there are enough resources available that you shouldn't have to wing it. Do what you can on your own, and then get support from an SBA, SBDC, other organizations in your area, or your accountant.

CHOOSING A COMPANY NAME AND LOGO

Your record label should have a name that people will recognize. Once you have artists doing reasonably well, people will pay attention when your label has a new release. Those who've enjoyed acts on your label in the past may want to see what else you put out. It helps if you have a name they can remember.

Do what you can to check that your choice hasn't been taken by another label. Some folks do a formal search to make sure that nobody's used a name they've chosen. There are trademark search companies and lawyers who'll do this for you. Or use a search engine. More avenues open as the Internet grows. If you're planning to operate on a small scale, you may not be as concerned about having to change your label's name if another label already has the rights to it. But if you're planning to run your label for the long haul, the more thoroughly you check now, the safer you'll be.

I'm a firm believer in having a nice logo for your label. It helps establish your identity more. A logo looks nice on business cards and stationery. It makes your label more recognizable. For example, after I had several successful dance records on Revenge Records, DJs recognized my logo on new releases and would at least ask to hear it. My records did especially well in Spain. The distributor said that, while most buyers there couldn't read titles in English, they knew Revenge as a label they liked and recognized my music through my logo.

A logo can be simple. It can be a piece of graphic art that presents the name of your label in a unique way. I designed the letters in Revenge Records to look like lightning bolts and gave a rough sketch to a friend who was a graphic designer. The name was in white, against a turquoise background. This color scheme worked on labels for my 12-inch singles, which had plain white sleeves; I used a turquoise rectangle with the white logo against it on packaging for other formats. People recognized my label from the logo. I even put it on T-shirts.

A nice logo adds to the professional look of your company, especially if you're going for longevity. An original piece of artwork, however simple, can give your label individuality. If you can't afford to pay someone to design it, try to find a graphic artist who'll do it free to build up his or her portfolio—like a student at a college with a graphics program.

TRADEMARKING YOUR LABEL'S NAME AND/OR ITS LOGO

If you trademark the name of your company, you'll have protection against someone else using your name for a record label. Logos and the names of recording artists can also be trademarked. If you have a name or logo which you may want to use on merchandise (hats, T-shirts, etc.), get it registered from the get-go to protect against bootlegging when your acts become well known.

Trademarks can be registered by state or nationally. Federal registration offers the best protection. You can reserve a name you want to trademark in advance by filing an intent to use it. Don't do this lightly. You have to intend to use it within a reasonable timeframe. Before filing for federal registration, plan to use the mark for interstate business transactions. Only using it locally doesn't qualify you. It's best to do a search to check that no one else has trademarked your name because if it's already trademarked, filing fees aren't refunded. The U.S. Patent and Trademark Office has libraries to do a search yourself, and now you can also search on-line on their website at www.uspto.gov. Once you do a search, they'll still do their own and determine whether you should get the trademark.

To register your federal trademark, file an application with the U.S. Patent and Trademark Office in Washington, D.C. It takes about a year for paperwork to come through. Costs run at least several hundred dollars for legal and filing fees. Registering a trademark in the U.S. doesn't protect the name or logo in other countries. If you plan on doing business internationally and want protection in other countries, apply for trademark status in each country. Trademark laws vary by country, so consult with a lawyer who's knowledgeable about international law for trademark registration.

CREATING THE APPEARANCE OF A SERIOUS BUSINESS

Numerous indie labels start each week. As I said earlier, it's hard to earn respect. If you have a reasonable budget and serious contacts, you're way ahead of the majority of new labels, which are small and unknown. If you have a low budget, no contacts, and little experience in the music industry, creating the appearance of a serious business can set you apart from other labels in the same boat as you.

Taking your label seriously as a business lets people know you plan on staying around and intend to make money from your label. So you're selling records out of a car. So you've put your social life on hold because your label is pulling in all your cash. So you live on tuna and mom's generosity because that's all you can afford. So you and your label share a small bedroom in your cousin's house. So you're scared because you're not sure of what you're doing. So . . . so . . . so . . . All of the above may fit your situation, but nobody has to know!

When I started my label, I ran it out of a house I shared. Boxes of records doubled for end tables, since I had nowhere to put them. I had no staff or office. I was a self-contained operation—*but* I took myself seriously enough to conduct my endeavor as a legitimate business. In the eyes of my business contacts, I was doing well. Nobody knew more than I shared. I didn't kid around when it came to Revenge Records. I might have answered the phone from the shower, but I'd turn off the water first. I'm sure callers pictured me in front of my desk in formal work attire instead of dripping wet, because I was so businesslike. I was running Revenge Records out of my living room, yet few people realized it.

WORKING OUT OF YOUR HOME

If you have a separate office, you'll generate a more a professional image. But many of you won't have one, at least not at first. In this case, be careful about details. It's hard to take yourself seriously when your business is also where you play and sleep. But you have to. Make the most of working out of your home.

If you share your space with others, it's better to have a separate number for business, although it's not imperative. What's most important is having a businesslike message on the answering machine and answering your phone in a reasonably formal manner. If you share the phone, have a generic message on your answering machine, i.e., "You've reached 444-4444. Please leave a message." You don't need to identify your business in the message. Supplying the telephone number lets callers know they've reached the right one.

Children shouldn't be answering a phone that's used for business. Nor should clowns. I have no patience for either. On too many occasions I've called what I knew to be a small business and had a very unprofessional response on the other end. When a young child answers and tries to make conversation instead of putting an adult on as I request, I eventually hang up. If your number is on a business card, respect your business enough to keep youngsters from acting as your secretary. No matter who answers your phone, make it clear that joking or being too informal takes the professionalism out of your business.

If other adults answer your phone, ask them just to say hello. They shouldn't discuss you or your business. I've had mothers, spouses, roommates, etc., tell me the person I'm calling is in the shower, at the movies, and even on the toilet—more than anyone needs to know! Treat your business like the business it is. Take yourself seriously enough to be careful about how your phone is answered. If all of this complicates your home life, get voice mail and return calls. Or use a cell phone for all business calls.

CREATING A SUCCESSFUL IMAGE

Make every effort to give off an air of success. When anyone other than a close friend asks how your label is doing, reply with a version of "very well, thank you." People want to help those whom they think are successful. Don't tell folks your problems. If you create a facade of success, there's a better chance of achieving it. From a spiritual perspective, you get back what you give out. If you treat yourself as successful, you'll have a better chance of it coming true.

I confess—I've sometimes stretched the truth. My dad took my first record to stores in Miami. Many took a few copies on consignment, maybe to humor him. When people asked if my record was out anywhere other than New York, I'd tell them a lot of stores in Miami carried it. It impressed them, and they took me more seriously. When a store in Minneapolis reordered records, I told people my music was doing well in Minneapolis. I didn't lie. I just stretched the truth a bit. It made folks more interested in my music. I'd be surprised if anyone ever checked these cities. No one cares that much. But when people hear that you're doing well in several cities, they take you more seriously.

If you have no staff, create the illusion of one. Some of you will start with a budget for hiring a staff. More of you won't. When I opened Revenge Records, I was the artist and knew it was unprofessional to represent myself. So I created the names of staff members, and signed letters accordingly. I had a marketing person, a publicist, etc. When someone called for one of my "other selves," I'd put on that hat. It got a bit schizophrenic, but it created the illusion of a serious business. To this day I use another name as publicist on my press releases. When someone calls for her, I say she's not in, and help them. Many folks use fake names to market themselves. Few care that much to notice later on.

Get into the habit of referring to anything about your company in terms of "we," instead of "I." "We'll get those records to you tomorrow." "We've had some great success with that format." "Someone will call you back tomorrow." "We've worked hard with that artist." Do you get it? It gives your business a fuller feeling and makes you sound more like a company. It's a mental thing, but people in this business can be mental. I still do it, even though I don't have to anymore. It has become such an ingrained habit that I can't stop!

If you keep putting out the message that you're successful, you create the best conditions for insuring that you will be. If you conduct your company as a legitimate business and take yourself seriously, others will, too. It took a while, but eventually I earned serious respect. No one's going to give respect away, but it *can* be earned. Taking yourself seriously as a business is the foundation. One day you'll wake up and actually believe what you've been putting out to others!

HAVING HIGH STANDARDS

This is my personal opinion, so take it for what it's worth. I've always tried to live by the motto, "If you can't do it right, don't do it at all." It takes a lot to get taken seriously. Don't sabotage yourself by only living up to the expectations of those who expect little from a new indie label.

If you can't put your best foot forward, wait until you can. When I released Powerule's video, people were impressed with its quality and took more notice of Revenge Records. My reputation got stronger. Had I put out just an okay video, I'd have been lumped with the other okay labels. The video wouldn't have received the airplay it did. I was told small indies don't get videos played on MTV. I did—regularly!

"Doing it right" doesn't necessarily mean spending a fortune. It means paying attention to details and making sure it's done well. Find a student to do creative work in exchange for credit or a reference. There are many great young people who'd jump at a chance to design your packaging, if they take you seriously. Focus your resources in the most important directions, making sure obvious facets are done well. For example, I never chose the least expensive vinyl for my records. Many DJs commented that they were a very good quality. I saved money by putting my 12-inch singles in plain, cut-out jackets. The professional art-work on my labels came through. Don't cut corners with visible quality.

SUPPLIES

It's not necessary to spend a fortune on business supplies but, again, putting up a serious front will get you taken more seriously. I'll repeat myself: Conduct yourself as a serious business and you'll be one.

I recommend having professional-looking business cards. Nice ones enhance the image of your company. It's your calling card, and often creates the first impression someone has of you. Printing 1,000 standard black-and-white business cards for under $25 isn't hard, but they don't impress. When you present a card that stands out, that says, "I take my business seriously," it sets a positive tone for how people see your business.

When I started my label, I got nicely embossed cards with my logo, printed on cardstock in my label's color. Almost everyone I met said, "Nice card." Most added, "You're doing well, right?" It's ridiculous how they jump to conclusions from a business card, but they do. I'd see people later who didn't remember my name but remembered my nice blue card. Once I went to a big music seminar with a batch of business cards for Revenge Records with the skyline of Chicago across the top in color, which a friend gave me as a goof. I watched everyone go "oooh" and "aaah" at them. When I saw these people later on, they remembered my card with the gorgeous skyline of New York. No one paid enough attention to see that it wasn't New York. It made quite an impression.

With computers so accessible, stationery is easy to create. It's good to have paper with your letterhead on it. I originally cut and pasted my logo onto the top of a blank sheet of paper, adding my address and phone number below it, and used that as a master to photocopy when I needed to send a letter. Nowadays, a logo scanned into your or a friend's computer will do. I like using good paper. You probably won't write a lot of letters, especially at the beginning, but it's good to have a few sheets on hand.

One way to show you're running a serious business is to have invoices. Many indie labels don't bother with them, but it's more businesslike. I've heard people from indies ask for a piece of paper when a store requested a receipt for product they'd just paid for. You can get a box of invoices in a stationery supply store. If you don't want to pay to have your company name and address printed on them, have the information put on a good rubber stamp. If possible, get a stamp with your phone number, because it should be on the invoice. Invoices can also be designed and printed out from a computer. Or create one and make copies.

DEVELOPING THE RIGHT ATTITUDE

You may not have lots of money or contacts. But no matter how much or how little you think you have, you'll get further with a positive attitude. Without this mind-set, I doubt Revenge Records would have done as well as it did, no matter how good my records were. Because I was very friendly, people responded in kind. I helped others and others helped me. DJs, people in record stores, journalists, etc., offered support because they liked me. People prefer someone with a smiling face and a positive outlook over someone who is moody or has an attitude. Develop a good rapport with everyone. It'll serve you well and doesn't cost a thing. Be friendly and sincere and you'll attract good people.

I personally believe that having a spiritual attitude attracts better people and more satisfying success. I'd never have succeeded without faith. It enables you to hang onto your belief in your music and go the distance. It also helps you to not deal with negative people in a negative way. What goes around really does come back to you. If you treat folks with respect, many will return it. Richard Ellis, manager of Aron's Records in L.A. agrees. "I think that's why so many businesses don't work. People don't realize that once you screw somebody they're not likely to business with you again." If people screw you, it's THEIR problem, not yours! Focus on maintaining your integrity, no matter how others act. Be real. Ellis adds, "If you walk into the store with an attitude and give a bunch of bull, we see through that and won't want to do business with them. Don't bullshit people and always fulfill what you promise. Those things are valuable to me."

Don't sell yourself short. Sometimes when we're getting started, we allow folks to take advantage of us. We undercut prices and terms of payment because we're afraid people won't work with us. But that's not taking your business seriously. When someone wants your product, they'll work with you. Once you create a market for it, you'll be dealt with more favorably. If you allow distributors and stores to manipulate you now, a pattern can be set that's hard to change. There are folks who'll try to dick you around even when they want your product. But if you hold out for fair terms, those who recognize your potential will come around. If someone believes your record will sell, they're less likely to take advantage. Someone who claims they're "doing you a favor" by carrying your records on unfair terms may not sell them anyway.

Respect yourself. Don't think of yourself as just a new indie label struggling to survive. Don't be apologetic when approaching people. Confidence makes a great impression (firm handshakes everyone!). Don't let retailers and distributors take advantage of you. If you have a good record and a way to let folks know about it, it will find its way into stores. Don't grovel to get an order or a deal. If you believe in your product and let that belief show, others will get the message. By respecting yourself, others will too. Carry yourself as a viable business. Know your music is worthy of success. Holding your head up proudly will make people take a second look at your label. To earn respect in this business, give it to yourself first.

ROAD WARRIORS: SUCCESSFUL INDIE LABELS

Can an independent label really succeed? Yes! Yes! Yes! While it isn't easy, it's possible. In this chapter, I've profiled healthy and happy indie labels. Some have a roster of artists, while others market one independent artist. While they won't argue that having major label resources behind them would make their label stronger, they're still making money and love their independence. I've included this chapter to show by example the variety of motivations and directions for starting and running a record label. Let these labels motivate you! Interviewing them sure inspired me. While they have different stories, their common ground is passion for the music they market and joy in being independent.

ARTEMIS RECORDS: DANNY GOLDBERG, CHAIRMAN AND CEO

Danny Goldberg has an illustrious music industry history: he had gone from being a journalist to a publicist and then a personal manager. He says, "When I got to be 40 I took a job with Atlantic, and from then worked for big companies." Goldberg became president of Atlantic Records and went on to be chairman and CEO of both Warner Bros. Records and the Mercury Records Group. He says he began Artemis in 1999, when Michael Chambers had a vision to start a new label. "I thought it was a good atmosphere to start one. We both had the same idea. He had the money, and I had the background, supposedly, so we were able to do it together." Goldberg explains that he worked a niche with great potential:

> We've been able to get good artists. A record company is only as good as the sum of the records you put out. I think we had enough funding and a team of people that could attract really good artists at a time when certain artists just aren't served

by the majors. So I've been able to fill part of that niche. I think we have a ways to go before I get where I want to get to be a solid company. And I want to operate with a longer-term agenda than you have when you're going year to year. But I think we've had some good records . . . We can offer artists more than some of the smaller indie labels, and we'll pay attention to artists that wouldn't get attention at some of the bigger ones. We have a niche where we can do well with certain things.

It's working. *Billboard* named Artemis the #1 independent label in the U. S. based on actual sales in both 2000 and 2001. Goldberg credits his great marketing team for their progress. He also emphasizes that the best marketing won't make a difference without the "right" music: "The most important thing is to attract good artists who'll make good records." Artemis' eclectic roster includes recording artists with longevity, such as Warren Zevon, Rickie Lee Jones, and Josh Joplin, and many accomplishments: the Baha Men's "Who Let The Dogs Out" went triple platinum; Jimmie Vaughan won a 2002 Grammy for the Best Traditional Blues album; and the label has gold albums from heavy metal band Kittie and rapper Kurupt. And that's just a sample! Goldberg adds:

I'd say two-thirds of what we do now are artists that were dropped by major companies and have a sales base—Boston, The Pretenders—where we know there's a certain amount of sales. The ballpark is a sales base between 100,000 and a million. Over a million, the majors are not going to drop anybody. For us, under 100,000 is not as attractive, although there are a lot of exceptions. A lot of it is dealing with established artists who were available and analyzing their creativity and value as a partner in promoting a record . . . On the newer artist, we look if there's a following, some press, a producer who brings some marketing ability, radio stations that like them. In other words, we're risking a lot when we put out a record, not only the cash. The smallest cost these days is the recording or the advance to the artist. The biggest cost is the marketing, and a substantial cost is the cost of staff time. We look at all those business factors as a filtering device.

When I asked Goldberg how he likes having an indie label, he replied, "I try to feel good about whatever I'm doing. That's just a philosophy of life. I love what I'm doing now. I enjoyed what I was doing then. If you can be successful at an independent, it's a nicer life. But being unsuccessful as an independent is no fun." Earlier in his career, Goldberg experimented with other indie labels, so he knows. Now Goldberg has a team of veterans to keep his label thriving. He sees advantages in being independent:

> We have the ability to focus on fewer things and more incremental types of sales. The good side is the ability to really focus on every record, to get to know every artist. The company is a more holistic entity and personal experience for me and the people who work here.

EVERFINE RECORDS: DAVE ROBERGE, PRESIDENT

Everfine Records was created as a vehicle for the band O.A.R. Dave Roberge began working with the band in 1999 as a fan, doing anything that was needed. When venues didn't take O.A.R. seriously enough to book them, they'd rent the venue and sell their own tickets. O.A.R. were freshman in college and determined to graduate. Roberge booked around their schedules. He says, "We drew a three-hour radius around Columbus and picked the markets that we could develop." He placed O.A.R.'s product in and around markets where they played. Roberge helped build a street team that went to stores to educate them on O.A.R. He read books to learn the industry, and opened Everfine Records in 2000:

> We started the record label in order to give the band higher visibility. They were seeking an identity with regards to having a label. More or less, it came down to a higher level of presentation in terms of the packaging and things like that. When we first came up with the concept, it was [to create] the impression that the band had a record label. From that, the record label manifested into a much more real situation. Right after we went into the studio there was major label interest in the band. At the time, it didn't make sense to align ourselves with a major label. There was still a lot of growth and development that the band needed

to do—maturing as individuals at 20 years old, but also musically and professionally, being understanding and knowledgeable about the industry.

By then they'd moved about 35,000 units of the band's first self-released CD and 20,000 of their second. They sold out big venues with no radio single or video. While not ready to sign, they developed a solid relationship with Lava Records, which led to a meeting with Andy Allen, president of ADA distributors. They entered into a pressing and distribution deal with ADA in February 2001. Roberge says Everfine Records went from being a concept to a fully functioning label with marketing, promotion, publicity, sales, consumer and trade advertising. They were functioning like an eight or ten department record label, though still a one-man operation. Roberge says that determination pushed them:

> O.A.R. is a band that was constantly told, "You don't fit what the industry standard is." They use this to add fuel to the fire. Tell us we can't do it and we'll prove to you that we can. That's my mentality, too. I'm not afraid to take on challenges and think of new ways to approach situations. If you fail, you fail, but you learn from your mistakes. We tell people that for every positive thing that happens for us, there's three or four mistakes behind it that we learned from. We just don't tell anybody about it. You succeed by failing at first, and it shows how resilient you are.

Everfine Records' model is based on artist development. Roberge says, "Everfine Records, in my mind, is almost like a hybrid company in that it's a cross between an artist management company and a record label. We try to develop an infrastructure that could truly support a career development model." Music and fans come first. Roberge doesn't worry about quarterly expectations or investor pressure. Instead he focuses on building the band. He knows it can take six months or six years. Roberge would like Everfine Records to be a developmental label for a larger one. He's passionate about helping young talented artists grow:

> I like getting hands-on at the beginning to help develop things because you get to set the tone of what the future is going to

hold. Our vision for the record label is having an artist development focus with this band and a grassroots approach in terms of building it up with a micro-marketing strategy, focusing region by region with the band's touring. We're motivated and trying to create a good infrastructure so we can eventually take on other bands and try to take that artist development approach that is lost at many major labels and employ that region by region. I love the fact of being independent. What we want to do is create an identity for the label . . . [so] that people who pick up an Everfine Record will know it's good.

As this book went to press, Everfine Records had entered into a strategic partnership with Lava Records.

BAD DOG RECORDS: JONATHA BROOKE, OWNER/RECORDING ARTIST

Jonatha Brooke says she began Bad Dog Records in 1999 for survival. When MCA Records dropped her in the middle of a tour with sold out shows, she chose to keep going. Since MCA owned her masters, she needed a new recording. Rather than go back to the studio, she recorded her live shows, which she knew her fans would love. She put the record out herself to keep momentum going. Her manager, Patrick Rains, already had a label and shepherded her through the process.

Rains knew they could sell a certain amount because of her fan base of 75,000 people. He convinced her to be aggressive in marketing by spending the kind of money that relates to those numbers. They spent money to make a beautiful package. She learned as she went and had good people around her, and, she says, "I wasn't bullheaded about knowing more than anybody else and having to do it my particular way." They made a distribution deal with Koch since Rains had a relationship with them through his label PRA Records, and she had a substantial profile for an indie. First they hired a publicist. Brooke says:

It's a ton of money but it's the kind of thing that can be invaluable to keep my name out there and keep the level of profile that I had established. We hired a publicist to spin the going independent, bucking the trend kind of deal. With Steady Pull, we got some very high profile television, and I think the publicity raised the bar a little bit. People were aware of me, and we were able to get Letterman, Conan, and Greg Kilborn. We were in the pipeline.

Steady Pull was the second release on Bad Dog Records. Brooke says she's not averse to partnering with someone with deeper pockets at some point, but she'd never make a typical artist's deal again. She has to own her masters: "I won't ever put myself into the position of not being able to put my record out." As of the date of our interview, Bad Dog Records had moved about 150,000 records. Brooke has come to appreciate being independent:

> When you make the decision to go independent, you have to say, "Okay, will this be enough? I know I won't sell two million records unless lightning strikes and I win the lottery. Can I readjust my sense of success?" We both said yes. If we only sell 100,000 records in the next few years, that will be okay. We can break even and have a nice little go of it. You're brought up for so long believing that you have to get a major deal and it's the big brass ring. It's the only way you'll succeed, and you want to be a household word. You have to say, "Wait a minute, what's a career? And what is success in a career?" It was pretty sobering and great to have to realign my thinking and say, "Wait a minute; I am successful and have an amazing career, an amazing audience and fan base." It's totally worth it. I have an amazing life and career, and it's all on my own terms. I just know I'll win the lottery someday!

VICTORY RECORDS: TONY BRUMMEL, PRESIDENT

Tony Brummel says he was involved in the underground, punk scene from a young age. An avid record collector and in a band himself, he developed relationships with bands around the country. Brummel didn't see many labels assisting these artists in getting their records out. So as a "hobby," he released some records. He began with nothing—no friends or family in the industry, and no money. Brummel figured things out as he went along. He says he had no choice since he was in Chicago, with L.A. and New York being the hubs of the scene. Victory Records started with a 7-inch single and built up fast. Brummel says:

There was one record after another. The wheels were churning at that point. I was 18 years old when I started it. I had to learn bookkeeping, maintaining an accounts receivable, collecting, paying people on time, vendor relations, overall organization of a business, sales, marketing, promotion. Even layout and design. I did everything. Now I have 25 employees and interns as well.

Victory Records first distributed through mail order and by finding stores in each market that wanted underground rock. Brummel says they also traded records with other labels and sold them at shows. After a year, boutique distributors picked them up. Within three to four years they were dealing with larger underground ones. RED began distributing Victory in '96. That's when they began penetrating chain stores. Brummel is pleased with what he's done:

I have a company and job that I love. My hobby turned into my life. I have 25 employees that are either younger or who have kids, and artists that tour the world. That's a pretty rewarding thing to have started as a hobby—as a fan.

Brummel sees the record business as a nefarious one and believes changes are necessary in regard to how business is conducted and how artists are treated. He's hopeful that Victory provides an alternative for their artists. Victory Records grows every year as some similar labels see their market share and gross sales decrease. "In our own little world, we're doing something right." Brummel acknowledges that having a label isn't easy in today's market. Since they control everything, having a major behind him could take Victory to the next level. He's been courted by them all but hasn't found an offer that works for the label. But he'd consider one. Brummel sacrificed to get where he is, which helps him appreciate how sweet success is. He proves you can do it from scratch:

When I started Victory, that was my only source of income. I had the choice—do I buy a bed or desk? For two years, I slept in a sleeping bag under that desk. I never had outside investors and didn't come from a wealthy family. So I put the money the company was making back into the company to keep it going. I'm very happy I had to struggle that way because I think it helped solidify the foundation for the company, and we've kept growing every year since.

NEW WEST RECORDS: JAY WOODS, SENIOR VICE PRESIDENT AND GENERAL MANAGER

Cameron Strang (president) originally had a one-man operation for New West Records based in LA. Jay Woods, senior vice president and general manager was with Doolittle Records. Woods told me they brought the two companies together in '99 because they had similar philosophies about how an independent record label should be run. Strang stayed in L.A. and Woods stayed in Austin, Texas.

Woods says they built their business on a two-tiered philosophy. Developing artists was an essential part of their plan. But they also wanted to sign established artists at varying levels. New West Records is passion driven. They like signing acts whose music they appreciate. In Billy Joe Shaver's case, Woods and Strang were fans. They also recognized his great history as a songwriter and his performance career. They signed Delbert McClinton because he'd been touring for 35 years, had a gold record, and still toured 150 days a year. They're known as a roots-rock label with a little bit of country, but that wasn't planned. Woods says:

> New West established itself as real music for real people. There was never a plan to be an Americana or roots-rock label. We wanted to do music that we believed deserved to be out there: good quality stuff. Cameron and I are rockers from way back. We wanted to do what we knew best. I grew up in Texas, so there's some country in me. We want to do good, honest music and to have an environment where all of us here at the label, the staff and the artists, can make some money and love what they're doing.

Woods says that before signing an artist, they look at that artist's marketing potential. Since Delbert McClinton had a gold record, they weren't trying to win over a bunch of new fans. If they could sell 75,000-100,000 copies, he knew they could all make money, based on their marketing dollars. Strang worked a deal to be distributed through RED. Now they do about 12 projects a year. Woods predicts that could grow, but knows his limits for now. They prefer to devote deserved attention to each project. Woods radiated enthusiasm when we spoke:

I love being independent! It's wonderful. I really do believe I'm the luckiest guy in the world. That's corny and cliché. But think about it. I grew up in Lubbock, Texas. I'm in the music business. I live in Austin and get to do music that I love. It doesn't get any better than that. I'm truly passionate about what I do. I love to come to work. Everybody should be able to say that in their lives, but most can't. It's hard work, a battle everyday. I bitch and moan as much as the next guy. But it's rewarding at the same time.

DEFINITIVE JUX RECORDS: EL-P, CO-OWNER/RECORDING ARTIST

Hip-hop artist EL-P says he was kicked out of two high schools and had to make a choice. He did; he decided to take music seriously. He and his friends decided to press up a single and send it to radio DJs to try to get the exposure to attract a major label deal. When they realized the cost of putting eight songs out was essentially the same as the cost for putting out one, they made an EP. EL-P says, "We (Company Flow) threw the record out and all of a sudden word of mouth was strong on us through the hip-hop underground communities and colleges." 30,000 copies sold immediately. EL-P says, "It was not something that happened at all on that level. At the time (1996), there was no independent rap scene, at least not the way there is now." Artists performed in front of friends and people in clubs who liked what they were doing. Their success was contingent on planning every action and doing whatever they could to make it happen. He says:

Our plan was to put something out, use it as leverage to get a deal with somebody bigger than us to give us exposure; use that as leverage to bring something back into our company and not have to use them for exposure. We mapped it out. We were getting so much money because we put none into promotion. We were working at [a mail order place] and sending our records out through their mail order department overnight to the radio stations. We were loving it. We'd been involved in every step of the way, and all of a sudden people were handing us sums of money. Directly to us! No bullshit. For us at the time, it was like, 20 G's—we probably don't have to make a record again. That was how you look at it while you're young.

Because they were doing so well, they were able to leverage a deal with Rawkus Records to put out one record (for more on this, see Chapter 4). It elevated them to a recognizable level in the industry, which was their plan. Once their record sold large numbers, it was time for what EL-P calls phase three: "Move on. Take what you need at the time, respectfully, let everybody know up front what it's about, and take control of yourself again." He left Rawkus and started his own label. This time he had experience, a name, connections, and a serious amount of weight behind what he'd done to attract a good distribution deal. They went to Caroline Records, the distributor for their record on Rawkus.

When I interviewed EL-P, his current record had been out for about four months, and sales were already well over 50,000, which is considered good for an indie. He laughed when he added, "If I said that at a major label office I'd have my ankle broken by some thug they keep in the closet. 50,000 records for us is great." EL-P knows that major labels need high six-figure sales to even crack a smile. All the artists on Def Jux are selling at least large five figures. He added, "We're making a living, a killing actually!" EL-P's plan is working. He's had many label deal offers but chooses to remain independent:

> I can't help but do it myself. I'm a controlling freak, and don't want to convince someone else to believe in me, or the people I believe in. I don't want to walk into an office and talk to someone who knows less than me about music and try to explain my vision, holding my breath, hoping that he relays that vision to whoever he has to relay it to in order to cut a check and support what we're trying to do. I love it. I'm proud of it . . . It's a lifestyle thing for me—I know that I feel better, stronger as a grown man, knowing that whatever is coming to all of my friends and everyone working for me and with me is *ours,* truly. We've gone the right way, with the right intentions.

RICH HARDESTY

Rich Hardesty earns a six-figure income by working his original music in the college market. He was finishing his eighth CD when I spoke to him. While studying business at a college in Indiana, he'd get his guitar out and entertain people. Hardesty wrote a song called "Never Wanna to F'n See You Again." Everybody in the dorm requested it, and he played that trademark song at open mic nights. He decided to try making money from his music, and began by performing acoustically in bars. Hardesty says, "It seemed too good to be true. I thought I was supposed to go out into the real world. I didn't know how long it would last but I had to do it. I had no idea that ten years later I'd still be doing it."

Bars gave Hardesty the cover money. Since he was popular, they gave him a lot. He figured if he performed three nights a week, he could work less and make more than he could at a real job. Fraternities called Hardesty to play at parties. He used his college education to structure his business and recorded live shows to pass around. People made copies. He learned that when they heard a live show on tape, they'd want more and come to see him. Word about him spread. Hardesty pressed his first CD for pleasure:

> Having a CD was all I wanted. I had no idea I'd keep recording and make money from them. I wanted to have my name on a CD—*my* CD. I was going to be the business dude. All of a sudden I had a CD I was proud of. That was more of a success to me in my heart.

People lined up to hear Hardesty play his trademark song. That song was a vehicle to invite people to shows and to sell his first CD. Hardesty realized what a large profit margin he had from selling CDs direct, and his business education took over. So far he's sold over 50,000 CDs with *no* distribution. He runs his business in-house, crediting his parents' support in handling mail orders and accounting. His most successful marketing tool has been encouraging people to steal his music and pass it around. He says, "I let people know that I write songs and like it when they steal them because it's a great way to get music out." That creates a bigger buzz. Hardesty is happy with what he's created:

> I want to make money—this is my business. I do everything now. I look at being with a larger label as a way to get extra help in promoting and marketing, if it's the right deal. There's so much involved it drains me. You have to be business oriented to succeed in selling albums. I don't want to just be an artist sitting under a tree writing songs. If you want this to be your full-time job, then you have to do business. People ask why I'm

not with a record label, as if that would be the greatest thing. They don't understand: I am my own record label.

REDEMPTION RECORDS: RYAN KUPER, OWNER

When Ryan Kuper felt his performing days were waning, he decided he still wanted to stay involved in the music he loved. After graduating from high school, he used his graduation money to start Redemption Records in 1990. His former band had put out a small vinyl record with a label, and he'd questioned them about how they did it. Armed with knowledge, Kuper advertised that he was accepting demos. After signing a band from Austin, Texas, he found one from New Jersey he thought was extremely good and quickly signed them. He continued signing bands, and it grew from there. Kuper made money from his first record:

> I put out a good band with a niche and knew how to exploit that scene. I continued making money until '95—the first time I took some big financial risks and had financial losses. I had to struggle. But because I took the risks, I got the most notoriety for the label and interest from other companies.

Kuper says he tried marketing pop records, but that required hiring promoters, spending a lot more money on radio, and bigger manufacturing numbers than punk and indie rock. Running the label became more expensive. He says, "It's no secret that a lot of radio is still about payola, and trying to compete with that as a smaller company was an eye-opening experience for me as far as the finances of a label that size. I got radio play because of the overall marketing and money I spent behind the band." He felt it wasn't a bad deal since it got attention for the label. Otherwise, Kuper says he is solely responsible for running Redemption:

> My staff is me. I have a sales team from my distributor and a publicist I hire. I have a designer I use for everything. As far as people that receive payroll from Redemption Records, you're talking to him!

Kuper already has sub-labels. He recently retooled to re-establish what he considers the Redemption sound. He wants to re-carve a niche for himself, a progressive indie-rock sound like he did with his first records, and be a solid development label for that scene. Kuper has talked to substantial companies about co-funding projects with Redemption and developing a few bands together. While he likes the idea of reaping the benefits of larger distribution, in-house salespeople, and in-house marketing, he says has to be in charge: "If I work with a major label, I'm not going to compromise on the artistic direction of the bands, how they're marketed, and I'd keep them free of the offensive corporate marketing that turns away so many die-hard fans." If the right relationship can be struck he'd definitely do it. Meanwhile Kuper loves being independent:

> It's an empowering feeling. It is an us-against-them mentality. A lot of people perceive indies as giant competitors. I pretty much reach out and ask advice and offer it to other indie labels. It's an interesting brother and sisterhood out there. I really appreciate being part of that because you don't get that same love at the major-label level. There's a credibility that will be there that will never be with major labels. I like being part of that.

FESTIVAL FIVE RECORDS: DAN ZANES, RECORDING ARTIST/OWNER

Dan Zanes began his career as a member of the band the Del Fuegos, who were signed to several majors throughout the '80s. When his daughter was born, he searched record stores for updated versions of music he grew up with, music with a homemade folk sound reflecting the times. Unhappy with what he found, he recorded his own versions of old songs and made 300 cassettes to give to enthusiastic neighborhood kids. Zanes says, "I wanted to make music that everyone could enjoy together."

Someone passed a cassette to a record company. They asked Zanes if he wanted to put it out. He says he had already made five records, owned no masters, and got very little. He passed because "I knew I had something good. I felt protective of it." Someone suggested starting a label. Zanes began Festival Five Records in 1999. His packaging helped. He didn't like what he'd seen for other records. His daughter liked something to look at when she got a CD. Zanes didn't like jewel boxes because of their environmental issues and because they break easily. He decided to package his music as a book with a sleeve in it, using recycled paper. People in manufacturing thought he was crazy. But Zanes was determined:

> I found . . . a printer who did books and a place that manufactures CDs. We came up with a design for our board book. It's full-color, 16 pages, and recycled paper. Many stores looked at the packaging and bought it without even listening to it. I'm so proud of it! There are no song lyrics. People go on-line for that. It's a better use of space if I put artwork in with text.

Zanes did everything himself at first. He took industry people to dinner and picked their brains for marketing strategies and contacts. He approached every store he found that carried kids' products, convincing most to carry his CD. He set up shows in schools and other kids' venues. Word spread among parents, and his performances were packed. Zanes worked the press and a *New York Times Magazine* article put him on the map. MRI distributes Festival Five through the Ryko/WEA system. He got the contact by networking. Ryko handles special sales, so he's getting into museum shops and other non-traditional outlets that make sense for his music. He also sells on CDBaby. As of this interview, he'd just released his third CD. Zanes says he's very happy being independent:

> I've spoken to all the kids' labels by now. When I say I'd like to license and retain ownership of my masters, conversations come to a screeching halt. Someone I know at a major discussed licensing my label through their machinery. It seemed like an exciting possibility. But once it got into business affairs, my stomach started hurting and I had trouble sleeping. Things that were clear in conversations were suddenly retracted. I couldn't have been happier to walk away from them and had a renewed appreciation for my situation. Slow and steady is right for me. As it grows, I learn. I never wanted to know anything about the business part before. I heard that Richard Foos from Rhino Records said he was able to understand every aspect of how the business worked because he did it all himself,. That's my case.

MC RECORDS: MARK CARPENTIERI, PRESIDENT / OWNER

Mark Carpentieri got his first taste of having a record label in the early '90s when his band put out a CD. He says it was reviewed in blues magazines and people liked it. Two years later, Carpentieri was doing management work and found an artist who was a good fit to work with. The first release on MC Records with a signed artist was released in '96. He credits the Association For Independent Music (AFIM) (called NAIRD at that time) for showing him the ropes. Carpentieri says:

> We went to their convention for two years before starting our label. We had the opportunity to meet with other blues labels, see the scene and what distributors were looking for. I was running a management company. We were organized and had a good expectation of what things were. But it's all great in theory until you release the record. For our first national release, we were well organized.

MC Records began with an artist who had a national but not huge following from another label. Carpentieri saw their need for something fresh after releasing many records. The artist wanted a label that would put new energy behind the record. Carpentieri says, "They thought even though we'd never released a record, I had done publicity work and management, so I was familiar with how things work." He had the business acumen and passion for music that leads to success. That's why he likes doing it on his own, he says:

> You can basically record what you think is good. You're not having to go through 50 million channels, and you have more flexibility to adjust to the market as you see fit, compared to bigger labels that have to go through leaps and bounds just to do the slightest change in their business practices.

Carpentieri used the lessons from when he released his own record to get airplay. He learned as much as possible by going to conferences and networking. MC Records got distribution through contacts made at AFIM and went on to get several Grammy nominations. Carpentieri finds tremendous satisfaction in that:

> Having an artist nominated for a Grammy is one of the best feelings. Our first nomination was in 1999 with Odetta. It was her first nomination in 50 years in the business. I told her when we made her CD that we would do everything possible to get her

a nomination. When that actually happened, it made me feel great that I did this for Odetta and that a record on my label could be honored by a nomination. Getting the second nomination was a confirmation of the path that we are on. This was also Kim Wilson's first solo nomination.

GROOVELILY: VALERIE VIGODA

GrooveLily has earned a living from their music since 1995. Lead singer/electric violinist Valerie Vigoda took her passion for classical music and decided to do something different. In 1994, the seven-piece Valerie Vigoda Band played locally in New York City. They were invited to be house band for an American comedy theater in Amsterdam in the summer of 1995. GrooveLily pared down to a unique portable trio: electric violin, keyboards, and drums. Vigoda says:

> It was the first time we had made a living solely from playing our original music. We realized that this was something we could really do and potentially make a living at, and that was very empowering. When we got back to New York in the fall of 1995, we knew we wanted to keep performing as much as possible, so we started looking for a booking agent.

That summer was a pivotal time for the band. Someone brought a college booking agent to see them, and they got signed. GrooveLily kept going. They began putting out their own CDs in order to sell them, book shows, and get reviews and radio play. A strong fan base developed, and now they have a street team called Petal Pushers working for them. GrooveLily has released three CDs and is earning a living from performing and from selling CDs and other merchandise. While she'd like help with her business, Vigoda is prepared to stay independent unless she gets offered the right deal:

> We're not inherently opposed to a record deal, if it were the right one. It would take someone who shares our vision of GrooveLily, someone who could take us to a significantly higher level of visibility and income. We're getting to the point now where it's rather overwhelming to be running all aspects of our business ourselves; each of us has way too much to do, and though we do have booking agents, a publicist, and a very active, fast-growing

street team called "Petal Pushers," there are many things that a good label could help us with, both financially and administratively. We wouldn't necessarily be interested only in a *huge* label, just a *good,* committed one with integrity, smarts, and a decent number of promotional dollars.

DAVID M. BAILEY

David M. Bailey played music throughout college, but put his guitar away to pursue a corporate career. On July 4, 1996, doctors told him he had a malignant brain tumor and would be dead by Christmas. Bailey says he turned to music as a healing process. He left his job and pursued his passion for songwriting. Eight albums later (as of this printing), Bailey, his songs, and passion are alive and well. His growing collection of CDs supports his solo career.

Bailey had no idea what he was doing when he released his first album in 1997 and learned the hard way, which he says is good. "You don't forget it when you learn it that way." Now he's determined to help others with his music. His songs tell stories of healing. Bailey inspires people not to give up on obstacles. People in his audience share and become part of his lyrics. Music has been his source of healing, but also a vehicle to give hope to others.

Bailey found a niche for himself in places with built-in audiences, such as churches, conferences, and colleges. He sells large numbers of CDs after each performance and on his website. Bailey tours full-time and continues releasing CDs. He's been featured on *CBS News, 48 Hours, 60 Minutes,* and much more. He's received many songwriting awards and accolades. Yet he's happiest when he's sharing music. I asked Bailey if the promotion and clout of being on a large label was worth giving up control of what you say and how you say it. NO!!! He's doing well, and plans to stay independent:

> There was a time when I thought getting a major record label deal was the pinnacle. Individuals who've been a part of it changed my mind. An artist friend signed to a subsidiary of a major got $12,000 up front and had to pay that back through sales. Then they made 60 cents a record, and that was good. I couldn't imagine after the time and expense of making a CD, walking away with just 60 cents per sale. But my things are going really, really well. I have more work than I can do. I'm working on my eighth album.

start & run your own record label

SADDLE CREEK RECORDS: ROBB NANSEL, OWNER

Saddle Creek Records started in '96 when Robb Nansel took over Lumberjack Records and changed the name. It began with friends who grew up together and played in bands. Rather than continue trying to get industry attention, they did it themselves, with guidance from friends who'd already done it. Nansel says the bands spend years touring and creating word-of-mouth buzz. Everyone works together to advance the label, and they keep it casual. He says:

> We don't have an A&R division and nobody looks for acts. We do what we want to do, how we want to do them. We know the bands well—exactly how they want their music marketed. When you work with a larger company, they would want to market the record in ways to sell it. Our bands aren't as concerned with selling it as they are with making sure that it is presented properly. 95 percent of what we put out is still with people we grew up with.

In May 2000, Saddle Creek did an exclusive distribution deal with Southern. Nansel says, "They liked how we handled ourselves and saw our potential. We let them handle it all so we don't have to worry about it. They keep track of accounts and pay us monthly. We just send the stuff to them." As bands gained popularity, Nansel says the label had to get more structured. But they avoid the majors because Saddle Creek is artist oriented and focused on the music:

> We've been offered deals for a while. I think that majors can do good things, given the right situations. But at this point, we're still putting out a lot of records that don't need that type of push. I think it would benefit some of our artists and would sell more records. But I don't know if the end result would be a positive thing. Acts that sell more records would probably benefit more than the smaller ones—the acts we put out because we like the records and they don't have a huge audience. Those records would get lost.

Nansel says they're growing. For a long time he did everything. Now they have four people on staff. They've discussed what they'd do if a

56

major label gave them lots of money, but they couldn't think of anything important. Nansel says they all work like mad and don't get paid well, but they're happy being independent:

> Music keeps most of us going. We get to come into a job we like. We get to work on music that we really love. We don't have to answer to anybody, and we don't have to do anything that we don't want to do. So it's great. We get to meet a lot of bands, hang out, and go to shows. That makes the music fun.

COMMUSE: ONNO LAKEMAN OF RED TO VIOLET

Commuse is the label created by Red to Violet, a duo (Onno Lakeman and EL) based in Holland. Their CD gets a lot of radio play and other coverage in the U.S. They got tired of killing time dealing with band politics and decided to a create a duo. After trying to get a distribution/promotion deal by sending material to a few labels, they were disgusted by the run-around they received. Lakeman says, "Having written the songs and done the recordings with so much love and dedication, we wanted something better than this." So he searched the web, discovered there's a lot you can do for yourself as an indie, and proceeded to do it.

Lakeman and EL wanted a complete package, so they made a video, too. They hooked up with CDbaby, CDstreet, and other webstores to sell their CDs and worked with an independent distributor to make the CD available at CDnow, Amazon, and some real stores. Lakeman contacted smaller radio, public radio, and web radio stations and was well received. Their track "Here I Am" got play on over 200 smaller U.S. radio stations, and their video was broadcast on public and cable TV shows all over the U.S. It won the Viewers' Choice on the largest cable TV network. Their CD's are now manufactured in the U.S.

At first, Lakeman spent most waking hours searching the Internet for resources—and working them. This small Dutch label gets exposure that eludes a large majority of start-up American ones. Using the Internet as his vehicle, Lakeman cruised the world and found outlets for his music. He says mistakes taught him to take one step at a time. He's relentless in finding ways to market the Red to Violet CD. His website is very active. Reviews are posted. Lakeman is focused on letting the world know about Red to Violet:

Richie Sambora said: "You can't polish bullshit." So you need talent and good material to start with. From there you need a good mental attitude. We've worked on mental strength as much as we did on our musical skills. You need this mental strength to be able to cope with the road going up and down. Persistence is very important too. People around me say I have that. I believe the impossible can become possible.

TROUT RECORDS: TROUT FISHING IN AMERICA

Trout Records is the label for the duo Trout Fishing in America—Keith Grimwood and Ezra Idlet. They began in the late '70s. In 1980, they pressed cassettes and vinyl to sell off the stage. Dick Renko, manager for Trout Records for over 15 years, says, "We were in the first wave of the DIY releases." They released their first CD in 1990. Idlet adds, "The main thing for us at first was developing a mailing list. When we played other cities, we brought our mailing list. When we'd go back there'd be a crowd. When we release a record there's an audience ready to buy." Trout Fishing also does kid's music. Grimwood adds "A lot of times you're not supposed to do that . . . This offers us the flexibility of playing different styles of music that we might not have with a record company." They alternate adult and kid releases. Renko likes their approach:

> It's still an in-house operation. Ezra's wife runs the label. I do management and booking. Because we're small, we've felt we have to be cautious in the development of Trout Fishing in America and the label Trout Records. We've been able to keep this tight and to make the agenda our own to serve the children's outlet and stay on course with their folk pop music as well.

Idlet is 6'9"; Grimwood is 5'5", which attracts attention. They've developed loyal fans across the country and overseas. Grimwood says, "Instead of focusing on getting signed, we focused on the music." About seven or eight years ago, they began selling more through distributors. Trout Fishing in America has expanded their playing to the performing arts area, festivals, and private functions. They work the Folk Alliance conference annually and have a broad appeal, opening for acts such as Richie Havens and Bob Dylan.

Trout Records has had interest from record labels. Renko says, "There's a chance we'd take a deal if all the elements were attractive enough." They've grown into a viable label, approaching 300,000 in sales with a Grammy nomination under their belt. Idlet enjoys what they've done. "I've always liked to do things independently—against the grain. I was a bad student in school. The idea of doing something on your own really appeals to me." Grimwood has a different opinion:

> I thought that you were supposed to sign with a record label. Doing it this way has been the most surprising thing I have ever done in my life. I'm not this kind of person. I travel by normal channels. I am very proud of the fact that we're independent.

FINANCING YOUR BUSINESS

One of the hardest questions to answer about starting a record label is "Where do you get financing?" There are no easy answers. Depending on your circumstances, background, and the strength of your business plan, financial backing is hard to come by. With so many people starting labels, people are wary of whom they invest with. Financing may be the hardest part for many of you. If you develop a great business plan, create a huge story for your artist(s), and implement an impressive marketing plan, people may take you more seriously.

GETTING MONEY FROM OUTSIDE SOURCES

Many of you will finance your label out of your own pockets like I did. I liked not answering to anyone. Many investors expect at least a say, if not active involvement, in your label, so be prepared for that if you get outside financing.

Banks are hesitant to loan money for start-up labels. If you get a loan, you'll need to put up collateral. Do you own something of value that can be taken from you if you don't pay back what you've borrowed? Unless you have a successful track record in the record business, I've been advised that a personal bank loan is easier to get than a business loan. Ryan Kuper (Redemption Records) advises that another type of bank loan is a line of credit. He says, "While it does take collateral like a lump-sum bank loan, you can pull from it to meet the needs of your company. However, there will be a monthly interest fee to cover." If you hope to get a large loan eventually, get your business started first and apply when you can show serious sales. Have a strong business plan.

Many people find private investors. Let's face it, the music industry is an exciting place, so it can appeal to folks with money to spare. By investing with a smart music person, they get a taste of the industry. I've heard of an amazing variety of types who invested in record labels. Some do it as a tax write-off. Some just want to get repaid with interest. Some want a percentage of profits. Some want involvement in what goes on with the label, which makes them the biggest pains in the butt if they don't understand the music industry.

Where do you find investors? There's no one place. People put ads in local papers or business journals. Be vigilant. Talk about your plans to everyone. You never know who may want to get involved. Someone may love your music and want to help get it out. The best kind of investor is one who gives you what's referred to as "angel capital." Ryan Kuper says, "It is funding that does not come with a heavy hand of interference, from someone who is willing to fund—like an angel—trusting you are doing the right thing." Love those angels! People laugh when I tell them to look for rich people who aren't connected to the industry for money. Rich people might get a kick out of being part of it or having a share in music that they like. The amount of money needed might be small change to them. Announce that you're looking for investors at gigs. Talk. Talk. Talk. Someone unexpected might bite. Be prepared with a business plan and an exciting pitch. Wait until you're ready.

Be careful about signing with an investor. Use a lawyer to structure the agreement so you maintain control. No matter who invests, have everything in writing. Spell out exactly what the investor is putting into your company, and what they'll get in return, and when. Even if a friend invests, sign a formal agreement. You can't be too careful when it comes to money. Have a lawyer look over anything you sign, no matter how straightforward it seems.

AFFILIATING WITH A LARGER LABEL

How do you hook up with a larger label? Folks with track records have it easier. Industry relationships help. If you have major success with an act, you may be able to get taken seriously by a label. But if no one's heard of you, doors won't open easily. You may have to kick them down with independent success. It may take several successful records or acts before anyone pays attention to you.

Nobody will give a deal to someone without proven success or an act that's very hot. Labels need to recognize the benefit in working with you. They want to see your artist in magazines and playing live to a full house. Most importantly, they want to see impressive record sales. Large numbers have the most impact. If a larger label knows you've sold many on your own, they can visualize the potential of the record with their clout behind it.

Concentrate on getting as big a buzz on your record as possible before looking to a larger label for support. The more you have to offer a label, the greater your chances of hooking up with one. EL-P (Definitive Jux Records) says success can put you in the driver's seat:

> Because a lot of record labels were knocking on our door, we arrogantly designed our own contract. I said I want 50 percent of everything, complete ownership of my masters, 100 percent creative control, and I'll sign a deal for one album. We held it out in front of us like the arc of the covenant. All the infidels fell and burned away. At the end of the day, Rawkus Records were the ones standing. Once my deal was done with them, it had brought us, and Rawkus, to a pretty recognizable level in the industry.

Large labels pick up successful indies to find artists and develop them. Gregg Latterman (Aware Records) got a joint venture with Columbia Records because he'd shown he could find and market good artists. He says, "They came to me. We broke Train, 5 for Fighting, John Mayer, and a bunch of new ones. I own our company, and we jointly own the stuff we do together. I think that's the best of both worlds." Major labels like indies that have shown successful grassroots marketing and that have a proven sales base. Brian Sirgutz, president of Elementree Records, Korn's label [started with their management company, The Firm], says Elementree was created with the concept that Korn could incubate other bands. According to Sirgutz, they do A&R and use the major's resources:

> We find different acts that we can work within a major label system. They handle Elementree's promotion, marketing, publicity, and distribution. We work alongside each other to do what's for the artist's interests as well as the record label's. We're a team, a joint venture. This is how Korn can help other artists. We work with the major label more on a grassroots basis, using marketing techniques that people may not have thought of. We're able to take risks that other labels cannot take because it's an artist-run label. A major label might say whoa, but we work within the major label system to do that.

Should you strive to hook up with a larger label? Many indies said they'd take a deal *if* the right one were offered. Yet they're still flying solo. It's better to work from the inside out—develop your company first so that you have more say in the terms of any deal with a larger label. Tony Brummel (Victory Records) is staying open to taking advantage of major label resources:

> We've been approached by everybody, multiple times. The right scenario hasn't been presented. Three years ago I'd have said there's no way we'd do that. But the way things are going, for our artists and from a realistic standpoint, there's only so much you can do unless you're part of that system. Multi-national corporations control this industry. You can't get past it. It's the same thing with getting your songs on the radio. We've had nominal success with certain artists at commercial radio, but we can't get past the tollbooth. We've done decent with several artists but not to where we have a full-blown hit. Look at the play lists—major label content. Indies can't pay the price. And indies don't have the relationships because they're not spending millions of dollars a year with the independent consultants.

The Music Business Registry (800-377-7411; www.musicregistry.com) has directories available if you want to approach labels. Their *A&R Registry* is updated every eight weeks with A&R people at most major and independent labels, including those in the U.K., with direct phone/fax numbers, e-mail addresses, and assistants' names. Pollstar (800-344-7383;www.pollstar.com) has *Record Company Rosters* which lists the entire staff of many record labels.

Nowadays larger labels aren't offering as many P&D deals. They prefer deals in which they own equity in the company. Below are common ways indies hook up with larger labels. I say "larger labels" rather than "majors" because you might want to go with a strong independent that has good distribution.

P&D (PRESSING & DISTRIBUTION) DEALS

A P&D deal means the larger label presses records and distributes them. An indie label's responsibility is to sign the artist, produce their music, design and prepare the cover artwork, and deliver the finished master and artwork to the P&D company. The P&D company manufactures the records and gets them distributed through their distribution system. The indie label is responsible for all marketing, promotion, videos, advertising, and publicity. The P&D company deducts manufacturing costs and a fee for distribution from record sales. The indie label gets what's left, except for money that's held on reserve against returns. That's a basic P&D deal.

John Luneau, head of business affairs at Palm Pictures, says that nowadays record companies are wary of doing P&D deals. They don't want to get stuck with huge returns and try to collect from a small label, which may be out of business. The larger label must be convinced the indie has the knowledge, money, and staff to market a record nationally. Without a hit record, it's unlikely anyone would want to distribute a label with no proven ability to market and promote. After all, why get records into stores in Iowa or Oklahoma if an indie located in New York can't promote nationally? Luneau adds:

> Companies only want to get involved with a small label if they believe that label is going to be savvy and make money. And be around in two years. Ideally, they should have a track record of being in the business before and having successful records under their belt—records that consistently sell what they project . . . If you're the smaller label, you should only consider this if you are a full—fledged label, with a marketing, a radio, and an A&R department, and a royalty department, because you'll be responsible for paying royalties to the artists and to the publishers.

The P&D company administers the deal and sends the indie regular written statements. The indie has a right to audit the books. While the deal is with a label that administers it, the distributor for the larger label gets records into stores. For example, if you had a deal with Atlantic Records, Atlantic would administer it but the distribution itself would be handled by Atlantic's distributor, WEA, which is a separate entity. They each make money on the deal. John Luneau says:

> The label that does the deal with the smaller label might charge them a percentage that would more than compensate them for what their distributor charges them. The average the larger label would take is 20-25 percent of gross receipts (based on wholesale price paid by record stores). The distributor's portion comes out of that. It might be more, depending on what the distributor charges the larger label.

Sometimes a P&D company will give the indie an advance on distribution to offset production costs, to make a video, for promotion, etc. John Luneau says, "If you're a successful smaller label, the larger label may seek ways of participating with you on a bigger basis, such as advancing money to you for marketing a record." This amount is then deducted from the indie's earnings and the deduction is shown on the next statement of those earnings. If the indie's act is hot, there's more bargaining leverage. Sometimes the P&D company provides a budget for various forms of promotion because it feels the indie has a better grip on where best to use the money. It depends on how badly the larger label wants the deal. Luneau warns they may want a share of the profit in return.

Sometimes larger labels just distribute indie product, without doing pressing. In this case, the indie handles all the manufacturing, and the larger label just gets the record out through its distribution system. In such arrangements, most of the terms are similar to those of a P&D deal, except there are no manufacturing costs involved.

JOINT VENTURE DEALS

Joint venture/equity deals have become more popular. Whereas in a P&D deal, the larger label gets a set fee per record sold, a joint venture deal involves the larger label sharing the profits. The label offering a joint venture pays all operating costs and usually handles promotion, videos, etc. Then it deducts all costs and a small percentage for overhead (to cover administration costs, etc.). A percentage is taken by the joint venture label's distributor, and the indie and larger label split what's left over, according to their agreement.

A joint venture deal is usually not structured as a partnership, in the legal sense of the word. One party isn't legally responsible for the other's obligations. In a partnership, the partners share in everything. In a joint venture agreement, when money is collected for the sale of records, all expenses are taken out first. Then the joint venture company and the independent label split what's left. This arrangement might not be the best one for you at the beginning. Since all operating costs are deducted from the top, you could stand to make less money in a joint venture if the record doesn't sell well.

In order to get a joint venture deal, you need something serious going for your label. It's unlikely for someone not known in the industry to convince people at a large label to invest in his or her dreams, however good they sound. Labels do joint ventures to take advantage of the talent, know-how, and street savvy of someone they know to have strong potential. But you'll have to prove yourself before a label will want to work with you on any level.

PRODUCTION DEALS

If you're starting a label with little or no experience, it may be easier to attract a production type of deal. They help establish a label without the expense and responsibility of marketing on a national level. Unless you have extensive industry experience, a sizable budget, and contacts, a production deal can provide knowledge of the business. According to Larry Rudolph, Esq., of Rudolph & Beer, an entertainment law firm in New York City:

> Something that some people miss completely when trying to get into the record business is . . . just making a great record and having a distribution deal doesn't mean that the public is going to ever become aware of the record and know to buy it in a record store. You have to create a market for it. Unless you can handle the marketing, promotion, and imaging of the artist, and everything that goes with promoting and creating public awareness of the artist, you're in much better shape getting your feet wet with a production type of agreement.

In a production deal, you as the label act as middleman between the artist and the larger label. You discover and develop talent. The artist remains signed to your label. It's a great arrangement if your main love is developing talent. Most commonly, an agreement between you and the larger label is structured similar to an artist/label deal. In a production deal, you get a recording budget, and royalty points (see Chapter 6) on the sale of records. Depending on your artist agreement, any money earned is usually split. You may be able to deduct certain expenses. You're responsible for getting a finished recording to the larger label. Most of the time, you set a recording budget based on what the larger label allows, and try to be prudent about spending it all. Whatever's left over is considered an advance, which the artist gets a portion of.

Production deals vary, depending on how much the larger labels want your artist. Once the recording is done, the larger label is responsible for almost everything else: pressing, marketing, distribution, videos, etc. You're free to do extra promotion since it ultimately helps you. But the responsibility is off. The record comes out on the larger label, with credit given to yours. If it sells and the costs are recouped, you get paid royalties.

THE NUTS & BOLTS OF KEEPING YOUR LABEL SOLVENT

Nuts and bolts hold things together. In this chapter, I'll share specific business functions, mindsets, and tools that can help keep your label solid. I'm presenting these here so you can keep them in mind as you plan your label. I'll provide *many* more details on marketing later, but here are some nuts and bolts for creating the strongest foundation for your label.

LEARN DA BIZ

The greatest obstacle to discovery is not ignorance — it is the illusion of knowledge.—Daniel Boorstin

Many people moan that they don't understand why their CDs aren't making money. They KNOW their music is perfect and KNOW how to market it. You can't tell them anything because they're *soooooo* brilliant. Excuses for why they haven't succeeded often have as many holes as their education. They've half-listened at seminars and to other advice and think it's enough. Don't let your ego hold you back! You don't know it all. Avoid the "I know what I'm doing on my own" trap.

There are loads of books on every business topic, so there's no excuse for not filling the holes in your knowledge. Peruse libraries and bookstores. Take adult education classes or pay for a consultation with someone who can explain everything until you understand. Ask all your "dumb questions." You'd be surprised how many people have the same ones. Being ignorant about business is normal. Not taking advantage of opportunities to learn is what's dumb! According to Cliff Chenfeld, co-president/co-founder of Razor & Tie Music:

Running an independent label is running a business. It's not just hanging out with some new music. There are bills to pay, employees to be responsible for . . . How you run your business is more important than the music you put out. You have to be really responsible and prepared to do that. If you're not willing to do that, you're not going to be able to adequately support the label, and ultimately it's gonna fail.

Dave Roberge (Everfine Records) always advises bands to learn and understand this business so they can develop realistic expectations about how much they have to work for success. The guys in the band O.A.R. educated themselves while surrounding themselves with a good team. Roberge says that while their team focuses on the business side to allow the band to focus on the creative side, they know everything about what goes on in the business because they handled things themselves first. They learned because they understood how important it was for their careers. Roberge himself did everything he could to learn as much as possible:

I had to learn a lot to be a responsible business owner and manager. You have to treat your employees well. So it was everything from applying basic HR principles to the company to developing a company handbook, to accounting and financing, to tax liability to eventual payroll, royalty payments, and spreadsheet maintenance. There's a totally unglamorous side of what we do. A lot of it is administrative in terms of number crunching, data crunching, and creating systems where we can share information internally. The accounting and finance was probably the most difficult aspect. Although I had a background as a business major, I'm not a CPA or a qualified business manager. So I learned those functions to the best of my ability until it outgrew me. You get to that breaking point and then hire a third party.

Jesse Fergusson, product manager for Definitive Jux Records, advises those wanting to start a label to take basic accounting. Even if you get an accountant, understand the process. Or, get someone to teach you. Dan Zanes (Festival Five Records) found mentors: "My process has been to find the best possible people I can that are interested in what

I do to give me advice." For example, one person showed him how to fill out an invoice slip. He'd take someone to dinner and pick that person's brain. Try to find a mentor. Don't pester that person, but ask if you can call occasionally with a question. Many people like giving advice. If you're friendly, someone may say yes. Tap into the Small Business Adminstration resources for general stuff. Find a way to learn. If you understand the biz, you'll make wiser decisions, save money, and have the best shot at success.

RECORD LABEL COOPERATIVES

Cooperative relationships between indies are becoming popular. Since there's strength in numbers, musicians are joining together to share resources. Some of the labels I profiled have a cooperative relationship with their artists, splitting profits fifty-fifty after expenses are paid. Their artists put more into their own marketing. Arrangements vary. Michael Hausman, recording artist Aimee Mann's manager and managing director of United Musicians, explains:

> When I founded Aimee's company, there were lots of things about the [record] business that are set up for labels that have multiple artists and multiple releases per year, like distribution, hiring staff. It helps to have more than one record. I thought that there were more artists in Aimee Mann's situation, who wanted their own label but didn't necessarily want to hire a full staff, have an office, and all the infrastructure, contracts, etc. to facilitate it. I thought, why don't we start something that helps artists have their own label? It's been building ever since. United Musicians is a distribution, marketing, and promotion co-op for artist-owned labels. We're not looking for new artists—they come through friends and family—only established ones that have the ability to produce their own records, tour, do publicity. They have their own label and we pick up whatever activities they're not going to do on their own.

United Musicians artists are distributed through RED. Hausman's staff helps with press, manufacturing, on-line sales, marketing, and promotion. They have very specific terms about what they'll do, and artists can do whatever else they want with the song or record. Artists retain all options, such as for TV/film. If they choose, they can take their copyright and go elsewhere. Hausman thinks this is a better situation for an established artist with a strong business sense or who has someone on their team with one. Musicians pool resources to hire staff and have other cost-effective advantages of a label with several artists. Hausman adds:

> We don't have the overhead and make money on a much lower sales number. We make sure to cover the bases for our artists [such as] press, club advertising in the market when an artist goes on the road, and stay on top of everything. That pays off with established artists because you know there's a fan base. We do lots of e-mail marketing, keeping lists of fans current.

Cooperatives can work for artists. Cropduster Records is a good example of a cooperative of musician friends. Co-founder Jeff Epstein says that many artists on the label had been on major labels and decided to go the independent route. According to Epstein, "It was a bunch of friends who decided there was safety in numbers. Everyone had a record done. Our motto was 'One for all and everyone for themselves.'" They pooled their knowledge and energies to turn Cropduster into a nationally distributed indie. Sean Seymour, another co-founder says, "With Cropduster, love of music, companionship, and camaraderie [were] a big part. We had such little expectations that it wound up bigger than we expected."

Cropduster began with six artists pooling their resources and whatever they could pull from their day gigs to benefit Cropduster. They chipped in for one publicist, which enabled them to get more publicity for the label than many do. Each artist also contributed to print advertising and swag (promotional give-aways). They did group shows to promote the label and individual acts. While it didn't begin that way, now each artist handles their own sales. Jeff Epstein adds:

> We did a lot of evenings together—Cropduster events—where we could share different people's fan bases and compile everyone's mailing lists. We send e-mails no matter who is gigging, even if it's not a Cropduster event. We want to try to build an audience. We also did a quarterly newsletter informing everybody what was going on at Cropduster.

If you're an artist and know others who are putting out a CD and seem to have a buzz, consider seeing if a group of you can work together for each other's good. Be careful with those you don't know well. Get to know their temperaments and ambitions. This is a big commitment—only work with like-minded people. And, make sure each has enough money and other resources to share equally. You don't want to fight over such things. Create a legal agreement, drawn up by a lawyer, spelling out everything that will be done and what each artist is responsible for.

COMPILATIONS

Compilations are CDs with a variety of artists. Many people love the idea of putting them out, but I'm told that nowadays they're not too profitable in the U.S. They seem to do better in European markets. Compilations can be good promotional tools if you have many artists, or you want to test some before signing. Gregg Latterman (Aware Records) started by putting out compilations to get his feet wet and learn the business. He says, "I didn't need a lot of equity to do it, and I thought it would allow me to meet everyone in the business, and get some cash flow as well." Latterman had a good ear for music and many great acts were on his first compilations, including Matchbox 20 and Hootie & the Blowfish.

Latterman chose bands with a following and put each on the cover. He gave free CDs to key stores in each band's region. Since fans recognized at least one band, the CDs sold and stores bought more. Aware Records grew from there. Eventually Columbia Records approached Latterman to develop acts with them. Recent artists to break on his label include John Mayer, Five for Fighting, and Train. Latterman still does compilations for promotion and adds:

> We still do them for A&R purposes and to introduce people to our new bands. We do one a year with two to four bands that we are signing or have signed. Then there's another eight that we have an association with but we haven't signed. It's good because it allows us to have a relationship with other bands.

Another label that likes compilations is 13 Stories Records. They're working on their seventh compilation CD. Founded by Brian Muni, Ann Ruckert, and James Rohler, they get most of their material from participants in Ruckert's Pro-shop, a weekly songwriter's pitch through the Songwriters Guild. According to Muni, vice president of A&R, they do thematic compilations, often based around holidays. Muni says they began the label because:

> We'd see many high-quality songs and wanted to do something with them. It was about empowering ourselves to make it happen. It's a cooperative. Everybody puts in to the cost of the mastering and pressing and must present a radio-ready production. We use a royalty-rate scale when we go over a certain amount of sales.

Muni says they do direct alternative retail marketing, including bookstores, museum stores, and gift shops. Music lovers buy them. Muni says it's a wonderful showcase, and he's gotten publishing deals from songs on these compilations. 13 Stories CDs aren't created for one demographic. They're family entertainment. They've been reviewed in *Billboard* and *American Songwriter*. The word continues to get out. Their writers help with marketing. This cooperative CD showcases songwriters in ways that can advance careers.

DEVELOP YOUR OWN INFRASTRUCTURE

The best way to make money is to get organized now—you and your biz. Whether you have an office or work from home, use a file cabinet to sort all paperwork. Get into good habits now! Otherwise you'll waste time trying to find or remember things. I keep a little spiral notebook nearby to use as a work diary. Each day I put the date on the next free line. Under it, I include *all* info from that day that's relevant to my biz: contact info for someone I speak to, who I left a message for, who I mailed something to, resources I want to check out, when I'm supposed to call someone back, etc. I used to lose my notes on bits of paper. It's easy to lose important info when you're crazy busy! I put that info in other places, too, but it's a relief knowing everything is in one place as back-up. Invest in a good database program. Mailing lists are one of the best tools for marketing, and if you use e-mail, it's the most cost-effective way to reach people who may buy your CDs. According to Charlie Cheney, founder of the Indie Band Manager (www.IndieBand-Manager.com):

A good database helps you remember things like how many CDs did we sell in this region last time we played; how much did we get for this gig last year; who's on our street team in that town; and when is the submission deadline for that festival? It helps you find stuff like who are key press contacts in this area; what likely radio stations are near that gig; and what record stores will stock our CD on tour? It helps you stay focused and on task when you ask, "What do I have to get done today? Who do I need to call? Who do I need to mail press kits or CDs to?" It helps you do all this a thousand times more efficiently than you could do it with paper and pencil.

A good database is a tool for storing info about marketing, promotion, touring, PR, etc., in one place. The Indie Band Manager is designed to specifically meet the needs of the music industry. It includes a booking calendar, contact manager, to do list, personalized mass e-mail tool, invoicing module, expense tracker, and more. If you don't use this, find one and *use it!* Being organized immediately leaves you more energy to effectively market.

Create an infrastructure for your business. What does that mean? A company's infrastructure is a supportive foundation and basic framework through which you operate, like the skeleton is for your body. Your infrastructure should support the goals for your label. I included Chapter 3 and tons of input from indie labels as models for you to learn from. Definitely start small. According to Dave Roberge, "A lot of people bite off more than they can chew. For me, it was a matter of taking on as much responsibility as I could at first, until I reached a breaking point." He did everything himself in the beginning. As Everfine Records grew, he expanded the label into functioning departments and gradually hired staff. He explains how his infrastructure developed:

> It made sense to have a sales function to acquire as many consignment accounts as possible. The next department was tour marketing—O.A.R. made a lot of strides through touring. For us that was having strong relationships with promoters and understanding the promoter/management relationship. Publicity was another. This band needed stories written about them to spread the word. We focused on high school papers,

local magazines, all the smaller publications. I tried to look at everything from major labels with twelve departments to what I thought were the strongest and coolest independent labels with maybe four or five departments to see what departments I needed to focus on first. When I say departments, [I mean that] I was basically every department—a utility player. I tried to focus on the most relevant areas to this particular artist and grow them. As the band grew, so would the label. We did it step by step. For everything we saw as growth for the band, we would try to translate in terms of growth of the label and add a new function. New media was one area we focused on: web development, on-line distribution to get product to people [in regions they weren't touring in]. I developed departments that made sense. [From there] we'd add and build things.

Target your artist's strongest areas and create departments that work for their needs, even if you run them all. It helps you focus on taking care of each area and highlights what needs to be done. Then, organize to handle responsibilities within each department. I advise you to create a list—on paper—for each department it makes sense to have now and later. List everything necessary to develop each, including long- and short-term goals. Break each down into small tasks to tackle one at a time. See page 75 for a sample. Use the tools provided in later chapters of this book to create your own lists.

Each part of such a list and would include the specific steps involved to accomplish each. Once you have distribution, you'll develop functions for working a record before its street date (more below) and working together with your distributor. Brainstorm with everyone involved. When you take things one step at a time, they don't seem as overwhelming.

LABEL STAFF/I'M STAFF

Should you be the whole staff or bring people in? Many of you have no choice if your budget is your wallet. But you may have to eventually use outside people at least for some departments. Ezra Idlet (Trout Records) says, "You get to the point where you can't handle the business you're bringing in, and it might be enough money for someone to take the management position. It evolves slowly and according to need." Trout Fishing in America developed a business around their own music. Keith

SAMPLE OUTLINE FOR A SALES DEPARTMENT

I. GET CONSIGNMENT ACCOUNTS IN STORES

    A. Create marketing material: posters, stickers, any
         appropriate swag

    B. Compile a list of every store you find that might carry
         your product
      List each known store
      Ask fans
      Search the Internet in that region
      Call or email each and get the name of the buyer
      Put all info—store name, address, email address, phone
         number, contact person—into your data base

    C. Approach stores in the strongest markets
      Talk to as many people at retail as you can to begin developing
         a relationship with stores that sell indie music
      Develop a street team in each market
      Give away promotional materials in those markets
      Get your artists to play live in those markets
      Keep in touch with stores and profusely thank anyone that
         supports you

    D. Move into adjacent regions and repeat the above

II. CREATE ON-LINE ACCOUNTS

III. GET A DISTRIBUTOR

Grimwood says when it got too big for them to handle *and* they were making money, they got Dick Renco as manager:

> We had to have somebody deal with this business stuff. We're not businessmen; we're musicians. We try to get away from the business as much as we can. We needed advice on the big business decisions and developed a team of people that work together to keep us on the road and making music.

Even with a big budget, start small. Let your staff grow with your label, as you identify needs. Jay Woods says, "One way to get upset in a hurry is having too much staff. If you don't have revenue coming in, or deep pockets, you're going to have a hard time justifying it." Hire an outside publicist, promoter, bookkeeper, etc., at first if you need them. Until you get your label going, you might not need full-time people. Use your street team (see Chapter 15 for more details) for what you can. Identify where your own strengths lie so you can compensate in the other areas when your budget allows. Dave Roberge says:

> I have four full-time employees for: tour marketing, new media, radio promotion, distributor relations, street-team marketing, publicity. We outsource functions such as booking and business management. I have a business manager that works both for the band and the label that handles everything from taxes to financial settlements, and deals with payroll issues for the band. I handle payroll for the label. We do internal publicity here and outsource tour publicity for the band. I'm a big believer in that.

Jesse Fergusson advises you to always have someone available who can be contacted for label business. Answer the phone, even a cell phone, all the time, and have someone checking e-mail, all the time. He adds:

> People e-mail and ask for information, and if you don't get back to them right away, they don't e-mail again. If you e-mail them right back, suddenly you may have yourself an interview or sponsorship or all kinds of stuff. People think that if you're unresponsive and not in communication with them, or that your door is closed to questions or comments, then you're not going to get as much done. Communication is key.

PLANNING TO MARKET

Be specific about your label's goals and how you want to set it up. Why waste time and money learning a harder way? It's hard enough if you have it together. Before shooting for huge sales, concentrate on selling the first records. Unless your budget can support a huge marketing campaign, baby-step toward your ultimate goals. Jay Woods (New West Records) says, "We want to sell a million records, of course. But you've got to sell ten before you can sell a million. We try to stay focused on what's right in front of us." Learn through experience to be realistic in your plans. Master crawling before running too fast. Woods adds:

> We learned from labels that had done things wrong, failed in various ways, or made difficult decisions that didn't turn out well. It's really easy for an independent label to get lured into "if I just spend this money, this is going to happen." In most cases, that's an illusion. You need a real solid footing in reality; in what it actually takes to sell. It's easy to get caught up thinking, "I need to sell 100,000 copies of this record" when you should be focusing on selling ten, then 100, then 1,000. You've got to sell all those numbers before you get to 100,000. You get caught in this "I've gotta hit this home run" thing. We felt confident we could sell a certain amount of Billy Joe Shaver Records. We stayed on the low side and knew we'd sell "this many." We based our marketing plan on that as opposed to the other way around—looking at the high side—what you "could" do. We did what we needed to do to see if the numbers made sense. Could we sign this artist and spend this much money and still be able to pay our bills and have the artist make money?

As I said earlier, *the key to running a successful record label is to target your audience and figure out how to reach them.* Sound simple? It may be the hardest thing you do. Great music won't sell if no one hears it. Making naïve assumptions like "everyone will love our music" leads to failure. Target your most likely group of potential record buyers and put all your energy into finding ways to let them know about your artist. What publications do they read that you can approach for press? What venues can you book your artist into? What radio stations do they listen to? What websites does this group like? What alternative marketing strategies can you employ to attract potential fans? Once you've targeted an audience and designed a marketing strategy to reach them, you have a shot at success. Create individual marketing plans for each artist (see Chapter 12 for more details). Dave Roberge agrees:

> We have a blueprint we used for O.A.R., but when we take on a second and third band we'll certainly look at the big picture. We'll individually cater every marketing plan, every approach, and every expectation to each particular artist.

If you're new to the biz, trial and error may have to teach you. Be prudent so the lessons don't get too expensive! If you study your market first, you'll get the strongest bang for your efforts. Dan Zanes says he flew by the seat of his pants when he started. Now he plans:

> I have in my mind a one-year plan and what I want to accomplish three years from now. I'm much more clear in my goals now than I was going into this. It had to do with seeing how people react- ed to what I'm putting out and what aspect people reacted to.

Expect active participation from your artists. A marketing plan is a team effort between the label and artist. Jeff Epstein says Cropduster had monthly meetings with all the artists to set goals. Jay Woods says they can supplement what their artists are doing by making sure that products are in the right places and the tools are there. But if the artists just want to sit on the couch and wonder why they're not on top of the chart, little will happen. If they're not creating visibility by touring or working other outlets, there's only so much you can do. He adds:

> We have to have people that are on the road. That's the key element to what we do on the developing-artist side and our estab- lished-artist side. We don't bank on radio airplay. Even when we get into that game a little bit, mainly on the commercial side, which we do, we like to be calculated about it. That's the fastest way in my opinion to throw away a ton of money. You have to be really careful. "Pick your battles wisely" has been my mantra.

Promotion can be an uphill battle. Figure out your artists' strongest areas and work them. Promotion isn't a crapshoot. Brainstorm with your artists and others who know the music to choose the first steps for getting more visibility. From Chapter 12 on, I give details for specific marketing and promotion tools and strategies. Right now, pay attention to everything related to your music to discover the most options. Create a full picture of your artists' assets. Plan to develop them slowly if you want longevity. Dave Roberge says:

> It's all about baby steps, unless you're an image-driven band that's planning to be around for just six months—one hit single and video. But my focus is on artist development and creating careers.

MONEY MATTERS

Budget—the big "b" word that can make or break any biz. It's a necessary function of running a label, but one that many of us aren't prepared to handle. This is where the accounting classes mentioned earlier are helpful. I HATE the money part of the work, unless it's working with huge profits! But, I grit my teeth and do it. Before marketing each artist, create a budget. Otherwise, you might waste a lot of money by spending it haphazardly. Jonatha Brooke advises:

> Set a very loose budget. Say "I know I can sell [X amount] of records." How much income is that? We can spend this much on the publicist, this much on touring, this much to buy positioning in stores and on radio. Do your best. You're spending before you have any money—totally gambling. I had to learn to not freak out each time I saw how in debt we were for the last year while we were waiting for our check from the distributor. You feel horrible knowing you can't pay them off right away, but that's how business works.

Many factors determine whether you'll make money. Like expenses! Having a great record and people to buy it doesn't spell profit. Most serious indies hire promoters/publicists, etc. Or, they have in-house staff, which requires paying salaries and more. I wish I could tell you specifically how much money you'll need, but there are too many variables. I've had people in my classes with budgets of $1,000 to $3,000, and people with $100,000 to $300,000 or more. How much you need to start your business depends on factors such as the following:

- *Whether you're working records regionally, nationally, or internationally*
- *What genre of music you're working with*
- *Whether you plan to hire independent promoters or publicists*
- *If you plan to do a video*
- *Whether you'll have a staff, a separate office, or work from home*
- *Whether you'll be pressing CDs, or vinyl, and what kind of packaging you'll be using*

The variables go on. My recommendation for developing your budget is to itemize everything you'll need money for and add those things up, as is recommended for a business plan. Create the ideal marketing budget, and then decide which things you can afford. You may not be able to do everything you'd like. Determine which things are most important. Onno Lakeman (Commuse) learned the hard way: "I spent too much money at first. I ordered too many videos for different countries, some even with subtitles, sent out packages of five T-shirts to many radios in the U.S., Canada, U.K.. I had to slow down and be selective. The money went out too fast." You can't jump when someone wants promotional material that's not part of your plan if your budget is limited. Creating a budget gives you a picture of your expenses. Put a lot of time into making sure you've got everything covered.

Allow extra for unexpected variables. Dan Zanes says. "The big expense that I didn't consider at all was mailing. I just spent over $200 yesterday, the first half of an AAA [radio] mailing." Fill in all blanks for anticipated expenses to develop your budget. If you're starting a label with real money, I suggest you work with an accountant from the beginning, unless you're good at handling budgets and accounting. Mark Carpentieri (MC Records) says:

One of the most important business functions is knowing where your money is going. What about radio? Retail? Money can just fly out—thousands and thousands of dollars in things like ads. You have to put budgets together and separate your expenses so you know where they're going. It quickly can get out of hand. When we started we did it ourselves, and now we have a book-keeper and an accountant but still give input. I think one thing about having a label is you have to be schizophrenic. You have to be able to talk about this great CD and the passion of the music and why it should be listened to. But on the other hand, you have to justify expenses. Maybe you can't hire a radio promoter on this one or just for [a limited amount of time]. You have to keep that in balance. If you can do that, you're in good shape.

Jay Woods advises:

Keep overhead low in the beginning. Do as much as you can on your own. The way distribution is set up—everybody gets paid before you do. If you don't have extremely deep pockets and somebody with a lot of faith filling those pockets, the best advice is to look at it like it's your own money.

Expenses affect how much money you make. I spoke to a musician who sold close to 100,000 CDs but complained he barely made money after paying everyone on his team. Then I met one who only sells CDs touring and on her website. She said she's doing well after selling 3,000 last year. I wondered why she considered that great until I did the math. She sells them for fifteen dollars each and they cost under two dollars to manufacture. That's thirteen dollars profit per CD! Thirty-nine thousand dollars a year, mostly cash. Plus she's paid to perform and also sells T-shirts and other merchandise. She's thrilled! So a lot depends on how much goes into marketing. Dave Roberge says:

A lot of it was learning and taking baby steps to where I felt comfortable and confident in my sales forecasting that the number of units [was] going to outweigh the cost to get [them] into the marketplace. ADA worked hand in hand with us in determining which sales programs we should target. We have the same opportunity to go into the Tower Records and do the national listening stations as any major label artist. It comes down to can you afford or are you willing to spend that amount of money at retail? We do a lot of sales analysis about if we spend X, what would be the return on the investment? We have to track that because of our micro-marketing strategy, almost market by market. We do a lot of analysis to see the effective-ness of the programs that we employ. It's really important to do that. You can spend a lot of money, but if you don't look back and see the results, you're certainly not helping yourself in creating the next marketing plan and budget.

If you're not solvent, create your budget around money AND resources. While you can't compensate for everything, there are many things you can do to get your label going without spending a fortune. You'll take longer to reach your goals, but if you want to achieve them badly enough, you can work your way to them. Ryan Kuper (Redemption Records) says, "The best way is to build slowly. I started with about 500 bucks after I bought a computer that I used for both school and biz. I built up my company making baby steps." And Kuper has a very successful label now. He's a great example of how small steps can bring large success.

In your resources budget, list all your resources as well as everyone you can call on for favors. Can someone run off fliers for you at work? Will a friend allow you to use her loaded computer? Can you park your website on someone else's domain and avoid that expense until you can afford your own host? Can you send sound files instead of CDs to some people; learn to do your own PR, and book gigs? Ask your street team what talents and resources they have. Put all components of your marketing plan on paper and figure out how to handle them. Prioritize what needs to be done first. Juggle what money you have with what resources you can turn to for support. Do one thing at a time to get one step closer to success.

RECORD KEEPING

I hate bookkeeping. I've always had an aversion to it. Tax time used to be traumatic for me. But I had no choice about handling money matters once I went into business for myself. If you can afford an accountant or bookkeeper, lucky you! Many of you, however, will have to do your own record keeping, at least at first. Even if you don't, you should understand the process. It's your business and money. I've learned that taking finances one step at a time makes them less complicated.

From the get-go, create a bookkeeping system that works for you. Don't get so immersed in your label that you pile the paperwork in a box. Organize your accounting at regular intervals. If you let the accounting function go untouched, soon you'll have papers piled all around you. Take time to organize your accounting. Anthony Orlando, C.P.A., recommends:

Keep it simple. If you can use a basic check-writing or home office program to keep track of your checking account, do so. Keep receipts and a diary for other expenses. If you can't handle a computer, use a pencil and a ledger sheet to track the checks written and other expenses.

I've been told that computer software programs make bookkeeping easy. Ask people with businesses for suggestions. I prefer a manual approach, keeping financial records in a bookkeeping ledger from an office supply store. There's no one way to keep records, but at least consult with a professional. My accountant showed me how to make columns for expenses and income. When I started my label, I also took a class on starting a business. I learned that writing checks for all business expenses makes it easier to keep track of them. If you pay cash for items, lump them together and write a check to yourself. Note what it's for. Then I list each check in my ledger and most of the expenses are covered.

I have a column for each type of expense: manufacturing, advertising, printing, office supplies, mailing/shipping, phone, salaries, fees for independent promoters, bank fees, studios, transportation, etc. Each check number is listed in the left column, and I put the amount spent in the column it fits into. If a check covers more than one type of expense, I write each figure into the appropriate column next to the check number. Periodically I tabulate totals to see how my expenses are running in relation to my income. At the end of the year, I total the columns and give the figures to my accountant to file my income tax forms.

When a store or distributor pays an invoice, I write the invoice number on the left and have a column for each record title. If there's more than one format, I have separate columns for each one. Include both the amount paid and the number of units sold. When I get returns on product that's been paid for, I list them in an appropriate column and deduct them. Starting a good system of recording your expenses, money intake, and returns from the beginning prevents headaches later. Whether your business is large or small, record keeping is essential. It makes doing your taxes and paying royalties easier. It also helps determine if your income is justifying your spending.

If possible, get an accountant or bookkeeper (one who knows the music industry) to do the royalty statements for your artists. Someone who knows what they're doing also knows the industry standards for deductions and base rates of payment (see Chapter 6 for more details). If you want to keep the books yourself, pay a professional for lessons about the basics, and then proceed. You, as the label, must figure out how many records were sold and compute the royalties owed after deductions (see Chapter 6 for more details on deductions) are taken.

FILING YOUR TAXES

Keep a record of all expenses, however trivial, that you incur in connection to your label. If your label makes money, these expenses can help lower the taxes you pay. If your label is a corporation, you'll file a corporate tax form, separate from your personal return. If your label is registered as a DBA, you'll file a Schedule C form with your personal tax filing. If your label shows a loss, it can offset taxes on other income you earned that year. New businesses can take a loss in three out of the first five years of operation.

I keep everything in my ledger so that, when tax time comes, it's easy—I just hand the ledger to my accountant. That's why writing a check to yourself for expenses you pay in cash simplifies bookkeeping. Don't forget small things like blank tapes or scotch tape. Anything you use for business can be declared an expense for tax purposes. Tony Brummel emphasizes, "If you're going to start a company, save all of your receipts. That was the one thing from the beginning that was very smart [to do] for tax purposes, record-keeping, [and] bookkeeping."

Since everyone's situation is different and filing taxes can involve changes in that situation or the tax code each year, I can't give more specific advice. Call the IRS at 800-829-3676 to get its tax kit and ask any questions you may have. I highly recommend using a good accountant to do the taxes for your label. Taxes get complicated if you take deductions and should be handled by a professional.

PREPARING FOR STREET DATE

This section provides the most important nut and bolt for giving yourself the best chance at producing a successful release. If you follow the advice in this section, you'll set yourself apart from a majority of indie labels. Indies are known for being informal and haphazard about releasing product. A majority press-up CDs when they can, and release them when they're pressed. If you want the industry to take you more seriously, pick a street date at least three months in advance.

Announce it. Promote it. Then, bust your butt to release the records on time. Jesse Fergusson says:

> We notify retail two and a half months prior to release. Caroline has a mailer, and then we follow up with retail calls and fax one-sheets (see Chapter 13 for more details). One of the first things that must be done on a record is a one-sheet: full track listings, title, artist, production credits, selling points, marketing strategy, the whole nine. After that, start your promotional tools in production—you want all your promotional tools ready at least four weeks before street date. Ideally the 12-inch is out four weeks before. Some people recommend eight weeks before.

The street date is the day records hit stores. Most successful indie labels begin promoting releases months before. They ship product to stores a few days early so it's available in stores on the targeted street date. Radio, press, distributors, and stores expect that. If you want longevity as a label, make sure your releases are available on their street dates! Andy Allen, president of Alternative Distribution Alliance (ADA) (see Chapter 11) says:

> We have some labels that begin promoting four to five months up front. It's terrific for us. When we go out with a release that's set up that well, people know who the artist is, what they can expect from the first week's sales. The longest possible is the best set-up. The press effort has the longest lead time. National monthly magazines have a two to three month lead time. To have articles appear at the time the record is released, you need to get on the phone two, three, four months in advance. We found that in order to have the record featured in a high-profile area of a store, you generally have to make those commitments two to three months in advance. Otherwise, you're likely not to get them.

You're competing against those who begin early. Many labels don't, however; you'll stand out like a beacon of light if you do. Send everyone you can a one-sheet about the record. Shock people at press, radio, and retail by showing them you know how to play in the "big league," even if you are a new indie! Give yourself an edge and plan ahead! Gregg Latterman advises:

Before you put something out, everything should be together—the album, artwork, photos, bio, and a plan of action. So many people get busy playing catch-up. But that doesn't work very well. It works better if you think ahead and have everything in place ahead of time.

Doing advance promotion shows that you're taking your label seriously. It also gives you a better shot at getting press and radio play. I talked to Aaron Burgess, managing editor of *Alternative Press Magazine*, about lead times. He said that a large number of indie releases don't get written about because they start too late. Magazines plan months in advance. When an indie sends in material early AND it's good, they're more likely to get press. Burgess explains:

> We're on a three-month lead time. Three months in advance would be ideal. Usually with major labels and indie labels with a lot of funding, it's not a problem. But for a lot of small indie labels, it's not a possibility. We get a lot of indie releases right when they're being released, which complicates it for us. If we write about them, we look like we're three months late.

Besides written material, send a sample of the band's music in advance, too. Burgess says he wants to hear the act, not just read about them. If you can get your material pressed way in advance of street date, great. But if you can't, burn or tape something to send. Burgess agrees: "Send out CD-Rs in advance. Even a cassette or MP3 that I can grab. Giving me something in advance is helpful. It's hard to do anything if we can't hear the music." I understand that it's hard to get product and then sit on it for months. But find a way to get advance music into the hands of people who might promote it if you want to make money. And make sure you're ready for your street date. Jesse Ferguson says:

> The biggest complaint people have is when records are scheduled to come out and they come out late. I would stress setting the deadlines and keeping them. Make sure you know the production schedule that your manufacturer and distributor are going on and stick to them. Build in big buffers so that you get things done before they're supposed to be done, so the records come out in a timely manner. Your promotion should correspond exactly with

the releasing of the record. Otherwise you just waste money. If you're wasting promotion money, then you're losing and you'll sell less records. Every record less is less to spend on the next record.

Do you need more motivation to promote in advance? Here's one word that should motivate you: pre-orders, which are orders made in advance of the release date. If you get a big enough early buzz on a record, stores may give you pre-orders. This means that they believe the record will sell at least X amount of copies when it's released and they order accordingly. Ryan Kuper says, "Getting pre-orders is a normal part of sales. All companies should strive for that. I do it with every record. We all want stuff sold before it is even out. It can mean a lot of returns, but it is usually 90 percent actual sales. It makes distributors happy." What would make stores order a record that hasn't been released from a label they don't know? Buzz—excitement in the streets about the record.

Get street teams to work your strongest markets. They can give out fliers, swag, and sample CDs and get people in stores and in colleges excited about your act. Book shows around your street date. Advance commitments for press from magazines are great incentives; get them if you can. The more you do to show a potential for sales, the greater your chance of getting pre-orders. Then make sure you have product on time and are ready with a bang on your street date. Jesse Fergusson says, "Records ship from three to ten days before street date. We always have a party, a performance, and an in-store. A week prior, we try to have local college radio appearances."

Richard Ellis, manager of Aron's Records, has seen many indies succeed while running his store and has suggestions for promoting your street date. He says he's had great success doing pre-orders—13 days prior to street. Labels offer something—a free poster, key chain, stickers, a one-song CD with a track that wasn't on the record or another promotion if someone buys the record in advance. He says this type of promotion can sell large numbers the week before the record comes out. He also says it's a good idea to "have a show on street date. Do a giveaway the week before, and everyone who pre-orders gets a free ticket to the gig." Prior to street date, Ellis advises offering to do a free show at a school, like your local junior colleges and universities. The key is getting the artist's name out.

BRANDING YOUR LABEL AND ARTISTS

When you begin your label, choose your brand and stick with it. Don't put out a country record one week and a hip-hop record the next. Something that indies have over majors is that people are attracted to buying their records because they have an idea of what to expect from them. According to Tony Brummel:

> That is one of the key assets for an independent label—that you actually have a brand that people care about. At the majors, because they're involved in every single type of music, the brand doesn't mean anything. There are people who will go out and buy every Victory Record, but not feel they need to buy everything that Warner Bros. puts out.

Nabisco is a company brand (like your label), and they have all those delicious varieties of cookies (like each artist). People have favorites but may try new ones that Nabisco makes, because they know they like Nabisco. You want people to associate your label with a certain kind of music so they'll eventually want to at least check out your new releases. Ryan Kuper learned the hard way, explaining:

> Pretty much everything on my label has been some form or another of rock. But I started as a punk and hardcore label and should have started a separate label when I did more pop and rock. Really analyze your core audience and do everything you can to stay in touch with them. I'm literally re-tooling my label now, and it's going to take a couple of years because of poor decisions I made in the '90s. I alienated the Redemption fan base. I'm so far from who I was when I began. I didn't stay true to it, but I'm trying to get back to it.

Artists are brands, too. The best way to attract loyal fans is to be consistent so they can expect a certain level of music from you. Then they stay fans! Pay attention to making great albums with all great songs. Music lovers are sick of paying money for a CD that only has a few good tracks. They'll be more loyal to an artist who has enough integrity to want their fans to love every song. You want to attract long-term fans. Branding begins with getting the name of the act out. Don't wait until your street date to spread the word. Begin NOW! Brian Sirgutz (Elementree Records) adds:

There [are] little things people can do before an album is even on the release schedule. I come from the philosophy that the longer a band waits to release a product, the better. The more their name is out in the public domain without having a product to sell, the better. You are able to build your brand. Bands are brands. Artists can help expand their brand recognition . . . If people become fans, they'll get involved with the artist's career by buying the records, going to shows, buying the merchandise, and being a vital part of the future, which is why you see a lot of bands on a lower level developing strong followings and having careers without major labels. They're able to get their music out and let people have it.

MONITORING PRODUCT

SoundScan is the primary tracking system for record sales for vendors that use UPC (uniform products code) scanning technology. It enables the scanner at record stores to read barcodes (more on this in Chapter 10) and record each sale. Trudy Lartz, vice president of sales and client service for Nielsen SoundScan, explains:

SoundScan is a tracking system that is used at point-of-sale cash registers in a little over 16,000 retail stores across the country. A CD is scanned at the cash register, and once a week it reports those sales to us. We calculate all those figures, produce a report on each piece of product in our system that's associated with that scan, and then do marketing reports based on industry numbers that come out of that conglomeration of numbers.

Billboard's retail music sales charts are based on data recorded by SoundScan. Other industry people also use the information. If you want your label taken seriously, you'll want sales of your product recorded. Jay Woods says:

Be it good or bad, SoundScan is the measuring stick that we have. We know it's a fallible system—there are problems with it—but it's as accurate as we will have. It's a tool for us. It helps tell the story. We try to make the most out of it. It's the industry standard so people want to know.

Jesse Fergusson adds:

> Charts in general build a story around a record for the corporate/industry people. They don't help with fans that much but if the industry gets excited about a record, then fans will, too. Whenever I send out an update to any of our contracted publicists, promoters, and salespeople for the distributors, I use SoundScan numbers to promote. Having an idea of what you're selling is important, but you can't spend your whole day tracking retail if you're a one-man operation. You'll never get anything done.

SoundScan offers sales reports for a variety of budgets. They have three packages. Check their website (www.soundscan.com) for more details. The reports enable you to see sales for the week in specific regions to check that your distributor is finding and taking care of hot spots and to make sure there's product in stores when your act has in-stores, gigs, or radio promotion. Lartz adds:

> It helps you to decide what cities are the important ones to do something in and which ones aren't, instead of feeling you have to canvass the whole country. There may just be pockets that are better for you and some that aren't. The basic package can help you determine that.

I'm not including prices because they can change. Using SoundScan services does cost real money, depending on which package you get. But the information is valuable and should be part of your budget in some way. If you're just beginning, you can purchase a one-time report on one specific album. Lartz says:

> For people with a small label—only one record out—I recommend that they don't get a package and track it weekly unless they have a specific plan in place. They can purchase the one-time report every three months so they can get a handle on where they are and what they can do next.

SoundScan now offers an option for touring bands to get credit for CD sales at venues if they're on a registered label. Lartz says, "We track venue sales, so if they open a venue sales account, they can sell their records at venues and make sure the reporting process takes place." You can show these sales even without distribution. You'd need a UPC code (more in Chapter 10) and must register with SoundScan to get an account number. Ryan Kuper explains:

> The band has a form to fill out. It must be signed by someone from the label and someone from the venue who guarantees that this is the amount of sales. They fax this to me, and I make a document that I e-mail to SoundScan. I send that as an e-mail attachment and fax them the signed forms. They compare them and register the product. Back in the days, major labels would not allow bands to sell their stuff on the road. They said it had to be in the stores because that's where SoundScan was.

This program is a blessing for touring artists whose sales on the road were never tracked. Kuper says there's a lot of paperwork, and they have safeguards to keep cheating to a minimum. Lartz says, "Verification is important. We do have investigative teams that verifies those things every week." Unfortunately, labels with one artist don't qualify. I asked Lartz if there were any other options, and she said that single-artist labels can ask the distributor for help in registering, or possibly co-op with other small indies and approach SoundScan together.

GETTING YOUR LEGAL AFFAIRS IN ORDER

Before starting your record label, find a good lawyer. This doesn't mean laying out money in advance. But before you do business, at least know who'll represent you when legal counsel is called for. *Never* make legal decisions without consulting a lawyer. Signing a bad deal can keep you from making the money you should be making, or it could kill your label. As Jay Cooper, Esq., entertainment lawyer and senior partner in the Los Angeles law firm Manatt, Phelps & Phillips, says:

> Find a good attorney to advise you. Don't presume you know something that you don't know. You've got to go to somebody . . . who's been doing this for a long time, who knows what all the pitfalls are. There's no way to educate somebody who's starting a record label about the business in an hour . . . or five hours. I once taught a class at S.C. on the record contract alone. It was a twenty-week course, three hours a night. It's a very complicated document.

CHOOSING AN ATTORNEY

People regularly ask me for the name of a good attorney. Sometimes they're frantic because they've just heard from someone offering them a deal, and they want me to tell them what lawyer to use. That's not the right way to choose legal representation.

It's always counterproductive to speak for yourself on legal issues. Someone may try to schmooze you, insisting you can informally work out a deal. No way! No matter how sincere that person may seem, you'll be outmaneuvered in a megasecond. I once had a lawyer from a major label say she wanted to discuss the terms of a deal with me. I told her to speak to my lawyer, but she tried to convince me that wasn't necessary. Upon hearing that, my lawyer went ballistic, saying that was totally unethical. Larger labels know that some indies may be so anxious for a deal, they'll forgo the lawyer to get it done, like many artists unfortunately do.

Don't settle for a lawyer who may not be right for you. Shop for appropriate representation *before* you need it. Now is the time to shop for one. Don't accept the first name you're given. Just as we all have different tastes in clothes and food, we'll prefer specific things in someone representing our legal affairs. I've encountered too many lawyers who made me wonder why anyone used them. They've struck me variously as unpleasant, unethical, or just plain dumb. Yet they had clients paying them competitive fees. There are lawyers for every taste. That's why you need to choose, and not rely on only one opinion.

It's imperative to use someone with a specialty in music or entertainment. Lawyers don't learn the finer points of negotiating record deals in school. They learn through experience. Many lawyers take my classes to learn the basics. If you don't have one who's experienced in music negotiations, you may get screwed, even if he or she has the best intentions, and even if that person is your father. Only insiders know music industry standards and trade-offs.

Interview several lawyers before choosing one. Some may give a free consultation or talk with you for a few minutes on the phone. Have questions prepared to get a feel for them both as professionals and as people. Some lawyers are friendlier than others. Some are more businesslike. Some may intimidate you. Don't use one whose personality irritates you. This is a business of relationships. If your lawyer can't win you over as the client, how will he or she get along with those whom they're negotiating with on your behalf?

Some lawyers may be interested in your projects. Those who appreciate your music are more likely to work well with you. Music lawyers know they probably won't put their kids through college from fees paid by a new label. But, if they see your potential to be successful, they may be flexible about fees. Look for enthusiasm. My first lawyer totally believed in me. She didn't mind if I called once in a while for advice, as long as I didn't keep her on the phone for too long. I didn't get billed for those calls. I got billed when I made money from a deal. It's great to have a legal person on your side!

How do you find a lawyer without calling me? Obviously, referrals from other labels are the best way. Ask around—a lot. Network—a lot.

Most legal organizations available to people in the arts (listed in my book *The Real Deal*) have referral lists available. If you cold-call someone whom you're thinking of using, ask for names of clients. Ask questions. There are all types of music lawyers available for all types of prices. When you do find one you like whose fees you can afford, establish that you'd like her or him to represent you when the time comes. When a deal comes your way, give this lawyer's name when you're asked who's representing you.

GETTING EVERYTHING IN WRITING

Don't ever make handshake deals, not even with people you completely trust. This industry can change people. I'm not saying it makes people cutthroat, but you must watch your ass! The best way to do that is to have a written agreement spelling out everything that you've agreed to.

Most people aren't out to screw you, but the details of an agreement can get fuzzy when money is involved. Your producer may forget the exact details of an agreement. Discussing something is not the same as putting all the specifics down on paper. A written agreement clarifies everything before the excitement of money factors into the situation. If you can't afford a lawyer for all business matters, you can help yourself by at least writing everything down in as much detail as possible. Include what you agree to give the other party and what you'll get in return. Be clear about which expenses can be reimbursed when money comes in.

I'm not crazy about using sample contracts, but if you have no choice, check out *The Musician's Business and Legal Guide* (Prentice-Hall) by Mark Halloran, Esq. It has a variety of sample contracts and explanations. *The Complete Music Business Office: Survival Skills for a Rough Trade* (Hal Leonard Publishing Corporation) by Greg Forest has templates for contracts and comes with a CD-Rom to get them into your computer. But be careful when using generic contracts. I've found that most agreements have unique circumstances. Modify what you get from a book to suit your circumstances. If you prepare your own contract, for your own safety, pay an attorney to look it over before you use it.

BUSINESS AFFAIRS DEPARTMENT

Larger labels have a department for business affairs. John Luneau, head of business affairs for Palm Picture, explains that at major corporations there would be an in-house legal department handling things like litigation, copyright registration, drafting of contracts, etc. The business affairs department, which is also staffed by lawyers, negotiates record deals with the artists and artist managers. Once they reduce it to a twelve-page memo, the legal department drafts it. Smaller labels usually use one department to handle all the functions, both drafting and negotiating artist agreements.

Indie labels often don't have a business affairs department at all. If you plan to sign artists to your label, John Luneau advises forming a relationship with a lawyer in private practice who has knowledge and experience in this area, to help you develop agreements that are right for your business. He explains:

> My recommendation for a small label that wants to minimize its legal fees is to pay the lawyer to train you to do as much of the negotiating as possible. You would then use the lawyer in the wings, advising and coaching you in the negotiations, and then doing the drafting. If the negotiations go for several drafts, someone at the label would call the lawyer between each draft and go over the comments that they received from the other side. In a half-hour phone conversation they can decide how to resolve those issues and what things to counter-propose to resolve them. Then the person inside the label would get on the phone and try to resolve those issues and get back to the lawyer. This would go on until there's a final signed contract. The reason it's so favorable to the label is that it's talking to the other side that takes the time. It can just suck up hours . . . If you pay a lawyer to do them, at four hundred dollars an hour, that can get very expensive. I represented a couple of small labels seven or eight years ago on that kind of system, and it worked to everybody's benefit.

ARTIST AGREEMENTS

If you're opening a label to put out only your own material, relax about artist agreements. I loved putting out my own material—no contract! But if you're signing another artist, it's imperative that you have a legitimate, binding artist's agreement between the artist and your label.

Earlier I talked about drafting your own agreement or using one from a book. But an artist agreement should come from a lawyer. There are no standard ones. A lawyer may start with what's called a "boilerplate" contract that includes all the basic clauses. But there can be many variables. For example, if an artist is the songwriter, the contract must cover publishing rights (see Chapter 7). Your lawyer will normally make the contract as much in your favor as possible. You can give up things later on. But the writing of such an agreement definitely requires a music lawyer's experience.

It's not uncommon for artists to try to break contracts with indie labels when they start becoming successful. After all, if a larger label wants to pick them up, why should they split royalties with you? By signing directly with a larger label, the artist gets more money and controls the production budget. I've heard of too many artists who ran to an attorney when a larger label was interested in them. And plenty of lawyers will encourage them to try and get out of their agreement with you. That's why you need to make sure your recording agreement is legal and binding, with no loopholes for your artists to crawl through.

Artists sometimes sign contracts without seeing a lawyer. Later, to break a contract, the artist may claim he or she had no legal representation and the agreement is unfair. I had artists swear they trusted me when I pushed them to get a lawyer while we were negotiating an agreement. Four months later, they got one to try to get them out of the deal (unsuccessfully) by claiming they originally didn't have a lawyer. You can't force artists to get legal counsel, but you can try to persuade them to use a lawyer before they sign anything. Some labels offer an advance specifically for hiring a lawyer to negotiate the artist's contract. Most lawyers who represent the record labels put a clause at the end of recording agreements saying that the label advised the artist to go to an attorney, and the artist chose not to do so according to their own free will. My lawyer created a separate letter to that effect, which the artist had to sign. You need to protect your interests.

An artist agreement should contain specific terms of longevity. Lock the artist into at least a minimum number of albums. Instead of signing for a number of years, labels get a commitment of X number of albums. This guarantees that you as the label won't get stiffed on albums if the artist stays out on tour or takes forever in the studio.

Get a commitment for as many albums as possible. If the artist does well, you'll benefit from releasing more under that contract. If the artist tanks, you have no obligation to record more. You can't lose by getting a commitment for several albums. If you don't put any out, the artist will try to get released from the contract. If he or she isn't doing well, that won't matter to you. Your lawyer should know how to cover these points in the contract.

IMPORTANT POINTS OF A GOOD CONTRACT

I highly recommend two books to have at hand. One is *This Business of Music,* 8th ed. (Billboard Books) by Sidney Shemel and M. William Krasilovsky, which is considered "the bible" of the music industry. Updated regularly, it's a great reference on the industry's structure and standards. Then there's *All You Need to Know about the Music Business* (Prentice-Hall) by Donald Passman, which provides easy reading on the business/legal end of music. Devour this book to get a clear picture of how it all operates. Passman thoroughly illustrates specific points you should understand before signing agreements with your artists. I don't want to reinvent the wheel by going into great detail about what these two books spell out brilliantly. But I will emphasize the points you must understand so you don't get ripped off or rip off your artists.

OWNING THE MASTER COPY

The master copy is the original copy of the recording. All copies originate from it. Most record labels make its ownership a high priority, and unless an artist has a big name or other bargaining power, it's common for the label to obtain ownership of the master copy as part of the artist agreement. But there's no standard about who gets these rights. You and your lawyer must assess how important such ownership is in regard to signing an act that's playing hardball over this issue. Jay Cooper, Esq., stresses that: "It's very important to own the master copy. It gives you control of what you do with it in the future . . . Most record companies recognize that this is an asset, and they want to own that asset."

ARTIST ROYALTIES

Your contract will specify the percentage (known as points) of the retail price of records sold that the artist royalties will be based on.

Royalties paid on retail average from about twelve to fourteen points, but they could go higher or lower depending on negotiations. Points paid to a producer are usually taken out of an artist's points, but there are no rules.

You can have a field day taking advantage of music industry standards that allow you to lower the royalties you pay artists. Many "customary" provisions used in recording agreements are based on outdated factors. Some are downright unfair. As a businessperson, weigh your sense of ethics against the money you'll save if you take the deductions that most record labels do. You can be a crusader for ethics in the music industry, or you can join the ranks and take whatever you can that saves you money. It's good to find a balance between being fair to the artist and being fair to your label. According to Larry Rudolph, Esq.:

> There are artificial ways that record companies can reduce the base price on which they need to pay royalties. If they can pay 14 percent of $7.00 instead of 14 percent of $14.98, obviously that benefits the record company tremendously. When you're doing a record deal, and [the artist] is getting a fourteen-point deal, it doesn't mean that [they're] getting 14 percent of the suggested list price of the record. [They're] getting 14 percent of some artificially deflated suggested retail list price.

Some deductions that are considered standard aren't based on factors that are relevant today. Several were originally instituted to offset problems caused by unsophisticated technology; these problems no longer exist. For example, labels deduct for records breaking. Records did break easily years ago. Today, labels still save some bucks by cashing in on this outdated custom. One deduction that artists' lawyers are fighting labels over is the reduced CD rate. Labels still try to use it, though the reason behind it is obsolete. Larry Rudolph explains:

> One deduction that I definitely disagree with is the CD reduction, and the deduction for other "configurations," which [means] the record company takes a deduction based upon the fact that they are selling a particular album, single, or EP

in the form of a CD as opposed to the form of a vinyl record or cassette. That deduction historically came about when CDs first hit the market, in response to the idea that the economics of CDs were not yet established. [Record companies] didn't know if it was going to be just a small niche market buying them . . . whether they were going to be spending a lot of money developing this product that wasn't going to make them a lot of money. They [CDs] were also more difficult to manufacture . . . the manufacturing process yielded a lot of waste. Now the economics of CDs are eminently clear. They are now by far the single biggest configuration going, and the manufacturing process has been perfected. Waste is not an issue anymore, so to say that the CD deduction should remain is absurd. There is literally no logical base in it. It's a historical provision that is very antiquated. Today, an initial offer from a record company is a CD rate at 75 to 80 percent. A victory for an artist is to get it 90 percent or above. We'd like to see it at 100 percent because that's truly where it should be.

Labels also try to get away with paying less than the full rate on singles, using the excuse that they're put out mainly to promote an album. There are other unfair reductions a lawyer representing labels may include. You, as the label owner, should expect that the artist will try to change or limit them.

Besides deductions from an artist's royalties, a label has the right to pay itself back for certain expenses, which are considered recoupable. These include things such as recording expenses, advances, tour support (money that you as the label spend to support an artist on tour), equipment, at least part if not the entire cost of making a video, at least part if not all the cost of hiring an independent promoter, and whatever other expenses your lawyer can get the artist to agree to as recoupable. Most expenses related to pressing, printing, advertising, publicity, and marketing are non-recoupable.

There are many other deductions, variables, and industry standards that you can read about thoroughly in the books mentioned earlier in this chapter and in my book *The Real Deal*. Make sure you understand these issues before discussing contracts with your attorney. The various ways that we as record labels can save money at the artist's expense can be compromised or eliminated. The artist's lawyer will try to get rid of as many of these deductions as possible, but unless the artist is hot, the ball is more often in your court. This is considered a business of pennies and, if you save even one penny per record, that can add up to a lot of money with a record that sells well. I recommend that you learn about different potential deductions, then decide which to keep. It can't hurt to leave them all in a contract that you initially offer your artist and use them for bargaining leverage.

PAYING ROYALTIES

Royalties are paid twice a year. You'll have a few months after the end of a royalty period to prepare a statement of earnings for the artists. It's best to hire a bookkeeper to do this. Once royalties are computed based on all deductions allowed in the agreement, you can deduct all recoupable expenses spelled out in your agreement before paying the artists a dime. Many never see a royalty check because they don't recoup. When you record a second album for an artist, any unrecouped debts are carried over and added to what needs to be paid back for album number two—this is called cross-collateralization. But if an artist never recoups, he or she doesn't have to pay back out of pocket what's owed.

As I said earlier, I'd highly recommend getting an accountant or bookkeeper to do your royalty statements. If you want to try it yourself, pay a professional to teach you how to do it. You need to know the base price on which points are computed, along with all the deductions and recoupable expenses.

COPYRIGHT AND PUBLISHING DECISIONS

After teaching classes on the music industry for many years, I've learned that copyright and publishing is an area that's fuzzy for many people. Confused souls say they don't worry about copyright and publishing—it's not important to them. That's ridiculous! Considering that publishing is one of the most lucrative arenas of the music industry, it's absurd to give it so little importance. Songwriting royalties can surpass artist's royalties on a hit album. Far surpass!

Owning a piece of the publishing royalties of songs on your artists' records can earn you money. I've had deals with larger labels for acts signed to Revenge Records. My share of the publishing rights on those acts' songs was a source of income for me when the larger labels released their albums. Even if you have a good lawyer, it's important for you to understand the basics of copyright and publishing issues. The more you manage it properly and take precautions to insure you're getting what you're entitled to, the more potential you have for making money. Is that convincing enough to deem the topic important?

COPYRIGHT PROTECTION

Copyright protects someone's original work. Taken literally it means, as stated by the U.S. Copyright Office, "the right to copy." The Copyright Act of 1976 establishes the right to protect all intellectual property that we create, and to have exclusive use of our songs for at least a reasonable period of time.

GETTING A COPYRIGHT

Do you assume that a copyright form must be filed before a song is copyrighted? Well, it's not so. Under present copyright law, any original work that's fixed on something tangible is automatically protected under the laws of copyright. "Original" means that the person claiming the copyright created the work as an original piece. A "work" involves something more concrete than just an idea in your head; it means something tangible, such as a written document or a recording on a tape. If you sing an original song to your friends, you don't have a copyright. If you sing it into a tape recorder, you do. It's that simple. Why should people formally register their copyrightable work? Because it provides written protection or proof. According to attorney Wallace Collins, Esq.:

> The filing of a copyright registration form with the Register of Copyrights in Washington, D.C., gives you additional protection in so far as it establishes a record of the existence of such copyright and gives you the legal presumption of validity in the event of a lawsuit. Registration is also a prerequisite for a copyright infringement lawsuit to be commenced in Federal court and, under Federal law, allows an award of attorneys fees to the prevailing party provided the form is filed within ninety days of when the work is first offered for sale or before the infringement occurs.

If you know what forms you need, call the Copyright Office's automated line at 202-707-9100 to request them. If you don't, call the information line at 202-707-3000 to ask questions. Or, go to the website for the Register of Copyrights at www.copyright.gov. You can download forms from the website. The Copyright Office receives and registers copyright claims—it doesn't evaluate them or make decisions about whether a song has already been copyrighted by someone else. If five songs with the same title come in, they'll all get registered.

PROTECTING THE SOUND RECORDING

The copyright form that songwriters use most commonly for registering the music and/or lyrics of a song is Form PA, which refers to works considered in the "performing arts." When the music and lyrics are copyrighted, it's indicated by a symbol of the letter C inside a circle: ©. You, as the record label owner, should register your recording of the song by using Form SR, which protects the "sound recording" of your product. This offers protection from people copying the sound recording and using it for their own purposes. When a sound recording is copyrighted, it's indicated by placing a symbol with the letter R inside a circle next to the title: ®.

When pressing a recording to sell, it's important to file Form SR. Owning the copyright for the sound recording provides protection from pirates and from people using samples from your record. Registering a song through Form SR also registers the lyrics and music. Copyright applications are sent to the Register of Copyrights with a completed form, a check for the fee for each form sent, and a copy of your song, which they refer to as a "deposit." It's not necessary to send a copy of the lyrics or music sheet if everything is on the format you send. Since registration is effective the day the Copyright Office receives your material, send it via certified mail, and request a return receipt. It costs a few dollars extra, but the receipt is proof of the date the material reached them. Hold the receipt until the Copyright Office sends your registration. It can take months for it to be processed.

COMPULSORY LICENSES

Whomever owns the copyright has the right to do the first version of the song, called the "right of first control." After it's been released publicly, others can record the song. No one can do a cover of it until the copyright owner has done a version that's been distributed to the public. The owner can give someone else permission to record and distribute it first, as long as that permission is documented in writing.

Once a song's been released and recorded, almost anyone can record it again. You must get a license to do this, but the copyright holder must issue one, as long as the applicant applies properly. Compulsory mechanical licenses are issued to those wanting to record and release a copyrighted work. The person requesting it must give notice of the intention to use the work and pay the appropriate fee to the copyright holder. It's perfectly legal for an artist on your label to do a cover of someone else's song, as long as the song has already been recorded and the recording released. Notify the copyright owner and pay all royalties to the appropriate writers and publishers of any songs you use.

In order to get a compulsory mechanical license, the person or label wanting to record and release the song must notify the copyright owner of the intention to release the work before it's been made available for sale. If the owner can't be found and the Copyright Office can't help you, a notice of intention can be filed with the Copyright Office. Monthly payments must be made to the owner of the copyright based on the number of records sold. The amount paid is a set fee called the statutory rate.

COPYRIGHT INFRINGEMENT = STEALING

Copyright infringement means using a copyrighted song without authorization (permission from the copyright owner). Someone can be guilty of copyright infringement if they: sample, re-record a song written without crediting the writer and paying appropriate royalties, use a piece of someone else's song within the framework of their own, etc. A person doing any of the above can be sued, as can most parties involved in the manufacture, sale, and performance of such work. For example, the pressing plant where the CD was made could be sued for manufacturing one with stolen material, as could the owner of a club where it's performed. If your artist uses someone's copyrighted song, you as the record label are in jeopardy. Copyright infringement is a Federal offense.

WHAT CONSTITUTES INFRINGEMENT?

Everything in a copyrighted work is protected. Not even a teeny piece of melodies, hooks, or lyrics from other songs can be used without permission. To establish copyright infringement, two things must be proven. First, it must be shown that the work is "substantially similar" to the copyrighted one. Access to the copyrighted song must also be proven. If someone writes a song that's similar to someone else's, but they have never heard the original, it's not infringement. Let's say Ruth in Dallas wrote a song similar to one written by Jim in Chicago. If she can prove that she's never been near Chicago, Jim doesn't have a case, unless he can prove his song was played somewhere Ruth had been. Coincidences happen. To prove an infringement, you must show that the person who produced something similar to the song that existed first had access to hearing that song.

Proving access means showing that this person or group had an opportunity to hear the song before writing their own. An example of obvious access would be if the original song had been played on radio. Even if the writer of the second song claims he or she never heard it, there's a good chance of winning the case. Other examples would be if both artists recorded in the same studio or lived next door to each other, or if the second artist could have heard it at a gig. If someone came to a show where the copyrighted song was performed, or heard a tape of it at a friend's house, or was in any situation where he or she had access to hear it, there's a case in which access can be proven.

The access factor is a prime reason why many record labels refuse unsolicited tapes from unknown artists/songwriters. They don't want to be sued because they have an artist singing a song that sounds similar to a song sent in by someone else. If their policy is "no unsolicited material," they have protection. Labels must be careful. There is no limit on what can be awarded in a copyright infringement case.

SHOULD A LABEL ALLOW SAMPLING?

Sampling is taking the sound of a recording made by someone else and using it in your own recording. Many musicians consider it an art and like to lift beats and sounds and hooks from other people's records to incorporate into their songs. But unless you get permission to use a copyrighted sound, you run the risk of being sued. Unauthorized sampling is copyright infringement.

I'm often asked how much one can legally lift from someone else's record. The answer is: nothing. If someone can prove that a single note came from his or her record, you can be sued. Most labels have a clause in their artist contracts stating that there's nothing in the finished products that infringes on anyone's copyright. Your artists should take legal responsibility for using uncleared samples. Unfortunately, as I said earlier, anyone involved in a record that infringes on someone's copyright is at risk—and guess who's the most seriously at risk, especially if your artists aren't solvent? Make sure any samples used on your product are cleared; if any are not, don't allow them to be used.

If you decide to use a sample legally, the percentage of songwriting royalties needs to be negotiated with the person who controls the copyright and use of the sound recording has to be licensed from the record label. There's no set licensing fee. Apply for a license before pressing records. Contact the label and ask for the person who handles copyright clearances. Someone will explain the procedure. Or you can go to a music clearance company. If you don't want to pay a licensing fee, get your artist to reproduce the sound in the studio and sample from that instead. Then at least the label isn't involved. You'll still have to work out a percentage of royalties with the owner of the copyright.

UNDERSTANDING PUBLISHING

It's not uncommon for a label to include publishing in the recording agreement. I said earlier that publishing/songwriting royalties can be good sources of income. That's why you as the owner of a record label should consider getting at least a piece of the publishing rights assigned to you.

CO-PUBLISHING AGREEMENTS

Many folks confuse the total songwriter's royalties with the publisher's share. Let me explain this for those of you who don't understand. The diagram below represents the total songwriting royalties, which come from three sources. A precedent was set years ago whereby the songwriter, who created the product to be sold, and the publisher, whose responsibility was to market the product and make sure all songwriting royalties were paid, split the royalties 50/50. Publisher's share refers to 50 percent of the total copyright revenues. The other half is referred to as the writer's share, which goes to the writer of the song.

A publisher deals with all business-related details regarding the songs in its catalog, since many songwriters can't effectively handle their business. Publishers usually have the copyrights of the songs assigned to them. The publisher's responsibilities include issuing licenses for use of the songs, finding other artists/producers to record them, and making sure royalties are paid. Real publishers are knowledgeable about different sources of songwriting royalties, and the best ways to license songs. Since they take care of the business side, they get 50 percent of the total royalties. None of this is set in stone, and agreements can be structured with different percentages, as long as everything is in writing.

Many independent record labels take 50 percent of the publisher's share. This is referred to as a co-publishing deal. It means that at least two people are sharing the publishing royalties earned by the song. A co-publishing deal doesn't have to be a 50/50 split. The publisher's share can be divided into whatever percentages are agreed to in writing. The songwriter, however, is entitled to the full writer's share of the royalties. It's unethical for a label to take any of it. In the diagram, the publisher's

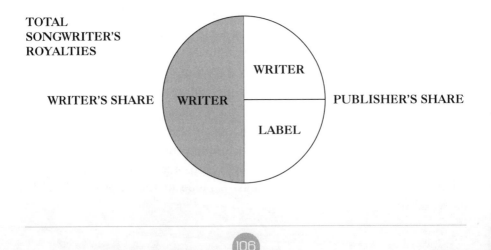

TOTAL
SONGWRITER'S
ROYALTIES

WRITER'S SHARE   WRITER   WRITER   PUBLISHER'S SHARE
                                  LABEL

royalties are split 50/50 between publisher and label. As you can see, the songwriter, in addition to the 50-percent writer's share of the royalties, also gets 50 percent of the publisher's share, for a total of 75 percent of the royalties. The label gets 50 percent of the publisher's share, which is 25 percent of the total royalties.

SONGWRITER ROYALTIES

There are several sources of songwriting income that get divided between the songwriter(s) and the publisher(s). One is mechanical royalties, which are paid by the record label for the right to manufacture (i.e., to mechanically reproduce, hence the name) and sell a writer's songs. The publisher holding the copyright on any songs recorded on a product sold by your label issues a mechanical license, giving your label permission to manufacture and distribute records for each song it controls. Your label must pay mechanical royalties on the songs for each record sold. John Luneau, head of business affairs for Palm Pictures, says:

> Lots of indie labels forget that as a record label, they owe mechanical royalties to publishers for the music on their albums and that they need to secure mechanical licenses for each song. If the songwriter is always their artist, the mechanical license can be built into the recording agreement. They would pay a separate royalty along with the artist royalty. But if the artist records songs that they don't write, or their own songs are owned by a third-party publisher, you can get into serious trouble releasing records without mechanical licenses in place. A lot of indie labels learn the hard way that you have to pay mechanical royalties. They might get audited by Harry Fox and get slapped with an invoice for unpaid mechanical licenses. If they don't pay, they get slapped with a copyright infringement lawsuit in federal court.

If you hold the rights, you technically issue yourself a license. As of press time for this book, the current rate is just over eight cents per song per record sold. Some labels cross-collateralize this royalty, i.e., use money an artist earns as a songwriter to recoup expenses in the way artist royalties are used. It isn't illegal if it's in the contract, and it can save you money. It is, however, unfair.

A second potential source of income is performance royalties, collected by the American Society of Composers, Authors, and Publishers (ASCAP), Broadcast Music Incorporated (BMI), or SESAC. These organizations issue licenses for use of music written or published by their members when it's played or performed in public venues such as clubs or on radio and TV. They charge fees appropriate to the particular venue and distribute the royalties to the writers and publishers.

A third source of income is synchronization royalties, which are paid for use of a song on TV shows, in commercials, in movies, etc. Payment for a "synch" license depends on the project and what you as the owner of the music rights will accept versus what the user is willing to pay. The publisher has to work out a reasonable licensing fee. Many variables can affect that amount.

All this income comprises the total songwriter royalties earned. A 50/50 co-publishing agreement between you and your artists/songwriters would give you 25 percent of all earned royalties. If a larger label picks you up, you'll probably have to give up some of your publisher's share rights. But keep at least a small piece, because if the album hits on the larger label you could make a nice chunk of change for doing very little. Larger labels give an advance on their share of the publishing. Smaller indies often don't. John Luneau says:

> Many indie labels neglect to realize how immensely profitable owning publishing can be. They neglect to make offers to their own artists to acquire their publishing. If you have a roster of artists whose sales are pretty predictable, you can predict how many mechanical royalties are going to be due to the songwriters and base your advances on those projections so that you never overpay. If you never overpay for your publishing rights, at the end of the day, not only will you break even, but you'll earn your share of the mechanical royalties, which can be very lucrative.

OPENING YOUR OWN PUBLISHING COMPANY

To collect the publisher's share of royalties, you must open a publishing company. Songwriters collect the songwriter's portion of the royalties directly, but they also must open a publishing company to collect a share of the publisher's royalties. Publishing royalties won't be paid to you directly. Even if you only hold a piece of the publishing rights, you need a company to collect royalties.

Opening a publishing company means submitting three potential company names to either ASCAP, BMI, or SESAC. Pick the society your songwriters are affiliated with. If you have songwriters affiliated with all three, you'll need to establish a separate publishing company with each one. The society checks to see that the name you've submitted isn't already in use. Try not to choose too common a name. Fees are charged by ASCAP and BMI to open a publishing company. SESAC doesn't charge one.

A publishing company is a business, and you're supposed to treat it as one. You are required to register it legally as a business, and it must have a street mailing address (as opposed to a P.O. box) and a bank account. You can start by either incorporating or getting a business certificate. Once you have established it as a business, you can open up a bank account for when royalty checks arrive.

CONTROLLED COMPOSITION CLAUSE

Record labels can be discriminatory toward singers who write their own songs, since they supposedly earn artist royalties. The feeling is they should take a cut in royalties paid for songs they write. As a songwriter, I can attest that this is unfair. Songwriting is separate from being an artist. But what you have in your contracts with your artists depends on you and the attorneys involved in the negotiations. Many people involved in the music industry consider the controlled composition clause unethical, but most labels use it. As a businessperson, you may need that clause to help cut expenses for your label. Do you to take advantage of the clause or be fair? According to attorney Wallace Collins:

> Under U.S. Copyright law, Congress established a statutory mechanical royalty rate for songwriters and their publishers based on an upward-sliding scale tied to a cost-of-living index on a per-song per-record basis. However, one of the many royalty-reducing provisions in any record contract is known as the "controlled composition clause," which contractually reduces the mechanical rate for a songwriter/recording artist and the publisher on songs written or otherwise "controlled" by the artist. Most such clauses also place a limit on the total number of

songs on which payment will be made and may fix the point in time at which the calculation will be done (thereby circumventing the cost-of-living index increase). For example, let's assume a typical clause, which might say that the songwriter/artist will receive three-quarters of the minimum statutory mechanical rate payable on a maximum of ten songs per LP. The mechanical royalty on the artist's entire LP has a cap so that, even if the songwriter/artist writes twelve songs for his or her own album, the artist's publishing [share], which should be worth about eighty-three cents an album at the full rate, is only allocated fifty-two cents under this clause. To further illustrate, assume the twelve-song album has six songs written by the artist and six songs from outside publishers. The outside publishers are not subject to the artist's three-quarters rate. So the six outside songs get the full rate and are entitled to a total of about forty-one cents. Since the mechanical royalty on the entire LP has a contractual cap of about fifty-two cents, the recording artist's publisher is limited to applying the remaining eleven cents to the artist's six songs, so that the artist's publishing |[royalty] is worth less than two cents per song. The most treacherous dilemma for the songwriter/artist is that, even if the record company does not expressly acquire the artist's publishing rights in its contract, the value of the artist's publishing may so greatly be reduced by the controlled composition clause that the artist may find it difficult to get a publishing deal elsewhere. This is particularly true if the mechanical royalties are cross-collateralized with the artist royalties, which means that, until the artist [royalties are] recouped, no mechanical royalties are payable on the recording artist's publishing [rights].

Just as your decisions about artist royalties require the weighing of ethics and economics, the same applies to contracts with artists who write their own songs. There are no laws about what you can or can't do regarding songwriting royalties. Industry standards are designed to put more money in the label's pocket. Almost anything is legal if it's in writing and signed by both parties. It's up to you to discuss these issues with your lawyer and decide what standards to follow. Let a combination of your conscience and your lawyer be your guide.

SIGNING ARTISTS TO YOUR LABEL

I was always my favorite artist when I ran Revenge Records. Why? Only then could I be assured that the artist would be on time to the studio, not complain when royalties weren't supporting a high lifestyle, and, in general, not be a big pain in the butt! Dealing with an artist's ego, problems, temperament, overblown expectations, and more, was often the main source of aggravation when I ran my label. If you're putting out your own music, be grateful that you do not have to worry about a lot of the issues that come up with artists. You won't need this chapter. If you're looking to sign other acts, read on.

WHAT TO LOOK FOR IN AN ARTIST

If you find an artist who you think sings as well, or better, than anyone on the charts, should you rush to sign her or him? No. Many factors should be considered besides just a potential artist's voice. It's easier to make money if you sign someone with more than one asset. There are many factors to keep in mind.

An artist who performs well live will sell more records. Some sound great in a studio, but may tank on stage. Live appearances are great promotion. A good live act has more potential for achieving a high public profile. And the bigger their following, the more sales they have from the get-go. Fans who come to the artist's gigs are likely to be the first buyers of the artist's release on your label. I know many A&R people at both major and independent labels who won't touch an act that doesn't have a decent-sized following. Ryan Kuper (Redemption Records) says:

> I need a band that has a stable lineup and is not tied down by huge commitments, like a salary day job. They must have a desire to get on the road and tour in support of a record. If they

won't tour, it makes it so much harder for a publicist, distributor, salespeople. If they're not available for a regional interview or in-store performance, it makes it tough.

Another factor to consider before signing an act is their material. Does the artist write great songs or have access to someone who does? That's always a plus. It saves you from having to find material, and you might earn money from owning a piece of the publishing. How is the artist's musicianship? Artists who are pros in the studio are a blessing. The recording process goes more smoothly when an artist has a professional attitude and great skills.

An artist's image is important. These days, a good sense of style is more important than good looks. Different genres have unique styles and nuances. The artist needs to fit in. One who works this angle well has the best chance of finding support from audiences, radio DJs, and the music press. An artist with a decent personality is more marketable. Friendly ones who handle themselves well with people get along better with everyone they work with, including the press when that time comes. Personality enhances an artist's image. Beauty isn't always a top priority, but an artist who radiates personality has a better "look." Personality comes across in photos and during live shows. That personality should also reflect in their music.

Artists who educate themselves about the industry are often more realistic about their money expectations and what it takes to succeed. That includes a greater understanding of how much they should do to promote their records. Do they have a press kit and local radio play? Have they been working it hard on their own? Danny Goldberg (Artemis Records) says, "Lisa Loeb is an incredible promoter and makes it much easier for us to try to get exposure for her record. That's a plus when you're deciding to sign somebody." Jesse Fergusson (Definitive Jux Records) says that after talent and skill, he'd look for:

> . . . flexibility and a willingness to work hard. It's not just about getting a deal and rapping. The artists at this label that I see succeeding are the ones that will work their asses off, before and after the record is out; who will do what it takes to further their own career, which is all we're asking them to do.

I preferred signing artists with finished, or almost finished, products. It obviously saves money on studio expenses, but that wasn't my main concern. If the material was at least close to its final state, I knew the artist could actually follow through in the studio. I don't like gambling. Those of you with larger budgets might feel fine about investing in a good producer who might make an act sound great on a recording. I liked knowing that the artist's material was great before we signed. Some acts can't bring what sounds killer on stage into the studio if the energy from an audience isn't there. I've heard too many flat recordings from artists who sound great live. I personally wouldn't sign an act without a recording that shows they can sound as good in the studio as on stage.

Be VERY careful about signing artists with a penchant for drugs and/or excessive alcohol. Even if they seem under control during performances, in the long run it can lead to substance abuse problems: trouble! Artists who over-indulge in drugs and alcohol are often unreliable. If you want help for a performer with a substance abuse problem, call 800-MUSICARES, a not-for-profit organization run through the National Academy of Recording Arts & Sciences (NARAS). It offers supportive services for people in the music industry with alcohol and drug problems and provides resources for dealing with such people. Although the music industry is known for the partying lifestyle, more labels are bypassing artists who appear to have addictions. As a label owner, an artist is your commodity, and excessive alcohol and drug abuse can damage that commodity.

Make sure that anyone you sign has at least a few key qualities that will help him or her succeed. The more of these qualities they have, the more you have to work with. That translates into record sales. *BUT*, don't allow your business sense to smother your passion. Sometimes you hear an artist and just know you have to work with them. Danny Goldberg says:

> The final element is equally important—intuition, an emotional connection to some of the music and a feeling about their new songs or where the artist is in the arc of their career or the recording is exciting. It's a decision that involves rationality as well as emotion—a balance of business considerations and emotion. Every once in a while somebody at the company will say they want to do something. Michael Chambers signed Kittie

strictly for the music. There was no business success at the time. It was just his gut feeling that they were great. But once or twice a year is the most we can afford to do that. That particular signing worked out for us, but those are definitely higher risk things. A lot of the indie labels come from people who are a lot younger than me and have a particular point of view about music and a passion. Their own taste really does become an identity for the label. They can become very successful. It's much more appropriate when you're younger, where your tastes can be part of a culture. A lot of the signings are my taste.

CHECKING YOUR ARTIST'S ATTITUDE

The last artist on my label was my favorite artist by far. Besides having a great set of chops, his main goal in life was to do music for music's sake. He was pleasant, polite, on time, and professional. If I needed him for a promotional gig, he was happy to do it because he loved music. Period. He wasn't moody, temperamental, or thinking about how much money he should have been making. He practiced so much before going into the studio that he was able to do his vocal track in one take! He focused on getting out and performing music, in whatever way possible. He was my dream artist!

I don't care how much talent an artist has. It's often not worth going the distance with an act that gives you a hard time on a regular basis. Unless you have resources for a large staff, you'll be living in some ways with your artists. Many take their problems into the studio, to gigs, etc. If they don't have managers, you may be the baby-sitter. I've had calls from artists during the night who'd lost a wallet and needed money, or had a fight with a band member. I've bailed an artist out of jail the night before a gig. Once you as the label owner invest money and time, an artist's problems can become yours. You may have to deal with them or lose the artist—and your time and money. I can say from experience that it can be very unpleasant. Be selective about the artists you choose to work with; make sure you can work in peace with them.

Some artists have bigger egos than others. Try to get a read on how self-absorbed an artist is. Of course you want your artists to think well of themselves. That's attractive. But when they think that because they have talent the world owes them success, that having a large following or getting good reviews gives them license to do as they please, they'll eventually look ugly to you. An artist with a bad attitude can affect work relationships on many levels, including those with producers, engineers, record store people, and other artists if they vie to be top banana. Difficult artists develop reputations that might keep some folks away. Unless they become very famous, few promoters want to take prima donnas on tour. Journalists won't want to interview them.

The issue of flexibility is related to ego problems. I prefer artists who are at least somewhat flexible about their music. An "I want my music my way because I know it all" attitude isn't uncommon, but it's a real problem. When everyone tells an artist he or she is terrific, the artist often thinks he or she knows it all and won't listen to suggestions. An artist should be able to work with a producer who may want changes in the original song or arrangement. An artist should show respect for the whole recording team. If an artist seems surly before being signed to your label, watch out. The situation only gets worse later.

I highly recommend signing artists who have some visible means of support. Too many artists have no financial security. You want them to be flexible for touring. But if nothing is going on at first, they'll look to you for income. As I said earlier, many artists make little from royalties. Decent-paying gigs may be scarce before an artist is established. Earning very little money in the beginning is a hard reality for many artists. When they see their records selling and receive adulation from fans, they may feel they should be earning serious bucks and get surly when their money expectations aren't met. Or, they may feel pressure from friends and fans who expect them to be spending money freely. These problems are especially common among young artists, who often have a hard time accepting a lack of money when they've achieved a certain level of success.

An artist who is realistic about his or her expectations is easier and more pleasant to work with. Be objective in deciding which artists to sign. Even if you're dying to sign an artist because you love the music, weigh the pros against possible cons. Interview potential artists about their expectations of being recording artists just as you'd interview candidates for jobs at your label. Make sure you're on the same page. Dave Roberge (Everfine Records) advises:

> You have to take the time to understand them and ask "What do you want? What are your expectations?" If you don't hold that as a preliminary conversation, you're doing [an] injustice to that artist.

Ask artists where they see themselves in a year and how much money they expect to make when their records are released. Clue them in to reality before they sign. Evaluate the artist's temperament, at least a little, to avoid anyone with serious attitude problems. You've been warned!

WHERE TO FIND ARTISTS

Most of you are probably starting your label with an act in mind. But if you don't have one, or if your label becomes successful and you need more acts, there's a lot of unsigned talent around. It's not too hard to find good artists, if you make an effort.

Begin your search in clubs where the genre you're looking for is performed. You'll find a variety of artists performing live every night in most cities, playing everything from rock to jazz to hip-hop to standards and everything in between. Go regularly. If you see performers you like, talk to them or their managers after the gigs. Network your butt off at live venues and ask for recommendations of acts that are looking for a label to put them out. Ask the people who work in clubs if they've seen any unsigned artists lately that made a great impression. Find out where they're playing live and check them out a few times.

If you live in a city with a paper that has a section for musicians, advertise for artists. When I was at Revenge Records, I needed an R&B artist to record a song that I'd written. I put an ad in the *Village Voice* in New York City asking for a singer with specific qualities. I got lots of calls. Some sent tapes. There was a lot of talent in the batch I got, and I found the guy I referred to earlier in this chapter as my dream artist. I also kept in touch with some of the other talented artists who contacted me for future projects. There might be music publications/fanzines for your genre that have a place to advertise. The Internet offers an unlimited resource. You can search sites that sell independent music. Indie artists are all over the Internet and some would like someone else to market them.

Word of mouth is often the best way to find artists. Put yourself into the music scene regularly and keep your ears open for news of acts people are raving about that as yet have no record deals. Let everyone you meet know you're looking for talent. Ask in clubs if anyone's seen an act worth signing. Talk to people in music organizations. Go to music showcases. Songwriters' organizations often showcase songs written by their members, who are often the artists performing those songs as well.

Become friendly with people who run recording studios. They often know of talented acts. By continuously putting the message out that you're looking, someone will point out an artist worth signing.

Artists who create their own material are more common in certain genres, such as rock and hip-hop. Other genres, such as country, pop, and R&B, tend to have fewer singers who write their own material. Although many artists have their own sources for their music, it's up to you or your A&R person to help locate and choose good songs. If you need material and networking doesn't help you hook up with an appropriate writer, call songwriters' organizations for recommendations. Ask around in music stores. Talk to people at recording studios and to producers. Put the word out if your artists need songs, and you'll find people who have them.

No matter where you find your artists, make sure they don't have any commitments on the side that you don't know about. Ask questions. Have they signed deals with producers? Have there been other indie label deals in their past? Do they have a management or publishing deal you should be aware of? After you've invested time and money in an act, you don't want someone coming out of the woodwork with a contract that's been forgotten or ignored. Sometimes an artist signs an agreement that doesn't work out. He or she may walk on it, thinking it becomes invalid by that action alone. But if an artist becomes known on your label, a contract he or she signed earlier with someone else may surface. Be careful. Ask lots of questions to find out where the artist's been in the years prior to your meeting just to make sure the person hasn't signed any kind of commitment with anyone else. If the artist tells you an old contract is over, ask to see it and show it to your attorney.

SIGNING SOMEONE UNDER EIGHTEEN

I once signed an artist who was under eighteen years of age. She was the daughter of a woman with whom I was friendly who had heard a song I'd written. I hadn't found an artist to sing it, and the girl's mom asked me to give her a chance. She was terrific, but my lawyer gave me a major argument. In most states, a contract signed by a minor (i.e., someone under eighteen) doesn't mean diddly. And if a parent signs it, the diddly doesn't get more valuable. Oftentimes you have to go through the courts to protect yourself legally when signing someone underage.

The legal procedures may seem like a pain in the butt, but laws were set up in many states to protect kids from being exploited by their parents. Depending on the legal jurisdiction, contracts offered to minors need to be validated in court. The court sets itself up as the custodian for the minor. The contract is reviewed, and a determination is made about whether its provisions are in the minor's best interest. If it's deemed that they are, the court validates the contract. From the standpoint of the minor, this is a safeguard. From your standpoint, it's a process you may not want to go through. There are legal expenses involved, and the time it takes may delay your project. And never forget: You should absolutely not invest one dime in an artist until you have a legal contract.

The mother of the artist I signed did use her daughter's age to screw me. She'd originally sworn that she'd honor the contract that she and her daughter signed. My lawyer started the court procedure. I put the record out and it did well, attracting a deal with a great label. But just before we signed that deal, the head of the label called my lawyer saying the artist's mother came to him behind my back to sign a deal directly with his label, saying that since our contract wasn't valid yet, she could break it. The label head didn't want to work with an artist whose mother was so unethical. So he nixed the deal and we all lost. My lawyer had to bite her tongue to keep from saying, "I told you so."

All this is to warn you: Be very careful if you consider signing someone underage in states with strict laws. Check with a lawyer in the state where the underage artist lives to see if there are laws governing what makes a contract with a minor valid. You may luck out and discover someone living in a state where you can sign him or her to a legally valid contract without going to court. But if your lawyer tells you that a parent's signature on the contract isn't enough, you may want to consider looking for another artist.

ADVANCES

It's good to give an artist a reasonable advance on royalties if you can afford it. My budget didn't allow for it most of the time. When I offered a contract to an artist, I put it to them straight. I couldn't give them money up front, but I'd do everything I could to promote the record well. Most artists were willing to take those terms. There are artists who'll agree to signing without much of an advance, just to get their material out. I did cover my artists' expenses for anything related to their records, and gave them immediate advances when I started getting money from record sales.

Labels with real budgets either give their artists a fixed recording budget with a built-in advance or what's referred to as an "all-in" deal. Nowadays, artists are more commonly given an all-in deal, whereby a recording fund is allocated to pay for all of the recording costs. The artist isn't given this money directly. You as the label owner monitor how the money is used and pay recording expenses out of this fund. Whatever money isn't spent on the recording goes to the artist as an advance. If you do all-in deals, it's good to remind your artists to be careful about choosing a studio and any people they hire to work on the album. You don't want them to cut corners on quality, but they shouldn't get carried away. Point out that any cost savings will mean more cash in their pockets at the end.

If you can afford to give an advance, it's the fair thing to do. How much is your call. Speak to your lawyer to decide on common ground between what's fair and what you can afford. Remember, since it's an advance on royalties, it's recoupable. If you believe in the record, you'll also feel more confident that you'll recoup the advance out of the artist's royalties. I always gave producers advances. If you have a different type of royalty structure for your artists that offers them more of the profit, your situation merits individual consideration. Discuss this with your lawyer and your accountant before making any decisions.

CREATING YOUR PRODUCT

Before stepping into a studio, put serious thought into planning the creation of your product. Make sure you end up with as good a recording as possible, before pressing anything. Settling for an okay recording doesn't sell records. If you don't believe in your product one thousand percent, it's hard to push it with enthusiasm: Don't cut too many corners in the studio. A killer sound makes more fans want to buy your record and will earn more respect from industry people.

CHOOSING THE FIRST RELEASE

Put thought into what would be best for your first release. If you're the artist, think carefully about which songs to include from a marketing standpoint rather than from a personal one. If you're signing acts, make sure your first release is as strong as possible to give your label the best chance of getting noticed.

Research helps. Get to know your music and study the markets. Devour trade publications and get a feel for what's selling all over the country and the world. Go to stores that carry music magazines and look through those publications. Learn about what trends are coming and going. The more educated you are, the better your judgment will be when it comes to making creative decisions.

Keep your ego in check. Just because you love the material you intend to release doesn't mean it's as marketable as it can be. None of us knows it all. Before finishing in the studio, play your rough mix for people who aren't friends. Get objective feedback from those in the thick of the music business, such as people working in record stores who sell music, DJs who play music, and even kids on the street who buy it. Don't tell them that you're the artist, songwriter, or producer or even mention you're in any way personally involved with it. You'll get a more objective view if potential critiquers aren't concerned with hurting your feelings or insulting your taste. For Revenge Records, I considered folks on the street my A&R staff, and I played material I was considering releasing on my boombox for them, without letting them know my relationship to it.

No one knows everything, including you. Get input from those who know what's selling in your genre. Ask for suggestions about making your product more marketable. Learn by keeping an open mind. Don't take all negative comments seriously. But if a number of folks make the same suggestion, such as that a bass line needs changing or a different drum riff would make the music sound more current, give it serious thought. Don't take criticism personally. Not everyone will like your music, and negative comments don't mean it's no good. That's why a wide range of feedback helps determine if the product needs work. Don't ignore anything that might make your recording stronger.

CHOOSING A RECORDING STUDIO

Choosing a studio for your recording takes research. Word of mouth is best. If you can't get recommendations, learn all you can. To make better decisions, read a book about or take a class on the basics of working in a studio. Studios vary in what they offer. You may not need the fancy toys offered by some. Ask what advantages each studio has. Learn as you go so that, when you do your second record, you'll be more confident about making the correct choices. Arty Skye, owner of SkyeLab Sound Studio in New York City and a producer and engineer with thirteen Platinum and Gold records who has worked with top artists including Madonna, Will Smith, Santana, 98 Degrees, and Sisqo, advises:

For an artist with little experience in the studio, the first thing to look at is, are you comfortable in the environment? Did you meet the engineer you'd be working with and do you like him? If you feel nervous, uncomfortable, or intimidated, chances are you will not achieve your goals in the studio and end up wasting money. If you're more experienced, the equipment becomes the number one priority. Do they have what you need? Will you be compatible with other studios or is their format so out of date or unique that no one else is using it? This could put you in a bind if you decide to remix or continue your project at another studio. Who is their regular clientele? Look at their client list and ask to hear samples of work that was done the in the style of music that you're doing. The equipment necessary for one style of music may be totally irrelevant for another style. Make sure you have a match.

When choosing a studio, price is a consideration. It doesn't matter how great a studio is if you can't afford it. But don't sacrifice too much quality. Many studios give better deals for using their facilities at odd hours. I recorded during what's known as "graveyard" hours. I hated beginning late and working until early morning, but got to use better studios for prices within my budget. No matter what you're told, try to negotiate a better price. Some studios give better rates if you book a block of time. Also, computers keep getting more sophisticated, which saves you money. Danny Goldberg (Artemis Records) says:

> Technology has driven down the cost of recording dramatically. It used to be more expensive to record. Today you can make a record with Pro-Tools and other digital systems for tens of thousands of dollars that would have cost a million or more 15 years ago.

Drummers hate me for saying this, but many producers have assured me that a good drum machine programmer can duplicate a great live drum sound. You absolutely need a real drummer for live shows, but it could be cost-effective to program drum tracks before going into the studio and use them for your recording. Getting live drum tracks down perfectly can take a lot of studio hours. You can add live drum rolls or other extras that are played live, but well-programmed drum tracks can save you some cash.

CHOOSING A RECORDING TEAM

Unless you or your band has good studio skills, you'll need competent people working with you. Don't count on a person who comes with the studio for everything. Just because someone has a great studio does not mean he or she is proficient as an engineer or producer. Anyone can buy equipment. It takes a trained professional to do the best recording possible. Be careful in choosing your recording team. Putting the right players together can mean the difference between a mediocre and a great recording.

GETTING THE RIGHT RECORDING ENGINEER

An engineer works the board in the studio and controls the flow of a session. Engineers can be pains in the butt or the key to great recording. I've had engineers who argued with artists, which wasn't productive. You should trust your engineer, since he or she is an integral part of the decisions that are made while recording. It's important to use one whom you respect, as well as one who works well with a team. An engineer executes the ideas of the producer. Be careful about whom you entrust this job to. Arty Skye says:

> Engineers are the ones responsible for the sonic quality of a recording. They record and mix the music and handle all the equipment and technical aspects within the studio. While being a technical wizard is a prerequisite for the job, a strong musical background and a creative mind are necessary as well. A potential hit song with a lousy mix will not have much success, while a simple song with an exciting mix might have more of a shot. A bad engineer can wipe your master tape (or disks), run up time in the studio, erase stuff they shouldn't, create tension, and basically destroy your session! Since the engineer is driving the session while recording, one who is fast will save time and money. A good engineer becomes the co-pilot to the producer and often has a say in the artistic quality of the music. A great engineer keeps everything running smoothly and makes your music sound better than you dreamed possible.

Angela Piva, an engineer/producer who's worked with artists including Naughty by Nature, Michael Jackson, and Toni Braxton, and co-owner of INFX Productions, Inc., adds:

> An engineer must have good people skills as well. Artists/musicians work better with someone they vibe with, who makes them feel comfortable and who understands their vision of the material. The best advice I could give someone choosing an engineer is don't just take word of mouth as a recommendation. Pick up a few records that person has worked on and listen to them. Ask for a discography and copy of the engineer's mix reel. Set up a meeting and play some of the project. Get a feel for what

the person is all about. Is he or she interested? What else is the person working on? And so on. Usually, gut instinct will tell you if this is a good candidate. But do your homework—just choosing a studio and hoping everything will go well may work for the lucky few, but most find themselves cheated in the long run.

Some engineers act like producers, whether you want them to or not. They may try to direct the way the songs are recorded based on what they themselves think rather than on what you or the producer wants. I've had engineers who tried to stick their two cents in when I didn't want it, which wasted time. There are loads of great engineers. Ask around instead of settling for one who comes with the studio, unless that person has a good reputation and reel. I've used house engineers who did a great job. But however you go about it, make sure you have the right engineer for your project.

USING A PRODUCER

Many people don't hire a separate producer, which can be a mistake. Many artists want to produce their music themselves, but few can do it properly. A producer orchestrates the flow of your recording, like the director of a movie orchestrates the action on a set, and makes critical decisions about your recording. A producer takes a song to the final level, makes sure the tracks are down properly, and decides when it's finished. How can you entrust this job to someone who may not have producing skills, or allow artists to produce their own material when they may find it hard to see beyond their own vision of what the material should sound like? I asked Arty Skye to explain the role of a producer:

> From an artist point of view in most styles of music, a produc-
> er's role is to understand the artist's vision and have the
> technical and musical ability to not only make it a reality, but
> [also] to make it shine. A producer should keep the sessions
> running smoothly, anticipate any problems beforehand, and
> get the best out of everyone from the artist to the engineer.
> The producer is responsible for everything while in the studio
> and their experience in the studio can save massive amounts
> of trial and error, thus saving time and money. A great
> producer should be able to take something ordinary and make

it extraordinary, or to take something terrible and make it acceptable. But don't expect a producer to be able to turn a turd into gold!

A producer helps to maintain good relationships between the engineer and others on the team. A producer needs a great ear and a sense of what's current in today's music market. A good producer can take a song that isn't working and make it fly by using the right beats and sounds. Producers get better by doing their jobs regularly. It's hard for a musician to have the seasoning a working producer has. Also, producers must sometimes play the heavy to get a recording done properly. It's hard for a musician acting as a producer to throw friends off the project or out of the studio or to set rules to get the job done efficiently. How do you find a good producer? Word of mouth is the best way. Ask people in the studio you plan to use, other musicians, and even music lawyers, who often represent good producers. Look on records you like and see who produced them. Arty Skye advises:

> In choosing a producer, there are several things to consider, because anyone can call themselves a producer. First, do you like them and trust their judgment? If not, walk away. If you don't like them, you won't enjoy being in the studio working on your music, and if you don't trust them, you're not letting them do the job you're paying them for. Next, what is the level of their experience? Ask to see a discography of records they've worked on and to hear some of their work. Do they produce part-time and have regular day jobs, or are they pros with countless years in the industry? Will you be working in a real studio or in someone's apartment? Will they be hiring an experienced engineer or doing it themselves? Basically, you're looking for producers with credentials and experience or you might as well do it yourself.

If your engineer wears both hats, he or she better know how to produce. Should you use one person to engineer and produce? It depends on the individual. Some engineers are good producers. If you find such a person, consider yourself lucky to have someone to do both jobs. Many engineers can't produce but think they can and would love to direct the recording session. Without a producer, an engineer can make whatever musical decisions he or she chooses. It may not be right for your music. It's a producer's job to direct the engineer, and sometimes to keep the engineer in check. Arty Skye advises:

> Many producers used to engineer, and it's not uncommon to find them sitting behind the console engineering while they produce. The engineering aspect almost becomes second nature when you've worked on hundreds or thousands of records. However, I do find problems when I see some producers with no engineering background trying to engineer. They may be wonderful arrangers, but the creative technical tools and tricks are only learned from years of hard work with countless producers.

Check the credentials of engineers/producers on both levels before committing yourself to someone who may be great at one job but not so great at the other. And keep in mind that having a separate producer and engineer means there are two sets of ears to listen for trouble or to come up with ideas or solutions to problems.

IN THE STUDIO

The studio is where your product is born, so treat it as an important aspect of your label. Success hinges on getting a great recording. Opening a record label means little if the recording itself isn't up to par. Plan for your project as much as possible to ensure the best quality. Make sure you leave with what you wanted.

PRE-PRODUCTION PLANNING

Pre-production planning is essential and saves money if you prepare before entering the studio; you'll save on the time it takes to choose a direction and order of production. It's good to have a meeting with the songwriter, producer, artist, and any other members of your team before the studio work. The producer orchestrates the planning.

Make sure you have your act together before the studio phase. Plans should be mapped out in detail prior to paid studio time. Decide the order of laying your tracks down. What kind of sounds do you want? Are you using samples? Have they been chosen? When will you bring in session players? Do you need the artist or whole band for every session? Sometimes it's easier to have the performers come in only when they're needed, rather than sitting around for too long and getting restless.

Your act should rehearse their butts off before reaching the studio. Sloppy playing wastes time and money. Encourage the singer to rehearse in front of a mic that's in a fixed position if possible. In the studio, they'll have to stand in the same spot and try to move as little as possible. Let them get used to that a bit before they're on paid studio time. Practicing saves time, which saves money.

WORKING IN THE STUDIO

I knew nothing when I first went into a studio, so I sat by the engineer watching everything that was turned, tweaked, and plugged, asking many questions. It's good to know what's going on. Don't feel funny asking about anything you don't understand.

Set rules about studio behavior. Will you allow friends to hang? Set limits on fooling around. Can the engineer receive phone calls during a session? Establish this beforehand. I've had engineers think that giving me an extra five minutes for each phone call could make up for breaking the flow of the session, and I had to put my foot down. One person should be in charge, and that's the producer. You as the executive producer have the right to make sure that the job's being done properly and your money isn't wasted. Discuss your role with the producer in advance to eliminate problems when you're on the clock.

Bring food and drinks for everyone (you can usually recoup the cost). It's your call whether to allow the use of drugs or alcohol. But when players get high, they slow down and get more hang-loose on your dollar. Some won't work without beer. But watch their behavior if you allow that. I recommend staying sober yourself to control things. If the session is long, food will keep the energy level up. A pizza can pick up spirits. Keeping your team happy helps get a good recording.

GETTING THE RIGHT MIX

Don't cut corners during a mix, which can take ages. Sometimes folks rush it when things end up taking a long time. It's not worth it in the end to invest in a record that's not done to your total satisfaction. I've worked on a song for over twelve hours. Some mixes go longer. With a good team, it can flow as smoothly and quickly as possible.

Let the engineer start by doing a rough mix on his or her own. Engineers usually have a feel for how a recording should be mixed. Starting with mix levels close to where they should be can save time. Once the engineer's done with this, the producer can adjust and fine-tune it all. A producer with good ears should work without interruption with the engineer. Once the producer is happy, the rest of the team can listen to determine if anything can be improved before it's complete.

When the mix is done, listen to it on several systems before you leave. Keep the board set up as your ears clear. Hearing music over and over at high volume for hours can desensitize your ears to subtleties of the music that might bug you later. Listen carefully to make sure the mix is exactly how you want it. Bring a walkman, a boombox, etc., to play a copy of the mix on several types of playback equipment. Does it sound as good as everything else you play on each system? If it doesn't, do another pass and make sure you're satisfied before the engineer shuts down the mixing board.

Are the vocals up enough? Play the song for someone who doesn't know the words to see if they understand them. If the vocals are low, do another pass with louder vocals. Take precautions to ensure the mix is done to your satisfaction before leaving the studio. Don't assume that if it sounded good when you were mixing it that it actually is good. An engineer can tweak the high-tech system and make it sound better than it really is because he or she wants you out of the studio! That's why it's important to hear copies in systems providing a more realistic sound. It's heartbreaking to get home after a long night in the studio and realize that some levels aren't where they should be. Then you must decide if you can afford to go back and do it over, or if you must put out a recording that you're not completely happy with, which will hurt you.

THE MANUFACTURING PROCESS

The manufacturing process has the potential to make or break your record. A good quality CD can make people want to play your product. A CD that is nicely packaged makes it more appealing to the consumer. Don't assume that all manufacturers will do the same job. Any format can get botched. If the sound quality isn't up to par, your music will get less play. If your artwork is lame, people may assume that the label is lame. In trying to build a market for your label, put your best foot forward in terms of manufacturing your product.

UNDERSTANDING THE MANUFACTURING PROCESS

Pressing up records isn't as simple as it sounds. I hear people say that they're starting a label and will "go press some up," as if it just takes a call to order records. Tony van Veen, vice president of sales and marketing for Disc Makers, America's largest CD and cassette manufacturer for independents, warns:

> Don't confuse value with economy. It's a common mistake to try to cut corners in manufacturing. While price is important, you get what you pay for. The cost of buying the best (as opposed to getting stuck with the worst) is extremely small when compared to the overall cost of recording, manufacturing, and promotion. This is your label's music that we're talking about, and it's got to compete with the majors on retail shelves and in the eyes of the buying public. Don't sabotage your chances of success just to save a few bucks.

The best way to learn about manufacturing is to ask questions. I'm not wild about technical stuff, but I managed to understand the process. Find someone you're comfortable with and ask for a mini-education. People working at technical jobs often enjoy showing the ropes to techno-infants like I once was. At least develop a working vocabulary about the manufacturing process to communicate on the subject without feeling totally ignorant about it. The minimum you need to know can all be made clear through the explanation of a kind-hearted expert.

Be aware that, when receiving your product and printed materials (labels, inserts, jackets, etc.), you'll rarely get exactly what you ordered. Issues of quality control are usually the reason. Not every record, tape, or CD will be perfect. Not every label will be right. Ink may smear, paper may tear, a printer may go out of alignment and copy may not be centered. Labels may also be put on backwards or off-center. Machines producing the components of your records can't think. They make mistakes and keep going. That's why people watch every step for defective pieces and pull out any that aren't done properly.

Manufacturers/printers anticipate damaged product. They do a run based on approximately the amount of material needed to fill the order, assuming some pieces will be trashed. Each run has a different amount. Industry standards allow them to be over or under what's ordered by ten percent. If they run out of materials within less than ten percent of the run, they'll stop producing rather than add supplies and risk making more product than you'll pay for. Conversely, if they reach the number you ordered and material to produce more still remains inside the press/printer/etc., they'll use it up. If you don't receive the full amount you ordered, you'll have to live with it. If you receive more than you wanted, most of the time you'll have to pay for it. Take all this into consideration when placing your order, and don't pay for more than ten percent over, unless you can use that much.

DECIDING WHAT FORMAT(S) TO PUT OUT

Determining what format(s) to manufacture is your first decision. Analyze the market for your genre of music. The decision also depends on where you plan to market your product. What kind of budget do you have? Will you use more than one format? Get input from folks working in record stores.

Are you putting out a full album (LP), not a full album (EP), or a single? Genre can make a difference in choosing a format. Without an album behind it, a rock or pop act probably won't get far with a single, whereas a dance or hip-hop record can break an act with one. Vinyl singles can be good for promotion, especially when you're working a more urban act. Some labels put out EPs if they don't have an album's worth of material but want more than a single. Albums are easier to get into stores because retailers are limited in space and prefer to fill it with higher-priced items.

If you're on a limited budget, start with the format that seems most practical. Expand to others if there's a demand for them. These days CDs are the format of choice. They have the best quality sound, which is important to music lovers. Retail prices on CDs have come down considerably. While some college radio stations may play cassettes and vinyl, most commercial stations won't. Club DJs still love vinyl. Putting out a 12-inch single is an inexpensive way to start your label. You can get a record going in clubs and create a buzz that develops a name for your label among DJs and then get the album out when you have created a demand.

A good pressing plant can usually handle all the steps to a finished product. It'll arrange to get your product mastered and to have labels, inserts, jackets, and imprints taken care of. If your time is limited, using such a plant is convenient. Most manufacturers farm out at least some components of their orders to other companies. Except for Disc Makers, most manufacturers don't have in-house printing, so labels and packaging are done by outside printers. Some manufacturers have mastering facilities; some don't. Loads of folks like one-stop shopping and are very satisfied with going to one manufacturing source for everything, especially if most of the steps are done in-house. I've been told there's not much difference in the price. The most important thing is developing a good relationship with the person who's orchestrating the process.

MASTERING

After mixing your recording, it should be mastered (sometimes called post-production), which fine-tunes the product. Mastering enhances the mix by further equalizing sound levels. You're selling your recording short if you choose not to master it. Doing so can perfect the quality by resequencing songs, adding or limiting compression to raise the level of the music, and using basic EQ to add to the lows, mids, and highs of a program. Arty Skye (SkyeLab Sound Studio) explains:

> Mastering is the process of taking the completed mix or mixes and sculpting it with compression, limiting, EQ, and more, so that it has the best possible sound quality for the specific style of

music. A rock record and a rap record are mastered much differently. The levels will be pushed to their limit so that the music comes screaming off of the CD at a much louder volume. EQ and levels will be matched between the various songs and put in the order required, with the proper spacing between the tracks. Great mastering can do wonders for an okay mix. Nothing sounds quite finished until it's mastered.

Use a mastering engineer with a good reputation because he or she will know what music for specific genres should sound like as well as what's needed to make a good mix sound great. Mastering makes all the songs on an album work and flow together. Some may have been recorded in different studios or with different engineers. There are subtle differences and tones that an engineer will recognize and adjust to make your songs work as one recording. Don't skimp on mastering—it can make or break the final sound. (I won't go into the technical end of mastering.) Contact Disc Makers at 800-468-9353 or www.discmakers.com for a free copy of their publication *Guide to Master Tape Preparation*.

PACKAGING

Your product should look nice. You can have great music, but if the presentation on the package doesn't reflect creativity and quality, people may not be motivated to buy it. Why spend money preparing a quality recording and not package it with the same respect? Remember what I said about putting your best foot forward. An indie needs to pay attention to the appearance of its product. If your packaging isn't attractive and professional, your label won't get taken seriously. Do I sound like a broken record? There's a reason!

Dave Roberge (Everfine Records) says "I get enamored with the packaging." Many fans will buy a CD if the packaging is special. That's why he puts effort into it. Eye-catching artwork makes people notice your product. It can create curiosity about an act and motivate someone to at least listen to the music. This is especially true of music that caters to markets in which the audience is young people who are particularly conscious of image. If a package shows the artist looking exceptionally attractive, cool, or trendy, kids are more likely to buy the music. If they like two artists equally, they're more likely to buy the one whose music has nicer packaging.

You're up against competition from a zillion labels. Visuals make your product stand out. It's human nature to be attracted to what looks good. Stores may display an interesting or clever-looking CD. A cover that looks like a lot of money went into its design might make a reviewer want to give it a listen. An A&R person at a label you're trying to get distribution from may give you the time of day if he or she sees you took yourself seriously enough to put a lot of work into how your product looks. Industry professionals get hundreds of new products a week. They can't check out everything. Do what you can to make sure they want to check out your product.

DESIGNING THE ARTWORK

Get your packaging together while preparing the recording. Printing takes time, so allow enough to do it right. It's good to have a graphic designer do your artwork. If you don't have a talented friend, ask around at art schools or put up an ad. Your printer or the sales rep at your manufacturer may have recommendations. There are good, young graphic artists around trying to start up their careers. Try to find one who'd like the opportunity to have the design of a CD cover for their portfolio.

If you can't find someone to design your cover but have some visual creativity yourself, take a stab at doing your own simple design. Photos are effective for artists who look great, but aren't used much these days. Be careful. A photo can turn people off before they hear the music. It's more important for the name of the act to be in large type that is clear enough to read, preferably with great, eye-catching artwork. Don't use artwork that won't stand up.

CHOOSING THE COPY

There's no set formula for what copy should be on your cover. Look at products in stores with music similar to yours for ideas. The front cover of a record in any format should show the name of the artist and the record title. The back cover usually lists the individual songs. What you include on the cover depends on whether you're putting out a CD accompanied by a booklet, which may contain other info. Include a copyright symbol (©) followed by the year of copyright, along with a statement that unauthorized duplication of your recording is a violation of the law. Some labels give credit to people involved with making the record. Some acknowledge outside musicians or thank friends of the artist. Many labels are choosing to put less on their covers these days, but it's your decision. However, don't forget to include the name of your label and your logo!

Designers must take into account information for the spine (side) of the product. Like the spine of a book, it should show the name of the artist, the title of the record, the name of the label, your logo if you have one, and your catalog number. A catalog number is the number you assign to each product. Choose it however you like. When I started, I was told to take a few letters from the name of my label (I chose REV) and add five numbers (REV00001). Each product after the first is then assigned the next highest number (i.e., REV00002, REV00003, etc.). But there are no set rules. Some people begin with a higher number than one so it doesn't look like they're just starting out. It's your call.

While it's obvious that the packaging should include the artist's name and the title of the record, I've been told people have forgotten them. The logo and name of the record label should also be visible. Information on CDs varies from simply listing the artist's name and the title of the CD to listing the names of individual songs, the catalog number, song publisher, and more. Again, it's your call. Look at other recordings within your genre. There's no wrong information to include.

Do you want a booklet to accompany your CD? It's always nice to have one, but can you afford it? Adding a booklet with more information about the music and artist makes the CD look better, but don't skimp on more important components (such as the artwork) in order to include one.

Include a contact phone number, fax number, e-mail address, and website on your copy so people buying your product can get in touch with you. I got a licensing deal out of London when my distributor in New York exported my record. Someone in London bought it, took it to his label, and the people there called me straight away. People may visit a city far from home on vacation, for a music conference or for business, and buy your record in a local store. Maybe they're DJs or own record shops. When they return home, they can play your recording for others and create a demand you wouldn't know about unless you were contacted. I used to get calls for orders from all over the country. It's amazing how a good record can get into a variety of people's hands.

GETTING MATERIALS PRINTED

Save money by giving the printer "camera-ready art," which means art that is ready to be photographed exactly as it is. Talk to the printer before you prepare your artwork so you know exactly what needs to be done. Even if you hire someone else to prepare it, understand the basics so you can keep track of the process. Having your artwork prepared correctly avoids problems and extra expenses later on.

Have the printer supply proofs once everything's ready for the press run. Before okaying the printing, go over the proofs carefully and show them to your designer. Make sure everything looks and reads exactly as it should. If you're using mixed colors, get a proof of the colors too. Make sure you check samples of the paper on which the material will be printed. Keep a tight rein at every step to prevent problems in the finished product. Then, if your printing doesn't turn out as you ordered, you have a reference for what it should have been, and recourse for demanding that the job be done over again correctly.

I recommend ordering enough printed material to cover a second run of records. Since it's considerably cheaper per unit to print up more at once, it's cost-effective if you expect to manufacture another batch. The major cost of a print run is the set up. At the actual printing stage, it may not cost much extra to produce a larger quantity. You don't want to waste time waiting for your packaging to be printed a second time when you have orders on hold. Many record manufacturers won't schedule your order until all the components—including the printed labels, booklets, etc.—are in their hands.

BAR CODES

A bar code is that rectangular series of horizontal lines with numbers under it found on most products sold in stores. Each bar code involves a series of twelve numbers called a Universal Product Code (UPC). The first six is the manufacturer's (your) ID number. Scanners used at cash registers are used to record sales, and many stores use SoundScan, which I discussed in Chapter 5.

To get bar codes for your products, you need to apply for a manufacturer's ID number through the Uniform Code Council (513-435-3870) in Dayton, Ohio. There are forms to fill out and a fee. The ID number is specific to your record label. I'm told there are computer programs which allow you to make bar codes yourself, once you're registered. But there are a number of companies that can make up the codes and bar code films, and they don't cost much. You'll need a separate bar code for each format. Otherwise store scanners won't be able to distinguish a CD from a 12-inch.

Should you get bar codes? If you plan to sell your product mainly at gigs, by mail, or by consignment in local stores, and you don't care about being tracked by SoundScan, bar codes may not be necessary. But if you're starting a label that you plan to sustain, you'll definitely want them. Many distributors won't touch a record without a bar code because most stores want them. If you want to show sales, get one. If you put out a product without a bar code and it takes off big-time, register your company and make bar code stickers as a temporary measure until the next pressing. It takes a while to get your number from the Uniform Code Council, so allow enough time. They charge more for a rush job.

THE MANUFACTURER

When choosing a manufacturer, shop around. Call for catalogues. Ask for references. Get samples. Shop for both price and quality. Talk to people at several companies. Do they seem willing to work with you? Will they put what they promise in writing? Don't just take the cheapest offer. If the quality isn't good, your label will lose credibility. If a cheaper plant takes much longer to produce, you may lose more than you save. What's their approximate turnaround time for a second run? What guarantees in terms of timing and quality do they offer? Base your choice on a combination of factors. I would never use a manufacturer that didn't show potential for a good working relationship.

I preferred a company close enough for me to visit in person, though that luxury may not be an option. Some companies have offices in large cities while their plants are far away. That's okay, as long as there's someone whose face you can get in if a problem comes up. Location is a consideration. When I started my label, I used a distant company and had a sizable shipping bill on top of the manufacturing cost. Then I switched to a company nearby and picked up my order in person. It saved money and time. With the first company, it took days to receive my order when I had some that needed to be filled immediately. If you have a distributor, the manufacturer can ship directly to them.

MANUFACTURING COSTS

There can be a big difference in price between manufacturers. Some offer package deals for different varieties of one format, such as CDs with and without booklets, or packaging in jewel boxes or cardboard. Some itemize for each specific expense. There are many variables. If you get a package deal, find out exactly what it includes.

Packaging has an impact on the total cost. For records, there are covers with artwork printed, or with black or white cut-out jackets, which save money. With a cut-out jacket, a well-designed label showing through works nicely. Jewel boxes are the most popular type of packaging for CDs. Another choice is a cardboard box that looks like a book, similar to a record album jacket. These can be more expensive than a jewel box if they have plastic CD holders inside. A cheaper version allows you to slip the CDs inside a slit, like a record sleeve. For promotional copies, you can save money by using even cheaper versions. Personally, I prefer cardboard. It doesn't crack like plastic, it's better in terms of ecology, it's usually cheaper to mail, and requires no assembly.

I'm not going to discuss manufacturing costs in terms of specific dollar amounts here. Prices change too frequently, and there are too many variables involved. Call a variety of manufacturers and ask for their catalogues or check on-line. Look in the back of trade magazines such as *Billboard* for names. Compare prices and talk to reps at several manufacturers before making a decision.

WORKING WITH YOUR MANUFACTURER

It's imperative that you develop a good rapport with everyone at your manufacturer. They have many clients. If they get to know and like you, you may receive better service and support. Be courteous and friendly, even when things go wrong. They'll love you for it! You also may get more realistic input concerning manufacturing decisions, rather than answers based on what they want to sell.

Before committing to a manufacturer, try getting a specific time commitment for the project to be completed. My manufacturers got to know me as someone who wouldn't let up until my order was filled. For a while, I used a small company with few machines. If one went down, work backed up fast. I understood that stuff does happen, but still needed my product on time. I was nice but persistent in my need for results. I think they pushed my order through just to appease me, which was fine. Once a company had a crew working day and night to catch up. The night they promised my records would be done, they weren't ready. I went down and stayed until 2:00 A.M. to take them with me. The workers had no choice but to stay and finish the job. I helped pack and put them in shrink wrap, while maintaining good humor. I developed a nice relationship with the guys in the plant. After that night, I was treated with even more respect.

One way I maintained good relationships with my suppliers was by paying my bills on time. Many folks don't. Manufacturers have to pay for materials to make your product, so they need prompt payment. I'd always arrive with my full payment. That's an endearing quality in a customer! All the companies I worked with always cooperated when I needed something in a rush, at least partly because they knew they'd get paid right away, no sob stories, no excuses, no bounced checks.

TEST COPIES

Get test copies of your recording before allowing the manufacturer to manufacture the full run of your product, even though you'll pay extra for it. Things can go wrong between mastering and manufacturing. Don't go through the heartache of pressing up 1,000 pieces and finding they don't sound as good as they should, or that they have a hiss, or that the vocals have an echo. Then you'll have to do them over at your own expense, or release an inferior product.

When you get test copies, listen to them thoroughly on a good system. I'd give copies to the major players in the recording—the producer and artists—and implore them, as I implore you, to listen to their copies very carefully, allowing nothing to distract their concentration from the first note to the last. Make sure that every second of the recording sounds the way it should. Take this very seriously. If there's a problem, you can rectify it before pressing the full run.

HOW MANY?

How many should you press? Ask six people and get at least four answers. It depends on your goals and how far you intend to distribute the first run. Do you already have a market? Will your main sales be at gigs? I'd advise going with at least 1,000 pieces. Under 1,000 is considerably less cost-effective. You'll have to give away a lot at the beginning, and you want to have enough left over to sell.

Some manufacturers have minimum limits. Those who'll do small quantities may charge only a small percentage less for pressing 500 rather than 1,000 pieces. Unless you're totally out of cash, it's worth it to make more. When choosing a manufacturer, check their turnaround time for re-orders (remember to have extra printed material on hand). Emphasize to your sales rep that this is an important factor. Keep your initial order smaller if you know you can get more pieces in a reasonable amount of time. As you see steady sales, re-order before running out of your product. Time will teach you how many you'll need.

Before placing an order, figure out approximately how many records you'll give away. Depending on your genre and scope of promotion, you may need at least one to five hundred promo copies. When placing your order, ask for whatever number you estimate you'll need as promos to be packaged without shrink wrap. I prefer to give my promos unwrapped. DJs, reviewers, people working in record stores, etc., may be quicker to pop it in their players if they don't have to remove the wrap. Since you may be charged for wrap, leaving it off of the pieces you plan to give away as promos might save a few dollars.

People you give promos to may sell them or return them to a store. Stores and distributors may return them to you for credit, which means you'd be buying back promos you originally gave out for free. To avoid this, promos should be marked to identify them as "not for sale." If you get back pieces marked as promos, you can refuse to issue credit for them. Rubber stamps may smear. Ask your manufacturer to put each of your promotional CDs in a jewel box with a hole punched in it. If this can't be done, take out the booklet of each promo and cut the corner. Or punch a hole in the bar code. That's a sure sign it's not to be sold. The corners of records can be cut too. Or punch a hole through your paper inserts. Even if it doesn't look nice, most of the people receiving your promos should be used to this practice.

HOW RECORD DISTRIBUTORS OPERATE

Good distribution is a necessity somewhere down the road if your goal is to maintain a viable record label. Those of you who are putting out a record just to attract a deal may not care so much about distribution. If you tour a lot and have a huge following, you may be happy making much more per unit than with a distributor, selling fewer CDs directly to fans. The level of distribution you need depends on your long-term goals.

HOW DISTRIBUTORS OPERATE

A distributor is a wholesaler of CDs, records, and tapes. It stocks product from record labels and gets it into retail stores. Some distributors handle videos, T-shirts, etc., in addition to recorded material. A good distributor gets your products into stores so they're available when your promotion kicks in. A not-so-good distributor might not get your products where they need to be, and may therefore return them all in six months.

People ask why they need a distributor. Why not sell to stores directly? If you get what you're striving for—a record that sells well—you won't want to worry about getting product into stores. At first it's fine to go straight to retailers. But once steady orders come in, you'll have enough to do without servicing stores regularly. When sales get strong and more stores want your product, using a distributor enables you to run your label efficiently.

There are currently five major distributors: EMD, WEA, BMG, UNI, and SONY. These distribute the major labels, as well as many established indies. As I said earlier, you'll probably start with the indie distributors. If you create a demand for your product, there are good ones available. Danny Goldberg (Artemis Records) says:

ADA, RED, Navarre, Caroline, and Koch are five healthy independent distributors that need independent labels and will meet with people. They don't accept every label, but they are in business to meet with small labels, and if they're excited or they believe in what's happening, they'll do the distribution and help those labels with their business in return for the fees they get. The access to at least make your pitch is definitely there. If none of them like what you're doing, there are smaller indie distributors.

INDEPENDENT DISTRIBUTORS

Independent distributors have good relationships with independent stores and chains that support indie music and are usually better than majors at targeting hot regions. They also get records to one-stops (see below). Independent distributors are often more knowledgeable than majors about specific genres. And, they can act quicker. Majors are more bureaucratic about getting product into stores. Independents can hit appropriate markets faster. They may give indie labels more personal attention, especially for records with good promotion.

When I ran Revenge Records, there were no real national distributors until Alternative Distribution Alliance (ADA) began. I talked to its president, Andy Allen, who qualified that while they're solely owned by the Warner Music Group, ADA was created in 1993 by Warner and a couple of indie labels to create a national distribution system, since there were none. Warner Music Group wanted to create a distribution system to serve independent labels and be involved with acts that were touring but that didn't have a big hit record yet. They wanted a more artist-friendly distribution system. ADA was completely autonomous until mid-2001. Now WEA does their pick, pack, and ship, and collections—their only connection. ADA distributes indie labels and selected projects for the Warner Music Group.

Today there are more national independent distributors. They want labels with a proven ability to market product. Some will guide you in marketing. But it's not their responsibility. A national distributor wants to see a national demand for your product. It also wants you to have the money and knowledge to promote a record nationally. A national independent distributor needs more product than a regional one, since they service more outlets.

Nowadays, independent distributors give P&D deals to many of their labels. They pay for pressing and recoup it out of the label's earnings. Jesse Fergusson (Definitive Jux Records) says, "Our distributor fronts the money for pressing. It comes out of the back-end accounting. They'll also front money for marketing and advertising." Labels with this arrangement say the distributor usually gets better prices on manufacturing because they do a higher volume. Andy Allen says:

> We manufacture about 70 percent of what we distribute. It's a service to the labels as a courtesy. The label can choose to use us as a manufacturer. We have a built-in advance for manufacturing in the way we deduct. The manufacturing charge is delayed until you ship the record, and then it's deducted from the revenue the record would generate. We take a distribution fee. The labels own their music here, and we're their selling agent. When we sell the record we report to them via statement what was sold and at what price.

Walter Zelnick, with City Hall Records, an independent distributor, says they'll consider a P&D deal under the right circumstances:

> They must be something we believe in strongly and think we can move the amount we invest in the pressing. We put marketing money into those programs too. There are a few ways to do those deals. One is to base it on a royalty. Another would be very similar to a distribution deal, but we'd put a fee on top of our pressing as an administration fee for handling the pressing and keeping the paperwork. If we believe in it enough, we'll give an advance.

One downside of using a large distributor is potentially large returns. No matter how many are ordered, there's no guarantee of sales. If a distributor sends product to many stores and one-stops, each account could return a substantial amount. You have little control over how many units the distributor sends to one-stops or large chains, where records can sit in a warehouse.

Chain stores may do nothing with a record. My first record sat in the warehouse of a large chain store while my students fumed about no stock at the local chain outlet. I called the store manager who swore he ordered it. The main warehouse gave me many stories. They acknowledged the manager's requests. No one knew why it got held up, but it took two months of calls to get a batch into the store, which sold out immediately. The re-order took just as long.

Whatever a store doesn't sell gets returned. It's nice to get a distributor who works with you by being more conservative about how many pieces they ship at one time. In the end, it's not the distributors who lose money if product comes back. They just return it to you for credit against what they owe for the order!

ONE-STOPS

One-stops carry every title. They charge stores more for the luxury of shopping for everything in one place. One-stops cater to what are referred to as mom-and-pop stores, often the small neighborhood record shops. Mom-and-pops can create a buzz on a record quickly and break one with a grassroots-buzz on the streets much faster than a chain store can. Chains do well with records that have high visibility. Fans come into those stores already knowing what they want. Mom-and-pop stores get the word out on records their customers *should* know about.

Mom-and-pops don't need large numbers of every record title. Only a few kids in the neighborhood may like a certain artist, or not many of their customers may buy jazz. They can't afford a whole box of a title if only a few units will sell. Larger distributors don't want to break up boxes to sell a few units of a single title to a store. One-stops buy records in realistic quantities and sell mom-and-pops the quantity they want. One-stops can be better to deal with when you begin. If you find one in the region where your market is, you only need to give them enough product for the market. It's easier to control quantity with one-stops. And often it's easier to get paid (see Chapter 13 for more details).

WHAT DISTRIBUTORS LOOK FOR

Should you be concerned from the start about getting distribution? No! Focus on marketing your music. You need a distributor to sell records. Distribution isn't the end-all, cure-all. You can ship 2,000 pieces and get them all back if you don't promote to your target audience. Distributors get records into stores. Most don't promote them. Finding one is easier when you have a good buzz on your records. If you don't, why have them sit in a warehouse? Danny Goldberg says:

I don't think getting distribution is the biggest hurdle. Getting the money to do some marketing is. Distributors don't do your marketing. They distribute records. They're reactive—being able to respond to orders, deliver the records, and do the collections. The biggest challenge is to find the money to do some marketing so that people know the record is out and to have some visibility. And having good enough taste to pick the right artists.

Andy Allen says, "Distribution is a warehousing function, a sales-and-solicitation function, a processing-returns function, and a collecting-the-money function." That's it! You do the rest. Records sell when people know the artist. Before taking in yours, distributors need to see that a large fan base is interested in buying them. The bottom line is that you and distributors have the same goal—selling records. Creating a demand achieves that. I'll repeat this over and over like a broken record—you must focus on creating that demand.

The best way to get a distributor is to put all your energy into marketing and promotion. Don't worry about getting distribution at first. When you create a demand for your product, distributors will pay attention. Do your groundwork first. Be patient and create a foundation to sell from. Until you identify your potential market and develop strategies for promoting your music to them, having distribution won't sell CDs. Distributors work with labels that have artists in demand. They don't care how good the music is if nobody knows about it. Andy Allen (ADA) explains:

> You have to create demand for your artist. In most cases, if you've successfully [created] demand, people are going to want to work with you. From a distributor's standpoint, the label that is successfully creating demand for an artist is the one that a distributor wants to work with.

I asked distributors what they look for in a record label. They consistently answered that they're looking for records that already have a market, with a label behind them that's working its butt off to promote them. Michael Bull, vice president of label relations at Caroline Distribution, a large, national distributor, says, "Very basically, we like labels with great records and the knowledge, desire, and means to market and sell them effectively." Michael Koch, president of Koch

International Corp., a North American distributor, says he wants a label with financing behind it. His decision to carry an indie label is based on how much funding the label has, its artist roster, and its management. Steve Pritchitt, senior vice president and general manager of Navarre Entertainment Media, a national distributor with offices in the U.S. and Canada, wants "Good product! But also good people running the label, plus financial capability to maintain their operations." Andy Allen says:

> We look for somebody who we think is going to consistently come out with great acts and will know what to do with them when they do. It's helpful if they've shown national sales. On occasion we've done a deal with a start-up, but not very often. I want to make sure that from a size or billing standpoint it fits in with the rest of the labels we're working with so they don't overwhelm the small labels.

You'll hear a lot about "developing a story." That's what everyone, from the media to stores to radio to distributors, looks for in an artist. A story doesn't mean a tale about the artist. Rather, it means the progressive growth and development of the artist as a marketable entity. A story refers to how much touring the artist is doing, how much radio play the record is getting, how much the press is writing about them, how many CDs they've sold. Distributors want to hear the buzz get louder as each page of the story unfolds. Nowadays, a reasonable budget for promotion is a big consideration. Walter Zelnick says:

> Right now we're looking for labels that hopefully have a marketing budget. In the old days, things could sell well on word of mouth. Now it's taking a lot more work and money. If someone comes to us with a really great record but no money and nothing to market it with, it's going to be tough.

It would be lovely if only the music were important, but marketing music is a business. Sales potential outweighs the importance of artistic ability. Sending an incredibly well produced, beautifully performed album to a distributor won't get you distribution if you have no fan base, media coverage, radio play, or promotion behind it. Alan Becker, vice president of product development for RED Distribution, a national music-software distributor and an affiliated subsidiary of Sony Music, says that while "the music speaks the loudest at the end of the day," distributors aren't A&R people. He explains:

> We look to work with people who are determined to be successful and have the wherewithal or experience in addition to the money to achieve success in a marketplace that's dominated by the major record companies . . . We have to be convinced that we're working with people who understand those factors and what it takes to overcome them. We look for aggressive people who are used to working at a very grassroots level and have the patience to stay with a project over a long period of time versus a company that has a pressure to have success quickly; [we look for people] who have a very clear artistic A&R vision—trend-setters versus followers. We look for creative people who, in addition to the music, can create clever advertising opportunities for us and create clever concepts that have not been tried before.

With so many indies around, single yourself out by getting your act together before approaching a distributor. Don't bring them your dreams. They've heard them all. Put together a marketing and promotional strategy and implement it, no matter how long it takes. Use the tools in the upcoming chapters to develop your own business into a reality. Make a distributor want to carry your product by offering a product that has an audience ready to buy it.

WHO PAYS DISTRIBUTORS?

Distributors usually take product on a consignment-type basis. They rarely buy it outright, although smaller ones might if they already have orders for it. When the product sells, they're paid by stores and in turn pay the label a price per unit that they agreed upon. If a product doesn't sell, it's returned to the label for credit against the amount the distributor owes for the order.

Larger national distributors mainly work on a fee-per-record sold basis. Steve Pritchitt says, "Mostly we take a fee as a percentage of receipts from customers (sales), but returns, discounts, advertising, and a reserve for returns are taken into consideration, too." Most distributors allow the label to set the retail price. Other distributors offer the label a price for each unit sold. The label bills the distributor with the price per unit that's agreed upon. Walter Zelnick explains:

> Some people think it's a fee. We don't work like that. The label decides the retail price. We tell them what we pay for that price range. Then they bill us whatever it is, and the standard invoice is 150 to 180 days. We tell them if we think they're not priced competitively.

Negotiate terms with your distributor. "Terms" refers to the amount of time the distributor has to pay the invoice. When payment is due, the distributor can return unsold product to you for a credit against its balance owed. Distributors don't always pay indies promptly, especially at first. Exercise patience. Until you establish yourself as a serious label, you probably won't be a priority.

Returns are an ongoing problem. After spending so much on manufacturing, records come back if they don't sell. Record stores return them to a distributor for a refund with few restrictions. Distributors send all returns back to the label for a credit against what they owe. Labels get stuck eating the returns in the end.

CREATING A MARKETING PLAN

It's imperative to develop a plan of action to get your artist known to the public. If you don't promote the heck out of your product, there may be no market for it. Your business acumen is critical when doing this. Create a marketing plan that will get your artist enough exposure to sell records and attract good distribution.

CREATING YOUR FOUNDATION

Develop marketing and promotional strategies with incremental baby steps toward getting more visibility, well before street date. As each component is added, the buzz on your artist can increase. Don't wait until records are piled in your office or living room to ponder how to market them. A strong foundation gives you the best chance for reaching your goals.

How can you strengthen your foundation? Start by living and breathing your music! Immerse yourself in the genre you're marketing. Learn all you can. When I marketed hip-hop, I listened to every rap radio show, went to hip-hop clubs, and read all the hip-hop magazines. When I marketed dance music, I was in clubs regularly studying how DJs mixed it, counting beats per minute (BPMs), and getting friendly with the DJs. Brian Sirgutz (Elementree Records) adds:

> If you're starting a record label, you want to associate that label with whatever scene you're in at the time. [Whatever the city], create alliances with the local record promoters, there and on the regional level. Sub Pop is associated with Seattle. What kind of music is associated with your label?

Learning all you can about the music you're marketing gives you an edge. If you're not part of the culture of your music, you'll miss the marketing boat. If you're not familiar with magazines that cover it, how can you know which ones to send material to? If you don't know the radio stations and DJs playing it, how can you get airplay? If you don't know what club-DJs set trends, whom can you approach? If you don't network in appropriate clubs and music venues, how can you make contacts to market to the max? Educate yourself NOW!

Gather resources. Get the networking process rolling. Talk to as many people as possible to get recommendations about ways to market your product. Read trade magazines such as *Billboard* to keep abreast of what's going on in the industry. Read music magazines to stay abreast of what's popular. Check the Internet, and see what other artists are doing. I cannot emphasize enough that you need to absorb as much information as you can about your genre of music. That's the foundation for marketing and promoting your product.

NETWORKING

Create the best chance for making a go of your record label by getting out, making industry friends, and developing as many people-resources as possible. Networking is available to all of us and doesn't have to cost much. A friendly smile can get more mileage than you might think. Showing appreciation for people's help attracts more support. This industry is built on relationships.

Networking means creating and maintaining a network of people whom you know on a variety of levels. To accomplish this, go to as many places as possible where you can meet music industry folks and begin the necessary interactions to build working relationships. Creating a network of people gives you more possibilities for support with your label. It increases the artist's mailing list. As you collect people's business cards, note relevant facts about each person on the back. Include the date and where you met as a reference, so you don't have a pile of cards that means nothing to you in a month.

Begin networking immediately. The more folks you know, the more potential recommendations for services, avenues of promotion, and resources you have. Someone may know a good photographer or a DJ at a radio station. Developing good relationships by networking can get your artist a good promotional gig. You never know whom you might meet or where contacts can lead you. A note to anyone who's helped you or whom you want to keep in touch with can solidify relationships. According to Florence Isaacs, author of *Business Notes: Writing Personal Notes That Build Professional Relationships* (Clarkson Potter):

> In a high-tech world where you can't get a live person on the phone and the world operates on e-mail, a personal note is a powerful tool. Because it's so rare, it's a way to stand out and get remembered. A thank-you note says there's something more to the relationship than the strictly business aspect. A follow-up note to a meeting strengthens a good first impression or an existing relationship. Stay-in-touch notes raise your visibility and help you stay connected to all your contacts.

When people like you, opportunities manifest themselves. Each contact is a stepping stone to another. A reference can get a distributor or club promoter to take you seriously. Building relationships with industry folks means developing a level of respect and comfort between you. Once that's established, they're more likely to take your call. A musician or indie label can be a source of mutual support and sharing of resources. Never be a snob and judge whether someone can help you. Everyone can be a good ally. You never know who'll help with your website or bring a crowd to a gig. Jesse Fergusson (Definitive Jux Records) says:

> I wouldn't recommend anyone start a label before spending time to get to know people in the industry. So much of this is about who you know and the connections you are able to make. I can't stress this enough, especially for artists trying to do it on their own. Try to get out and meet people. You never know who you'll meet [who] could be a down-the-road person. I've had that happen many times.

People resources are great and cost nothing. I talked earlier about the resources of people working in record shops. They're often involved in the creative end of music on their own time, as producers, DJs, etc., and/or work in stores because they love music. They know what's going on, which distributors are better, and other helpful info. Get friendly with people who work in stores. And don't forget to give them a sincere thank-you. I'm truly grateful to them! My friends in stores guided me every step of the way in starting and running my label.

Get out to clubs, industry events, and live performances of acts similar to yours. If you like an act, invite them to your artist's gigs. Indies support each other, and clubs are a good place to meet them. Music conferences are big and impersonal, but bring together many folks to network with. There are music industry conferences all year long. Check the *Billboard* calendar regularly to find those best for your genre. South by Southwest (SXSW), held every March in Austin, Texas, is considered the biggest music conference. I like the more specialized conferences. For example, the CMJ Music Marathon (see Chapter 17), oriented to college radio, is held in New York City every fall. Be friendly to everyone you meet. Keep in touch with everyone possible. The Internet makes this easier.

EVALUATING YOUR OPTIONS

Techniques for marketing and promoting vary with the music. Part of your direction depends on what your artists have generated on their own. Do they have press, a following, and regular live shows booked? Create a marketing plan around what the artist has started. Learn what resources are available, how much they cost, and the potential for sales if you use them. Then realistically determine what, if any, you can afford. Put serious thought into your marketing because there are many options. Danny Goldberg (Artemis Records) explains:

> You need to try and gauge in each situation what works. Some need a radio strategy, some a press strategy, [for] some it's about touring. Some people get enough momentum going through radio and press that it makes sense to make a video. With others it makes no sense. Josh Joplin was getting to AAA radio on the first record. That's how we got that record to 100,000. In the wake of that he did some touring and built fans . . . Kittie was able to lock in with a moment when new metal was happening. They opened for Slip Knot. Their ability to do well in front of Slip Knot's audience was a big, big part of it. They also got more press than a new band usually gets, in part because of the rarity of females being in a hard rock or metal band. So *Spin* and *Rolling Stone* covered them early.

Be flexible and pay attention. Prepare to roll with situations. Jay Woods (New West Records) says, "It's a reacting sort of business. You can be pro-active to a degree. But you've got to be ready. If you catch a break, be ready to jump on it. Maximize it and exploit it in whatever way you can." If your artist gets press, jump on it to get more. If a radio station gives it good airplay, work it to other stations. Make sure stores are stocked. Don't spend money too freely but create a marketing plan with breathing room. Ryan Kuper (Redemption Records) says:

> I like a loose, fluctuating way. Some people fail because they lock themselves into an ultimately rigid system: "On this day we go for adds on radio; this day it's available in stores." You can't do that. The coolest thing about indies is that we're flexible. Today we can pick up and run, or close down. If we're spending too much money on something, we stop the bleeding. That makes us different from majors. I've seen people who've worked at majors think they can operate an indie like that on a smaller basis. That's not the case.

PROMOTING DIFFERENT GENRES

I've found that music played by live DJs in a club, from techno to hip-hop to reggae to rock, sells well on its musical merits. Club DJs are music-driven and aren't as concerned about who the artist is or their label, as long as the music rocks. They usually don't care if the artist is gorgeous or thin. They want records with good beats or a groove people enjoy dancing to, that mixes well with other records. Music appealing to club DJs is easier to market if the music is great. Folks in stores catering to DJs give it in-store play. DJs buy many records at one time. If a record takes off in clubs, you can sell many for minimal promotional costs.

Artist development isn't as crucial with music-driven music. The music can sell itself. Artist-driven music requires artist development and visibility. People need to hear it, read about it, and see it performed live. The artist's appearance affects sales. Videos are effective for selling artist-driven music. Artist visibility in magazines and touring increases sales in all genres. Live shows are crucial for many genres. Radio play feeds the success of most artists.

To avoid wasting time, decide your direction for marketing your product way in advance for each artist. How will you make its presence known? Prepare press kits for reviewers and journalists (see Chapter 16). Compile a list of radio stations that might play the music (see Chapter 17). Book gigs. Target club DJs (see Chapter 18). Do you have a budget for a video? Most importantly, solidify relationships with people in the industry so you have support when the release date arrives. Mark Carpentieri (MC Records) says:

> Every artist is a little different. We decide if we're going to use an outside publicist or radio person or do everything in-house. That's going to affect what we do. We go through the artist and their touring schedule; decide what we think is unique about them, whether it's their age or something that they do that no one else does, or a former claim to fame. So besides the great music, we can make it an interesting story as well. Great music is always objective, but a story is a story.

VIDEOS

Is a video worth the investment? Having a good video with regular airplay on TV can increase record sales. But it depends on whether your audience watches video shows. Making a video can be a gamble for a new label. You may invest your last penny to create it, and get little or no airplay. Videos are a promotional tool. Sometimes you can get a store, a club, or a roller rink to play a video, or put it on your website, but this may not generate enough sales to pay you back for the money invested in it. Ryan Kuper says:

> I'd really need a story behind my bands before I could get [a major show] to play it. Typically your band's got to be selling in excess of 30,000 units to get that kind of love. If it's not, you'll end up on some cable access shows. When you start factoring in all the duplication and postage and everything, it may not be worth it until you have a story behind a band.

If you're thinking of making a video, figure out your goals. Don't just make one for the heck of it. Will your audience see it? Can you put it on your website? Have you found alternative shows to play it? Mainstream video shows may not air it if you don't have a promoter. Will the promotion be worth the expense? Onno Lakeman (Red to Violet) has used videos to promote from Holland:

> We contact cable and public television that have music video shows. We send out to film festivals playing indie videos. We got

five days national broadcast on inDemandTV and on two NBC compilations. It helps build the name and sound of Red to Violet. We have been broadcast in about ten states now, and the video is still being requested.

If you have access to equipment for shooting a more home-grown video, it might be worth your while. Rich Hardesty sometimes has someone follow him around with a video camera, and his fans love the films. He says, "I've always made fun videos. I may eventually put them all together and give them away to fans." If your artist has a good live performance, you might want to make a less expensive video to put on your website as a promotional tool, just to show how they look. Dave Roberge (Everfine Records) finds this useful:

> I'm a big believer of having a video in an electronic press kit, so whether you're trying to acquire college gigs or something else, it's there when they need a very short three to five minute snapshot of what the band is. We haven't been able to go out and do a professional level video. You want to do that when you're doing radio.

Many factors should be taken into account before deciding to film a video. What kind of budget do you have? You don't want to do one on the cheap if the quality won't inspire video shows to play it. Remember what I said earlier about doing things right or not doing them at all. A video has to be able to compete with many others. A creative young director can do a killer video for a fraction of what major labels pay, but you have to find the right one.

Now here's the good news. New technology is making it much cheaper to create videos. Up till now it's been expensive to make a video. Filmmaker Darren Doane (www.darrendoane.com), who's done videos that run the gamut, from many small indies to Blink 182 and Jimmy Eats World, says things are changing quickly. He clarified by saying that since everything is digital now, a good video should be shot with 24P technology—a digital format that shoots the digital at 24 frames per second, which is what film does. It eliminates film and about ten processes. Doane says this technology substantially lowers the cost of a video. His last three MTV videos were shot with a new camera that Panasonic just released called the DVX-100, which as I write costs only $3500. He explains:

Everything goes from my camera to my Mac. I do the edits into my computer and spit that out to a tape, which goes to the label to make a dub for MTV. It takes out film developing and transfer costs. Soon we are going to see the Wild West of film production because what you'll be paying for is truly somebody's talent. A sixteen- to eighteen-year-old kid can show their work and get hired. He'll go with his camera and make the video. With a computer and the camera, you have everything you need to shoot a video, minus lights.

Ask indie labels for recommendations for directors who can make a quality video. Doane says most of the ones he does for indies cost $3,000 to $15,000, adding, "I never give a label a price. A label will tell me what they have to spend." One way to save money is to find a college film student who can use his or her school's resources. But if you go this route, you may not have as much input as you'd like, since the student may see it as his or her own project. Doane suggests:

Find videos that you like. Do some research. A lot of indies have video compilations out. Look at the work. Find two or three directors whose work you like. Track them down and tell them how much money you have to spend for a video. Ask if they can do it. Find someone you can outsource the whole project to. From an indie's standpoint, that's the best way to do it.

Videos, like records, need to be promoted. You can hire a video promoter or do it yourself. Doane says that it costs many thousands of dollars to hire a promoter and make/send copies to get a video onto the many local video shows all across the country. Larger video shows want a story, like everyone else. Send press info or a one-sheet (see Chapter 13 for details) with your tape. Find out what format they want first. If you're serious, consider subscribing to *CVC Report* (cvcreport.com), the music video trade magazine. According to publisher Mitchell Rowen:

Information available in the publication [includes] playlist reports from 150-plus venues around the country, most of them national, multi-regional, and local music video programs—everything from MTV down to someone who might air once a week in [a small town]. We cover all formats of contemporary music . . .

we also have a fairly extensive nightclub and closed circuit distribution section. We do music video reviews, news, industry updates, columns . . . we have four different charts based on television airplay.

CVC Report comes out twice a month. Subscribers receive a master contact list with addresses, phone numbers, programming people, the hours they take calls, and the tape formats they require for screening and programming. The magazine provides contact updates. Rowen says it's valuable because you save on calls to stations for this info and you don't waste money sending them the wrong format.

Before shooting a video, watch video shows for several weeks. Get a feel for what's working in your genre so you know what styles and effects to go after. Talk to the producer of the video. It's your money—don't be afraid to give input. If something doesn't feel right, get it fixed before moving forward. Videos are very effective marketing tools if you can afford to create *and* market one. Tony Brummel (Victory Records) says he does one for almost every artist:

> We go after all the major outlets. If you don't get success at the major outlets, there are regional shows across the country. There are a good 200 to 300 of those and international outlets. We get our distributors excited about our videos. There are many ways in which your videos can be used where it makes sense (as long as you have a sensible budget), such as MTV2. We have a video promoter internally. We're fully staffed and bring an indie on when my people are over-burdened. It depends on our release schedule.

Doane says "If you do four to six releases, you can put out a video compilation for your label. With DVDs being under a buck to make, there [are] huge profits." That can make it worthwhile to invest in the initial promotion.

CHARTS

There are many types of music charts in a variety of publications. They indicate radio play, retail sales, and club play for overall national rankings, geographical regions, and genres of music. There are charts for different levels of commercial and noncommercial radio and charts for video play. The variety of charts can seem endless, depending on how many publications you look in.

Some charts are more influential than others. Having a record on the charts for commercial radio stations in major markets will increase sales more than charting on college radio. Because of its longevity and the accuracy of its information-gathering systems, charts in *Billboard* have the highest recognition, according to Geoff Mayfield, director of charts for *Billboard*. Mayfield says:

> *Billboard*'s been charting music for more than 50 years . . . Part of the reason that we have stayed ahead of the pack is that we have, during this decade, embraced new technologies that weren't available to us before, so that we can do what we do in a much more scientific manner. The universe of sales that we can use to project our national charts is more than 75 percent of the U.S. retail marketplace. When you consider that [famous polls such as Gallup] make handsome livings dealing with a fraction of one percent [of the populations they are surveying], you can imagine the luxury of having a sample that large on either the radio side or the sales side. We have it on both sides. On the radio side there's a division of our company called Broadcast Data Systems (BDS). It actually does, from a scientific point of view, the same thing for us on the radio side that SoundScan does for us on the sales side. It has listening posts in more than 100 markets. It measures 85 percent or more of the radio listeners in the United States.

Mayfield says the system listens to the radio 24 hours a day, seven days a week. It can get very specific data, such as the number of times a record was played or the audience size. There's lots of information indies can get, according to Mayfield:

> The companies that provide us with our chart information can offer detailed information to the labels that's even more significant than what the national charts can tell you. They give you local information . . . You'll be able to see which radio stations actually impact sales . . . There [are] a lot of meaningful things that you can get out of looking at the detailed data that these companies provide that is of equal if not greater significance to the importance of the national charts.

Only *Billboard* uses SoundScan and BDS. Charts in other publications are usually compiled from a panel of reporting stores, DJs, radio stations, etc. Charts are based on playlists/sales figures from these reporters. Radio stations and club DJs put their playlists together and send them in at the appropriate time.

Indies have a much harder time getting on the most significant charts. It takes much work/resources to promote to reporting stations and stores on a national level. In order to chart, you must get serious play and sales in the right markets simultaneously, which is hard to coordinate. Promoters have relationships with the players that most indies don't. However, studying the charts provides info that can be useful in determining what markets might be right for your artist.

FINDING PROMOTERS

If you don't have radio, retail, club, and video promoters on staff, hiring a professional who has relationships in the area in which you need to work your product is one way to go. Promoters are expensive. Some give indies lower rates than larger labels. But often you get what you pay for. Promoters logically put more energy into those paying more. But if you find a good one, they can be a big asset to your label. Onno Lakeman says:

> I learned that one person can do a lot, but you need insiders, who can approach people at *SPIN* magazine, *Music Week,* record stores, and larger college radio stations. Indiego did this for us in a series of promotion packages. Besides the exclusive promotion for the CD "Red to Violet," the Indiego samplers, with well-known featured artists like Nils Lofgren or Edie Brickell/New Bohemians, plus 13 new indies, are a great vehicle too. Being one of the indies on these samplers gets a lot of attention.

Be careful not to waste money on someone who can't provide what you expect. Promoters can get only so many records or videos played. If you decide to hire one, check their track record. Ask for references and information on what chart positions he or she achieved for other labels. The best way to find a good promoter is through recommendations from other indie labels. Otherwise, talk to the people in the music industry you're trying to reach—music directors at radio stations, club DJs, etc. Ask if they can recommend a promoter with whom they like dealing.

PLANNING A MARKETING STRATEGY

Decide what regions to hit first. Unless you have deep pockets, it's more prudent to work a small area initially, and grow from there. Working your product nationally means you'll need to manufacture a lot more. However small your first run is, you can get more as you work your way to other regions. Baby step from region to region. Be patient and you'll create a much larger market. Dave Roberge successfully used a micro-marketing strategy with O.A.R. He explains:

> When that band first started to create a buzz, it was in specific areas of the country—South Carolina, Arizona, and Ohio. When we first tried to acquire consignment accounts, we looked at it as a micro-marketing strategy. It made sense for us to spend ad dollars on a region-by-region level. With that approach, we kind of look at it almost like a spider web. You start in the center somewhere and go part by part and build it, almost like a web. If an artist's strength is in the Carolinas, we're going to employ a micro-marketing strategy that focuses on the Carolinas. We'll develop the Carolinas before we move into Atlanta and as far north as Virginia. It's about mastering that one market and creating a presence in that market, because without that one market, you're not going to be able to get to that second and then the third market. A lot of stores we spoke to in the beginning were only impressed when they heard about that second store carrying the product [and so on]. A lot of it is going out there and proving yourself. We started small, with baby steps. You're not going to go from X to 4X overnight. You have to start somewhere and go from X to Y to Z. We weren't in a position at that time to spend two million dollars at radio to push a single to make the band go from Columbus, Ohio, to a national phenomenon. It had to take time.

PLANNING WHERE TO MARKET YOUR PRODUCT

If you're marketing regionally, start in cities that you have access to, where the artist tours, or those with the best potential for selling your music. I worked New York first because I live there. Then I went to Philadelphia and one or two other cities I could visit in a day. I then got distributed in the Southeast, because I was there regularly. Choosing a region can depend on the music. Your hometown might not be a good market for your music. If your artist has a story building in a specific region or is playing live there, that's where to start.

If your record doesn't work in one region, it may work everywhere else. My own motto has been: "Don't judge the rest of the country by New York." What works well here may not sell anywhere else. What you'd have trouble giving away in your own hometown might make you a fortune outside that region. My hottest dance track sold across the country, but couldn't be given away in Chicago—they liked music that was very specific to that city.

COMPILING RETAIL STORES

You'll have to work stores in order to get them to carry your product. If you already have distribution, get input from them for a retail strategy. If you need to attract distribution, create a base of stores that you can sell to directly. I identified as many stores as possible that sold my style of music in regions I planned to work first. When starting with little or no distribution, every store counts, especially if you need the cash flow that comes from direct sales.

How do you find stores? Start with the Yellow Pages. Some stores are specialized. If you're not familiar with a store, call and ask what they sell. However, not all stores are listed in the telephone book. Sometimes they must be found by word of mouth. Talk to people in stores, DJs, and people at other indie labels. Pick their brains for the locations of stores that may help you. Some record retailers are located inside video shops or electronics stores or at flea markets. Check out trade magazines specializing in your genre.

REACHING YOUR AUDIENCE

Your marketing plan must reflect a combo of working your artist's strengths and your budget. What is your artist prepared to do? How much support can you afford? If you have some marketing money, what are the most realistic areas into which to put it? Budget with your energy, too. I ran myself ragged at first, jumping whenever someone called for a promo package or an idea for me to try. It got exhausting fast and scattered me so thinly that I wasn't as effective as I possibly could have been at anything. Plan what you can realistically do yourself. PR? Radio promotion? Street marketing campaigns? Budget your energy so that you have enough for what's essential. Focus on reaching your audience. Ryan Kuper says:

It's different for every act. I base it on what I think I can get from the band—can I get them on the road for months? If so, will I go heavier on street team promotion or a publicist? Or am I going to just put this out with print ads and hope the band gets some love? Sometimes I tag-team releases with another label. We say, "This is what I do best and can bring to the table. This is what you do best and can bring to the table. This is what we can do together."

Tony Brummel says that some artists can potentially reach other demographics and fan bases. People who like X, Y, and Z artists might be into yours if they knew about them. He adds, "You might sticker the product with a clever press quote that might allude to an artist that people might be aware of." Do what you can to reach the fans of other artists who are similar to yours. The Internet is another vehicle for reaching them (see Chapter 19). Street teams (see Chapter 15) can get the word out at concerts and other events featuring the established artists.

Make postcards to advertise your artists. Put an album cover or photo on the front and contact info, quotes if you have them, and your website address on the back. They can be used like flyers and handed out. David M. Bailey says, "For every new album, I get 5,000 postcards printed. I may or may not mail them. I hand them out like water at shows." If you order from 1800Postcards.com and mention *The Real Deal*, you get 10 percent off your first order. Postcards can be as cheap as flyers, but they look nicer. Jay Woods (New West Records) says:

> We do a lot of postcards because we've found it to be a fairly inexpensive way to send the message. We mail cards to fan lists and writers on the press side if we've got a new development we want to let people know about. We do mass mailings to radio stations and retail stores.

Don't spread yourself too thin chasing markets. For new indies, the micro-marketing strategy works best. To the best of your ability, get your artist's name out one market at a time. Jesse Fergusson suggests choosing whatever number of markets you're going to work. Allot X amount of fliers per market. He's found cost-effective ways to increase awareness:

Pick a key market and concentrate on awareness through affordable print advertising. A lot of distributors will offer multi-cut advertising. They take out an ad and charge [ten percent for each of ten cuts that will be used in the ad]. So you pick your key markets. If you're a hip-hop artist, make sure you're in all the hip-hop magazines.

"I can't get anywhere in a market!" Stop complaining! If you have great music, you'll find a way to market it successfully by working hard. Don't look to the bigger publications or clubs at first. Start small. Have a many-tiered marketing plan. Concentrate on ways to sell your first 100 records. Then work up to larger numbers. Brian Sirgutz insists that there's always a way to reach an audience if you look for it. He's found very creative directions in which to market the artists on Elementree Records and says you can absolutely do it, too:

> If you say you can't penetrate a market, I could give you ten examples of smaller things. It's like microeconomics. You'll do better hitting the market you want in smaller publications than one hit in a larger one. Get the public talking about your record. Word of mouth is still, and will always be, the most powerful marketing tool in the music business. You can't buy or fabricate it. What you can do is build around that. Make sure that if you have a good product, people will talk about it. Research. E-mail regional people—periodicals, radio stations, ma-and-pa stores for records—the smaller the better. Build a network of people to start out with.

If the music is fantastic, you can find an audience for it to speak to, one step at a time! Be patient. It can take time to find a marketing plan that works, but if the music is there, you'll find one.

GETTING PRODUCT INTO STORES

Getting distribution isn't as easy as just wanting it. Unless you have an act buzzing loudly, it takes time. Distributors want labels that appear to be striving for longevity. You must convince them they'll make money with your label. Relationships developed in retail stores help with initial sales. As stores sell your product, your artist's story increases.

GETTING INTO STORES

Developing and maintaining relationships with retail folks provides great allies. When I started my label, I'd load my bag with promotional copies and visit all stores that might sell my product. I introduced myself to everyone. Many people listened to my record on the spot. If they liked it, I'd ask if they'd carry some. Most records are left on consignment.

If a store thinks the record can sell, they'll take some. Even chains may take CDs on consignment. According to Richard Ellis, manager of Aron's Records, a large, indie-friendly store in L.A., "Most people who run indie labels are in it more for love in the beginning, and that comes across. Enthusiasm always gets my attention." John T. Kunz, owner of Waterloo Records, an indie-friendly store in Austin, Texas, warns, "It's as much work for [us to stock] someone who sold one or two CDs as someone who sold a few thousand. Artists need to understand this." Show respect and appreciation for stores that support your music. They don't have to!

When leaving records on consignment, give the store a copy of the invoice. Whether you bring them in person to a store or to a distributor, write "received" at the bottom of the invoice. Have the one who accepts them sign that they were received. Otherwise there's no proof. If you ship the records, save the receipt. A signature ensures that, when it's time to get paid, the store can't deny having received them. I've had stores try that ploy, but a signed invoice was proof.

Make a good impression on the folks in record stores. Be courteous. A friendly smile earns mileage. If they like you, they may push your product harder. Smaller stores can get people interested in buying something. Richard Ellis advises being organized and prompt—a lot of labels aren't. He likes to get a price list. Decide on your retail price beforehand. John Kunz says, "Some people want to price their merchandise so cheaply it makes people wonder what's wrong with them. They need to have a developing artist price." He also wants bar codes, explaining, "Otherwise it's more work for us." Ellis adds, "If they don't have bar codes, it's a nightmare from a retail standpoint. We have to enter all the information manually." Show you have your act together. Ellis says:

> Many people start an indie label without any business sense what-soever. They don't even know how to fill out an invoice. If I say we want to be net 30 (refers to terms of 30 days), they don't know what it means. They need to have all that stuff figured out before they approach stores for orders.

John T. Kunz recommends you come up with a package that has things retailers want. For example, "Make sure their name is very legible at the top 30 percent of the cover, not at the bottom." Richard Ellis says that some labels aren't aware of how retail works to the point that they impede their own progress. He warns:

> A lot of indie labels think it's cute to do unusually sized packages for CDs. What they don't realize is probably 75 percent of stores in the country use some sort of security packaging. They have no idea of the extra labor it takes to put tags on stuff. Sometimes an indie will put things in beautifully designed packages that won't fit into any security packaging. Labels stand in their own way of getting their product out. A lot of things that are a pain may wait three to four days to reach the floor. We may have to mark them up a dollar for that.

When I released my first record, I went to every store within driving distance and established relationships with record buyers. After meeting in person, I'd follow up by phone. I found stores in other states through trade magazines. Call the store, ask for the buyer, introduce yourself, and ask if he or she would like a promo copy with a one-sheet (see below). Send it and call back in a week. Start with markets where people will be aware of the artist, such as regions where there's radio play or the artist does live shows regularly. Be realistic. No one's going to carry your record if they've never heard of the artist and there's no promotion. Dave Roberge (Everfine Records) says they sparked interest from distributors because they were making an impact at retail on their own:

> We understood that you need to get product into stores. The first way to do it is by making champions of retail stores and entering into consignment accounts—proving you can move product off the store's shelf. Retail is becoming more and more competitive. You can have major label distribution but it doesn't mean your product will be on store shelves. It's become very tight. So our focus was independent stores first and making an impact with the people that we really felt understand and care about music.

GETTING STARTED WITH A DISTRIBUTOR

Your records are beginning to sell in stores. The story on your label is building. You're tired of sending product when stores run out. You want distribution in place, thinking you'll be set. Not true. Don't for a second think that a distributor will make your label run smoothly. Brian Sirgutz (Elementree Records) says:

> Distribution is not that important initially. If you just go out to get a distribution deal at the beginning, you'll get horrible terms, they won't push your product, and you're lucky if it even ends up on the shelves. After a few months it gets sent back to you anyway. Are you doing anything in that market to promote the act? Are you ready for it to be out there? You can't just put it out there, even if it's on the web and you're getting spins on college radio stations. Take it slowly, market by market, and build relationships.

Finding a distributor that gets product into stores efficiently can be rough. Some stay on top of orders better than others do. It's frustrating to arrive in a town for a well-promoted gig and discover that stores have no product because the distributor didn't ship them. Some actively alert stores to your product. Others just fill orders if stores request it. Finding a good distributor requires patience and shopping around until you click with a good match. Persist in building a big enough demand to attract a good one if you want your label to grow.

There are no sure-fire methods of obtaining good distribution. Start with a great product, an identified audience and a way of reaching it. No one has to carry your product. If they believe your material will sell, they'll work with you more. Depending on the genre and demand, it's better to start with several small distributors in markets you can promote in than to start with one that covers a larger region.

WHEN TO GET DISTRIBUTION

What's the point of pressing up and shipping records that may not sell because you haven't done enough marketing? If you want national distribution, you need a solid marketing campaign on a national level. Since there are different levels of distribution, don't let your ego push you to pursue one you're not ready for. Start small and work your way up.

Keep in regular touch with stores. If they say the record is selling, ask if they need more. When your re-orders are steady, contact local or regional distributors, unless you have a national thing going. Explain where the product is selling. Have promotion in place at this point. Be confident. Find ways to market the record yourself until a distributor accepts your label. The more sales you show, the easier it is to attract one. Michael Bull (Caroline) elaborates:

> We look for labels with an excellent roster of artists that fit more or less into our strongest genres, a clearly defined aesthetic vision, some history of prior success (as a label, and/or among its artists and key staff), good connections, an understanding of the distribution side of the business and what a label's responsibilities are in relation to that, good catalog, a strong and consistent release schedule, an understanding of consumer and retail marketing, and adequate financing. Of course, labels with all of these qualities are relatively rare, and exceptional strength in one area can offset weakness in another.

ONE-SHEETS

A one-sheet is one sheet of paper that describes your product with details that tell the artist's story. It's a concise summary of pertinent information including specifics about individual members of a group, a short description of the music, reviews and other press, where the artist is touring, radio play, and any other promotional information that will create excitement about the artist. All this should fit succinctly on one page. Walter Zelnick (City Hall) explains:

A one-sheet is important. That's what a lot of customers want to see. Even though they're getting a new release book from us, they want a one-sheet. It's a tool that's very handy for some customers. A well-laid-out black-and-white one-sheet—a simple sheet with all the information—is more important than a beautiful glossy which leaves stuff off.

A one-sheet should include the label's name, the artist, the name of the release, the release's UPC code, its catalog number, the release date, and the suggested retail price. Andy Allen says a one-sheet is what ultimately sets the record up in all the data systems throughout the industry:

It's what initially communicates info about the act and that particular project to the buyers. In the case of a brand new band, it may be the only thing you have to introduce the music. It should be accurate and easy to understand. Most buyers have asked us to have a one-sheet that's clear and concise, with the information presented in a way that can be easily digested.

Ask stores or distributors for samples of good one-sheets from other labels to see how they're organized. Some are done in a more high-tech way than others. Most include a copy of the album cover. Some are in color on glossy paper, but distributors and retailers assure me that the content is much more important than fancy presentation, and that plain black-and-white faxes better. Richard Ellis adds:

A good one-sheet goes a long way. I go for one-sided and love those with a three-ring binder punch so I can file them after I've ordered stuff. I'd like to know what radio are you hitting in my area? What magazines? What kind of advertising plan do you have? Provide information about the band. Who's important? Where do they come from? Why will I like this, and how will I sell it to somebody else? I love bar codes and [you should] list price information on the one-sheet, and a good representation of what the cover art will look like.

Distributors prefer working with labels that provide them with enough sheets for the retail stores they service. Providing them shows you're serious.

FINDING DISTRIBUTION

When you begin, using local distributors to get into stores gets people familiar with your label. Steve Pritchitt (Navarre) advises, "Take time to really understand your target market(s), and the business overall, and then develop a plan and stick with it." Jeff Epstein (Cropduster Records) says they got their national distribution through their press:

> The distributor came to us through a contact. We sent them a press kit. Any distributor wants to know that someone has some sort of track record. We had accumulated 100 pieces of media coverage and they looked at us as a viable outlet to sell CDs.

As you develop a track record with sales and promotion, shop for larger distributors. Start in one region and expand from there. Work it! When you feel ready for national distribution, Michael Bull (Caroline) advises, "Do your homework. Identifying which distributors are strongest with the type of music and type of label you've got BEFORE soliciting will save time in the long run." Be prepared with a marketing plan and a picture of your finances. Andy Allen says, "We have to make sure that they're in a position to market the records effectively. We ask probing questions about the financial stability of the label, where their money comes from, and whether they're adequately prepared to market things." Call and ask how to approach them. Michael Bull says:

> We're approached in about as many different ways as humans can communicate, but the best is: first, a simple introductory e-mail sketching the label's general concept, roster, key past, current, and upcoming releases, and sales history and expectations. It will often be readily apparent to the distributor whether the label might be a good fit for them, in which case the conversation can become more detailed.

How do you find distributors? Ask for suggestions from buyers in stores. If a store uses more than one distributor, get an opinion about which one they think would work best for you. Individuals working in stores often know which distributors work well with indie labels or which ones they hear other labels complain about. Pick everyone's brains. Alan Becker of RED Distribution says:

> There are many ways to find distribution. If you're looking for a national distributor, you better have the ability to create the activity that can keep the attention of a national distributor. You better have an act that has the ability to get on the radio, have a tour that's going to run from California to New York . . . to create that kind of national profile. Otherwise, it might be best to work on a more local or regional basis. On a local level, you could be a local phenomenon at your college or in a vicinity that could support you without having to take it in a more regional or national basis. So build up a local following that can then be leveraged to a regional distributor; then on up to a national distributor to make that entry a little bit smoother. I think in looking for a national distributor, it's best to start out locally—build up a following—create some results. Create some activity that you can bring to a larger distributor so that you're not put at the mercy of being one of the few starter, not-very-well-looked-after labels. In any distribution system, the distributor can't do everything for everyone. [Distributors] spend a lot of time with the labels who are creating the most activity . . . I think it's better to start out at a more manageable level, at a less high maintenance type of distribution company until you're able to create the kind of activity that can keep a national or regional distributor focusing on what you're trying to accomplish.

I began by calling buyers at local distributors and sending promotional material and the product. It's good if someone at a store lets you use his or her name as an introduction. Steve Pritchitt wants to be approached "either through an established industry channel, directly via our website, or by mail." He wants to receive a business plan, samples of product, release schedule, and financial statements. Dave Roberge says after he talked to ADA, he met with Andy Allen:

I went to New York with my business plan, my catalogue, sales figures for the band, every piece of press, anything you could think of to sell him on the fact that we were a legitimate, one-artist label, and that we had pieces in place in order to maximize that relationship. Based on that meeting, he was impressed enough to give us that shot. At the time it was a very unique deal in that the record label was one artist with three pieces.

Roberge had proven that O.A.R. could sell records, and he had his act together for marketing. Creating demand attracts distribution. If you get a reasonable buzz going on your act, however local, write a letter to distributors. Include pertinent information about your artist's story, what stores sell your product, and a one-sheet. It's not even necessary to send the product at first. Hard facts are most important. Ask if the distributor would be interested in receiving the music and promotional material. If you've created a market, it isn't that hard to get a small distributor to stock at least a minimal amount of your product. Once the distributor sells some, it'll order more.

WORKING WITH YOUR DISTRIBUTOR

You can have more than one local or regional distributor in different locations. Choose several that complement each other in terms of regions and specific stores covered. Go to as few as it takes to cover the necessary ground. National ones want exclusive rights to distribute your product. An agreement should include specific payment terms.

Send invoices with all shipments to distributors. List exactly what you're shipping, the unit price of each item, the terms of payment, the number of cartons being shipped, and the Purchase Order (PO) number that was supplied when it was ordered from you. Most invoice forms have sections clearly marked for each of these items. The invoice is placed in an envelope marked "Invoice Enclosed" and taped to the outside of a carton containing your shipment, or mailed directly to the accounts payable department of the distributor. You can buy invoices in an office supply store. You can also buy "Invoice Enclosed" envelopes or write the phrase on a plain envelope.

Some invoices have a packing slip—a list of what's being shipped, without the price—as the last page. A packing slip includes the number of cartons sent, number of units, and a Purchase Order number. It goes to the shipping office. If your invoices don't have packing slips, make your own. Either cover the area where prices would be on the last page of your invoice so the carbon doesn't go through or on business letterhead, write "Packing Slip" and list what you sent. Just as with your invoice, put a copy of the packing slip into an envelope marked "Packing Slip Enclosed" and tape it to the outside of a carton in your shipment. Don't put the invoice and packing slip in the same envelope. They go to separate departments when the shipment reaches the distributor.

Once you have distribution, don't assume the distributor(s) will do more than stock your record. Develop relationships with the sales reps. Call or visit them. Ask if they want promotional copies. It shows you're actively trying to market the record. Call regularly to see how your product is doing. Distributors carry a lot of product by many labels, and yours can get lost. By developing relationships with reps, your product may be one they push. Ryan Kuper says:

> A lot of labels have distribution and they whine a lot. They say, "My records don't sell," but they're not doing anything proactively to get those records sold. Sometimes I'm on my distributor saying, "Hey, you've got to give me more love. When you make your sales calls, I want to make sure that you're pitching that product because this is what I've done. The band's on tour with a national act. I placed print ads in . . . magazines. These are the reviews we're getting back. Interviews are happening. Radio is going on." You have to stay on it. A lot of people expect a distributor to do everything.

Keep in touch with stores. Let them know which distributor has your product and thank them for pushing it in their stores. Notify a sales rep at the distributor about any stores showing interest in carrying your product. Michael Bull says:

> Understand your role in the label/distributor relationship, and make the distributor aware of how you will make their job (putting the right quantity of records in the right stores for each release) as easy and productive as possible.

I always had promos with me when I ran my label. If I was visiting someone and saw a store I'd never been to, I'd go in, introduce myself, and

give the people there a promo and a one sheet. If they expressed interest in my music, I'd call my distributor and tell the sales rep whom I
spoke with in that store. Distributors like a label that works its product.
It earns you respect, and possibly greater priority in how hard the distributor works with you. Walter Zelnick advises:

> Keep supplying us with important information: Is your artist
> touring, getting airplay? Give us copies of important press and any-
> thing we can use as a tool to give to our sales reps so they have a
> story to tell buyers. With e-mail, update us weekly if there's new
> information. We send out weekly messages to our reps about
> increased airplay, charting information, and other stuff.

Let the distributor know if you're working radio and where your artist is
playing live. Send them copies of any press write-ups. All such information can help the company move your product into sales outlets. Build
good relationships. Andy Allen says:

> Most of it is about communication—letting us know about the
> artist, the set-up of the project, and the continuing update
> about what's happening so that we can pass that information to
> our sales force, and they can pass it through to the buyers of
> the accounts.

RELEASE DATES

I asked Andy Allen for the best time to release a record. He says, "When
you're prepared for it and the label feels that they have everything to put
together the best possible marketing plan is the best time to release a
record." There are certain times that can be advantageous. Labels tend
not to release records during Christmas season, although I released my
biggest selling dance track then and had less competition with club DJs.
Do what seems best. Allen clarifies:

> From a seasonality standpoint, there's no good or bad time any
> more. We've found that our indie labels tend not to release things
> in the fourth quarter because programs are a little more
> expensive, and the onslaught of the major artist's releases tends to
> come out in the fourth quarter. Any other time of the year can
> work fine.

Labels traditionally release records on a Tuesday. Walter Zelnick says it's a customary day for new releases. Once you have distribution, they can direct you. Many send out material to stores way in advance of the street date. Talk to your distributor for guidance on your schedule so that it works with their mailings. It can help attract pre-orders. Zelnick explains:

> We like a label to give us two months notice and work with us in our release book. We've cut it back to once a month. They get at least two months of publicity in our book. For example, in December we send out the February new release book. The customers will have all of January and the beginning of February to order.

GETTING PAID

It's said that the only way to get paid by a distributor is to follow your first record with a second. The explanation for this is that distributors will pay for the first release when they have another record on which money is owed. Then they can credit any returns from the first release against what's owed on the second. This is true to an extent, but a record label can get paid more frequently.

DISTRIBUTORS AREN'T BAD GUYS

Distributors don't have the best image in the music industry, especially in regard to paying. This reputation comes with the role of being middleman. Distributors aren't trying to cheat labels, but they have to protect themselves from a lousy system. If they don't get paid, neither do you. Record stores don't always pay bills on time, so a distributor can't always pay quickly.

Returns can come back for a long time after a record's been shipped. A distributor then gives the store credit, and gets credit from the label. Therefore, they must be prudent about paying, especially with newer labels. Distributors like keeping an open invoice (one that hasn't been paid yet) as a safety against returns. Why? For example, if a new label is paid in full by a distributor and fifty pieces are returned a year later, it could be hard getting money back from the label on those returns. Indies often change distributors or go out of business. Would you give a distributor back money if you closed your label and then got returns? Most wouldn't. Therefore, distributors always want to owe you something. An open invoice ensures they can get credit for late returns.

MAXIMIZING YOUR CHANCES OF GETTING PAID

There are ways to give yourself the best possible shot at getting paid. If you use regional distributors, don't spread yourself too thin. The more companies you use, the more you'll have to collect money from, and the more from which you can get returns. Don't get carried away with orders. Memorize my motto: **Orders don't pay bills; sales pay bills.**

Too often, we get caught up in the thrill of getting large orders. Trust me, the thrill disintegrates quickly as returns arrive. It is exciting when people agree to carry your product. You may work hard to convince lots of stores and smaller distributors to do it. But orders that you push for don't mean you'll see a dime later. Don't leave large numbers of product on consignment to anyone who will take them. Be as selective as possible about which distributors and stores you place product with. Use as few as needed to cover the greatest area of stores and distributors in regions where you have promotion in place. And you should leave as few units as is necessary. You can always send more.

Distributors pay faster if they take a record label seriously. As you get established and release more records, your label is more appealing to work with you. Getting paid is a little easier when the artist's demand grows and you seem more likely to stay in business. You get more leverage as sales increase. Don't despair if things are slow at the beginning; they can get better—as good as you make your label! The best way to get paid is to release records that sell.

The terms (length of time) of payments from distributors can vary. Get the terms in writing. It doesn't mean you'll get paid, but it gives you something on paper to argue your side of the matter if you must go to court to recover money that is owed to you. Sometimes larger distributors wait longer, unless your product is selling fast. They handle larger amounts of product and get returns from stores, chains, and one-stops. If you know the product sold well in retail stores, ask your distributor to return any stock and give them credit on the invoice. Then ask for at least a partial payment on what they owe you. If they pay 75 percent of that amount, they can keep the 25 percent open until they get more product from you.

Much of how you are paid will depend on your relationship with your distributor, and how much the distributor respects your label. Distributors do need indie labels, so they're not looking to screw you over. But the system forces them to be cautious about paying too soon. Walter Zelnick advises:

Make sure they've got something that sells. We'll even pay people early if we're sure it's selling, to take advantage of early discounts. The main thing is we don't want to pay for things that aren't selling. Hopefully the distributors are ordering what they need. Go for small orders and look for re-orders instead of loading people up. That will be better in the long run.

I recommend smaller distributors at first. Getting paid can be easier. They can work with you by taking fewer units at a time. I've had local distributors take as few as twenty-five units. Stifle the impulse to convince them to take more. **Orders don't pay bills; sales pay bills.** If they sell out, they'll order more. Some local ones will work with you by paying from order to order. Once they reorder, they pay the last invoice as the new one arrives. At the initial meeting, ask that the terms be made invoice to invoice. If you're dealing with a smaller one that's out-of-town, try to arrange for C.O.D. orders only. If they won't pay up front and you want them to carry the product, send the minimum number of units they'll accept. When they re-order, insist on sending the shipment C.O.D. for payment of the first invoice, plus shipping. If there's a market for the product, they'll work with you. If there isn't, you don't need the distributor.

When I ran my label, I tried not to give any distributor too much product at one time. When I'd get a big order, I'd ask if the distributor would take less. Why? **Orders don't pay bills; sales pay bills.** Distributors sometimes order more than they need, to be certain they have enough—they can return what doesn't sell. As you establish relationships and they learn to trust that you won't run out of product when it's needed, they'll be more flexible. I'd assure them that if they re-ordered, they'd receive product fast. Often they agreed to cut orders. A small order sells through faster, leading to re-orders. Then you can ask to be paid for the first invoice. If you have product a distributor wants, refuse to ship more until the previous invoice is paid. Alan Becker (RED) advises:

In our business fortunes change, so when we're hot, we're getting paid very regularly by our customers, and when we're not it's a little bit more difficult to get paid. Therefore it's harder to pay all of our distributed labels . . . Enter into a deal—have a written contract—and still at the end of the day, unfortunately in this business, sometimes you have to sue to get the money that's normally due you. Still, have some sort of legal document. If you have a contract and you're working with a stable [company], you're going to get paid . . . My advice on getting paid: Have a contract. Have a good lawyer.

If you have trouble collecting, small claims court is an option. You have a right, when the terms are due, to demand either payment or return of your product. The catch is that if you cause too much trouble, you may not find distribution for your next record. I limited the number of my distributors that weren't close enough to take to court. Distributors located far away from you know that the chances are you'll never come to them and sue if they don't pay.

If a distributor comes to you, of course things are somewhat different, and you can get more of your own terms met. My rule of thumb was that if a local or regional distributor called me, we did it my way, which usually meant C.O.D. shipments. When distributors call wanting your product, it's usually because they have a demand for it. Sometimes it's an overseas order. I used to insist on C.O.D.—paid right away. They often agreed. I loved it when distributors called me. It provided leverage for getting paid.

The picture I painted may discourage you, but it's reality. If you're serious, get motivated to be one of the labels that gets paid because you sell records. That's why I advised that you concentrate on developing a demand. You CAN do it, if you have an act with great music and persist in working it. I asked Steve Pritchitt how he sees the state of indie labels. He says, "Tough and getting tougher, but a great opportunity exists for labels with focus and the right set of skills." *So,* get focused and develop those skills!! You CAN achieve success if you want to.

THE INTERNATIONAL MARKET

Do you want to get your product out "overseas?" Do you think that American music flies out of the box once it gets there? The "overseas" market has a very alluring reputation. Let me fill you in on what could indeed be a lucrative market if you take the time to understand it.

BREAKING DOWN THE OVERSEAS MARKETS

Where is overseas? People refer to "overseas" as if it's one big place, which is ridiculous. The overseas market is comprised of all the countries in the world that are across an ocean you. Yet we lump them all together when referring to foreign markets. Do that and you'll probably drown trying to cross the ocean. Tom Ferguson, international editor of *Billboard* magazine explains:

> That there's no such thing as "the European market." Don't be fooled into thinking that, because a number of European countries now have a shared currency, it's suddenly become one country. There are huge differences in economics and culture— not to mention language—between the individual countries in Europe. Sometimes there are even differences in culture and language within the same country, like Belgium, for example. Likewise, there are real differences in working practices from country to country. And we might have various directives from the European Union being put into place in our individual countries' national legislation, but the legal systems in the various countries within the EU are still wildly different. In particular, remember that copyright law in much of Eastern Europe is, to put it mildly, not strictly enforced! Overall, do your homework, talk to other U.S. indies who have experience of

Europe, and rely on the guidance of a good local distributor. IMPALA (see below) is also definitely worth contacting.

Each country has distinctive likes and dislikes in music, just as there are regional preferences in the U.S. Ferguson adds, "Bear in mind that Europe is such a diverse group of markets, that what's popular in the U.K., say, might go down like a lead balloon in Germany or France."

Michel Lambot, The Independent Music Companies Association (IMPALA) chairman, says of his company, "IMPALA are light footed, rapid, supple and graceful. Independent music companies have the same qualities but like impalas they are also vulnerable to predators. Let's make sure that the similarity does not lead independents to become extinct species." Philippe Kern is Secretary General of IMPALA (www.impalasite.org), based in Brussels, a non-profit organization that aims at promoting the interests of the independent music industry with governments, international organizations (WTO/WIPO), and European institutions (European Union, Council of Europe). He says, "[The European marketplace] is very diverse. Trading in Germany is different than trading in the U.K. or Spain. Each market has is own specificities and should be taken as one—there is no such thing as one European single market." Having an accurate perception of foreign markets helps you make realistic promotional decisions. Tom Ferguson says:

> Obviously, a lot of major American acts are just as successful in Europe as they are in the states, although certain styles of U.S. rock in particular just don't seem to travel. The John Mellencamp school of "mainstream" roots rock, or the blander rock acts like Matchbox Twenty and Dave Matthews, just don't seem to strike much of a chord in Europe. The more mainstream country acts also don't tend to do so well here, for example, but we do like the real mavericks—Lyle Lovett or Steve Earle can tour and pull sizeable crowds, although their albums aren't likely to trouble the upper echelons of the charts. And obviously, a lot of hip-hop won't play too well in non-English language markets, unless you're Eminem, of course.

Many folks are under the misconception that people in foreign countries love all American music. No way! There will only be a market for your music in a specific country if it conforms to their musical tastes. But there's hope. Susan Rush, head of label management for Pinnacle Records, the biggest distributor for independent labels in the U.K., says, "It's not an easy time at the moment, but there [have] always been niche markets [in the U.K.] for U.S. artists, especially in alternative, punk, metal, hip-hop, and urban genres." Tom Ferguson adds:

> It's impossible to generalize about "indie American artists" in Europe, unfortunately. There's a long tradition of acts [that] couldn't get arrested back in the States yet [that] can sell tickets and shift a decent number of albums in Europe. Currently, acts mining the "Americana" seam are doing pretty well on the indie scene in Europe. Lambchop, for example, can play the Royal Albert Hall, in London, which holds about 5,000 people. That's more than they'd play to back home in Nashville. There's always going to be some interest in the latest flavors to come out of New York as well, and acts like the Liars or Yeah Yeah Yeahs have picked up a lot of press recently in the U.K. and in some European markets.

How do you approach international markets? Ask your distributor(s) for advice about which countries might be good markets for your label. Read magazines and trades with charts from other countries. Go to magazine stores with foreign publications and read music magazines from different countries. Reviews include specifics that can provide more insight into what people there like or dislike in music. Know your own music well enough to recognize similar acts. It gives you clues about which markets might welcome your product.

So what's selling as I write? Susan Rush says, "At the moment, the U.K. charts are dominated by Pop Idol and Fame Academy artists, but there has always been a pop market. There are fewer bands becoming massive and staying at the top because the public seems to move on more quickly." Peter Thompson, managing director of Vital Distribution, an independent sales, marketing, and distribution company says, "The Irish tend to like American music. France is very insular. They tend to promote French music." Tom Ferguson points out:

> Rather than genre shifts, the main movement in Europe over recent years has been towards domestic repertoire over "international" (i.e., U.S.). France in particular has strict quotas

limiting the amount of non-French music being played on radio, so U.S. acts face tougher competition than before in getting airplay. Otherwise, there's been a swing towards pop music in most European markets over the past couple of years, but there's still a big market for rock in Germany, and metal goes down well in the Scandinavian markets. The U.K. is probably the most "trend" oriented market in Europe, but it's currently heavily weighted in favor of straight pop acts.

Philippe Kern adds:

> Nordic countries are more receptive to metal and country music but it is difficult to generalize—the trend in Europe is the success of local repertoire over international repertoire—classical is hav ing a hard time, but it is much stronger than in the U.S. (ten percent versus five percent in the U.S.A.). Jazz is popular in Denmark and Nordic countries in general.

Holland and Belgium have always been receptive to American music. Kern says that the market concentration in radio, retail, and distribution make it difficult to break new artists, as is the case in the U.S. "In France, independents have hardly a five percent market share in distribution, whilst representing close to twenty percent in production market share. In the U.S., indies have a twenty-percent market share in distribution."

GETTING DISTRIBUTION IN INTERNATIONAL MARKETS

Getting distribution in foreign markets is similar to getting it in the U.S. You also need to create a demand or strong story for your record before foreign distributors carry it. There are distributors that work within individual countries and regions referred to as "territories," and there are larger ones that distribute in several territories or across all of Europe. Peter Thompson says:

> The European markets are saturated at the moment. There are a lot of labels out there, and I think people are focusing on the key labels. It's hard to get new labels distribution everywhere. But there are territorial differences. We have a lot of contacts throughout Europe—companies we can use—and we try to find the best possible ones for the labels that give us the rights to do so.

Most U.S. independent distributors don't distribute overseas. One-stops often do. When I ran my label, some automatically sent product to countries where they might sell. Most distributors with access to foreign markets are limited in terms of how many outlets they can get product into. They usually send a few copies to their account in potential countries to test interest. Dance music can still be the easiest to sell in many international markets through one-stops. Just like in this country, DJs all over the world love new music. It's a huge undertaking to actually go after a distributor and work your record in foreign markets. Susan Rush says:

> Whether it's U.K. or U.S. based, we need to see them build their profiles either through smaller distributors or our main competitors. The market at the moment is not conducive to labels putting records out just to "see what happens." There are too many labels and too many releases, and the consumer has too much choice, so retailers are expecting labels to deliver more, as they do not want to take risks.

It's difficult to attract distribution if your record is cold. Peter Thompson says, "It helps if we're familiar with the label or artist. In a swamped marketplace, we question whether to take them on. If we're familiar with the artist, we try to find a way to make it work." If your artist is doing well here, it might not matter to foreign markets if they're not known there. Tom Ferguson says, "It's vital to come to the European markets in person. If a U.S. act isn't prepared to show its face over here, to do press and tour, then forget it." Just like here! Susan Rush adds, "If they don't, there are fewer options to get promotional coverage and therefore less profile. Making key appearances should consolidate what your promotions people are hopefully beginning to build."

Distributors want to see a story behind the artist and how it relates to their market. Your artist must establish a presence in markets in which you want to sell and promote. Touring is a great way, but takes time. Peter Thompson says, "If they come over once, they would make a few inroads. After two or three times, they'd probably start getting a lot more interest." IF the artist is good! If you want to make money in a territory, market and promote! Susan Rush says:

Having a demand for your releases in the U.K. is important, so we look to see if labels are building up their profile via imports, or whether they already license to U.K.-based labels and might be considering doing it themselves. If that's happening, we would expect a label to set up U.K.-based promotion and marketing partners. Ideally, you would also have someone in the U.K. managing the day-to-day distribution activities, but if that's not possible, you certainly need someone who is contact-able every day and understands what's required for the U.K. market. E-mail makes things much easier, but it means things move quicker and everyone expects faster responses.

As Rush says, the best way to market a record in a foreign territory is to hire a representative for your label in that territory. Peter Thompson explains:

From our perspective, having somebody we can regularly speak to in the U.K., during business hours, is key. It may not be so bad for a New York label, but it would be very difficult to communicate properly with the West Coast because of the time difference. Things can move very quickly in the U.K., so you need to be able to react very quickly. We like to feel that a label we're working with is serious about what it's doing and investing in that by having someone in our territory, on the ground, who understands our territory and how it works, and the frustrating nature of what we do. Often the biggest problem is trying to explain to somebody thousands of miles away why they haven't sold as many records as they think they should because they're selling a lot in America. They're not selling any records in the U.K. because no one's heard of them. I don't want to spend all my time on the phone explaining the basics of the marketplace. It's easier if we can speak face to face with people and build up a proper rapport. Then we work together to achieve our aims. It's building up a relationship.

If you have someone based in the territory, that person should know the marketplace well. It's expensive, but something to consider for the future if you want to work foreign territories. Perhaps you can find other indies in the same situation and hire one person together in a cooperative arrangement.

The press in some countries can be generous with U.S. acts that they like. I got quite a bit of media coverage in the U.K. for myself as the "rappin' teach" and for my other acts as well by going there and developing relationships. Networking can put you in touch with radio stations that might play your record if you send them a copy, and with magazines that might review it. Peter Thompson says, "There are more nationwide specialty shows in the U.K., and many are very supportive of American acts at the moment. But things change quickly."

Visiting a potential market can solidify those all-important relationships, which you can later maintain with phone, fax, or e-mail. I got my records on radio in Europe when I went to the DJs. The press is also friendlier in person. Write-ups in foreign magazines establish a foundation for your market. It's harder to make those first contacts long distance. But once people got to know me, I mailed my later releases and followed up from home. Jonatha Brooke says she's making inroads in the European market:

It's really daunting to do it yourself there. You have to go territory by territory and have a separate deal with each territory. We decided to hit the countries that love singer/songwriters: Denmark, Belgium, and Ireland. We've actually built a little audience over there. We do short tours and keep pounding away at the press. We've got one distributor in Denmark and a different one in Ireland. We're just hooking up with a German distributor. I started in Denmark and went from record store to record store asking them if they'd buy some on consignment. I had a couple of gigs set up. My first gig was through the conservatory. I did a songwriting workshop and performed at the end. In a year's time we went from an audience of 50 to 1,000, the second time back. I sell a ton at gigs in Europe. [They don't know if they'll find it again, so they buy it then.]

It *is* possible to hook up directly with a foreign distributor. If you identify an audience in specific countries, find ways to reach it to get the story started. Get your artist touring in those markets. Use the Internet to find contacts. If your market increases, Susan Rush advises, "Consider manufacturing in Europe and shipping from a European base. But I would only do it if it [were] obvious there [were] a growing demand for the labels, rather than pushing just to feel like it's ticking distribution boxes in each territory."

How do distributors pay? Peter Thompson says, "We take a percentage of the dealer price of the record and try to set the price as a U.K. dealer price. We [support our labels/artists]—advise them on everything from how to format the record, how to price it, to what stores to pitch it [to]." He told me that major labels come to him, too, because they have their marketing down so well. The programs for foreign distributors are similar to those here. Susan Rush says:

> Certainly the U.K. market is similar to the U.S. market in that retailers have the power, and sales to the chains are generally sale or return. Labels also pay for retail marketing (racking, co-op ads, etc.) and returns can be heavy. This means manufacturing and shipping can be very expensive, so the label needs to make sure it has a viable business for it to work. Otherwise it should just sell on import.

Choose a distributor with care. Sometimes having just one for all of Western Europe doesn't work, sometimes it does. If a distributor doesn't have separate marketing people in each country, the record may not have the sales it should. One can't treat all parts of the international market with one big strategy and hope to be successful. Philippe Kern points out that U.S. music has a 30 percent market share in Europe, while European music (including U.K.) has a seven percent market share in the U.S. He adds, "It is time the U.S. public opens its ears to European music."

OVERSEAS ROYALTIES

Artists don't get the same royalty rate for foreign sales as they do for sales in the United States. For acts signed to American labels, the overseas rates are always lower than here, which your lawyer should include in the artist agreement with your label. Many of those reductions are considered industry standards, like the clauses in artist agreements I mentioned earlier in the book. They all favor the record label, of course. According to attorney Larry Rudolph:

> An independent label needs to take a very close look at how they're handling their international distribution . . . at what they're getting in various territories, and try to mirror that in their deal with the artist . . . They don't pay the same rate in the

United States as in other countries. Usually a label will start out at 50 percent [of the normal U.S. artist royalty rate for worldwide sales], which I think is unfair. A starting point should probably be something like 75 percent in some of the major territories of the world, like Japan and Australia, some of the countries in the EEC [European Economic Community] and Canada . . . [and] sometimes [even] 85 percent in Canada.

Here's a nice bonus for marketing music in other countries: They pay higher rates on publishing. While in the U.S. a flat rate is paid for the mechanical license, in most other countries the rate is based on a percentage of the price paid to dealer (PPD). This can end up being considerably more than what would be earned here for the same sales. Artists get credit for use of songs they perform in each venue. Publishing is a lot more valuable. If you, as the label owner, have a piece of the songwriter's publishing, you'll enjoy this benefit. Philippe Kern explains:

Licensing fees for songwriters and music publishers are much higher in Europe than in the U.S. This is mainly due to the *droit d'auteur* tradition that put authors in a stronger bargaining position than on the other side of the Atlantic. Performance royalties and mechanicals are higher than in the U.S.

LICENSING

An easier way to get your product out to foreign markets is to license it to a foreign record label. Licensing gives the foreign label the right to manufacture the record on its own label instead of just buying the record from your company for distribution. When independent labels license their records to foreign companies, they often give those companies the right to manufacture and sell records in all parts of the world where the independent labels have limited or no distribution anyway.

A licensing agreement can cover a small territory such as one country, a larger territory such as all of Europe, or the whole world except for the United States. Indies lacking good distribution outside the U.S. often do a worldwide deal, except for the U.S., since they'd have trouble doing it on their own. According to Larry Rudolph, "International licensing is a great way to open up the world as a market. Today the market is worldwide . . . Either you do a worldwide distribution deal as an indie label, or you can do it territory by territory, or group some territories together." Attorney Wallace Collins warns:

> You must make sure that your agreement with the recording artist (or with the owner of the masters if you are purchasing a master recording) provides for a worldwide right of distribution and sale, and permits you to use licensees to exploit this right. Otherwise, the artist or the owner of the masters has the right to do the foreign licensing deals directly.

When a single or album you've licensed is released, your label is acknowledged on it. The label with the license should give you an advance. In some ways, a licensing agreement is similar to one signed between a record label and an artist. When expenses and the advance are recouped from royalties earned, you'll receive royalty checks, from the label. Depending on the terms of your own artist agreement, your artist shares that money. Wallace Collins says:

> As for your royalty rate, in foreign deals it is often a percentage of the published PPD. This is usually something between the retail price and the wholesale price, depending on how PPD is defined in your agreement. You must be very careful because percentages can be deceiving. It really depends on what number your percentage is applied to—and the definition of PPD is often a heavily negotiated issue in any deal. I always try to get the royalty percentage applied to the highest number possible. I also make the licensee state the actual dealer price or PPD dollar amount so I can do a "penny count" and know exactly how much my client receives per record sold. Also, I always make sure that my client, the indie label, gets a piece of any flat fee or third-party license made by the licensee.

Sometimes if a foreign distributor wants to carry an American label's product, it tries to arrange for that label to get a licensing deal with a record label it already distributes in the overseas territory. Rather than relying on the U.S. label to get a story going for an artist, foreign distributors prefer involving a local label that knows how to market and promote in its own territory.

Warning: Don't even think about licensing a record without using a lawyer. While what you earn from licensing may seem like found money, don't sell your label short by not getting all you should from the deal. The owner of a label who had received an offer from an English label insisted he believed their story about being too small to give much of an advance. The American was dying for a deal. The English label knew it and pushed him to sign quickly. Just as quickly I insisted he get a lawyer. A month later he sent me a gift because the lawyer negotiated him a much better contract with a lot more money.

Be careful dealing with businesses in foreign countries. They know it's unlikely you'll come over to audit their books or take them to court over royalties owed. Make sure you get a reasonable advance—it may be the only money you'll see from the deal. Check them out thoroughly before signing. A lawyer experienced in foreign markets can help.

If you do a licensing agreement, you'll probably be offered a publishing deal for the songs on the record. I always got an advance on royalties when licensing a record. Usually the licensing record label has it's own publishing company and prefers that you use it. You don't have to. It's easier, but you might get a better deal from another. As I said, these royalties can be lucrative outside the U.S. Use a publisher that will earn you the most money! Your lawyer should handle this, too, and be knowledgeable enough about international biz to advise you properly.

INTERNATIONAL CONFERENCES

When I asked industry folks for the best way of hooking up with international companies for a distribution or licensing deal, the most common response was "Go to MIDEM." Larry Rudolph says, "MIDEM is where all of the international companies are coming for exactly the purpose of picking up licensing deals in their particular territories." Tom Ferguson says:

> The big European markets, Popkomm and MIDEM, are very indie-oriented, and deals are done at both of them. So it's worth attending if you can afford it, but probably not essential. At least they give indie labels a chance to meet overseas distributors face to face.

MIDEM, an international music licensing/publishing/distribution conference held each year in January in Cannes, France, is probably the largest gathering of international music industry folks. Music publishers, distributors, record labels, etc., come from all over to attend. According to Bill Craig, its vice president of sales:

> MIDEM is by far the most important music industry conference in the world. MIDEM has continued to grow for over 30 years because it [provides] an atmosphere where business is accomplished. Although MIDEM is a five-day event, the business generated can take months of work. Meetings planned in advance are the effective way to manage your time at the market. Once [you see how much] business is accomplished at MIDEM, you will find that it is a necessary event to attend every year.

Wallace Collins says, "MIDEM is four long days of meeting and greeting and miles of running around deal making and bread-breaking. 'Schmoozing' is too gentle a word for it!" It's an incredible networking opportunity. It's also incredibly expensive, so don't go unless you know you have music with a reasonable chance of attracting international interest. Going does save money on sending product to folks overseas and phone calls to establish contact. It also saves time. If you attend, try to borrow a copy of the directory from the last year to make advance appointments. Hit up everyone! For information, look up www.midem.com on the Internet or call 212-689-4220.

The most valuable thing you may get from MIDEM is relationships. People take you more seriously in the environment of MIDEM than they would if you were just another indie label sending an unsolicited package. Once they're in place, these relationships can be worked for later releases. You might not get a deal initially, but the relationships get you in doors later.

Another European opportunity is Popkomm, an annual communications trade fair held during August in Germany. It involves a trade fair, congress, and festival. It offers a presentation platform for the international pop music industry. The folks at Popkomm say it's the largest music industry get-together worldwide, and represents the largest concert event in the world. It includes public concerts in clubs and on outdoor stages, presenting over six hundred acts to huge audiences consisting of the trade fair's attendees and the general public. The concerts offer music that spans genres across the entire pop music spectrum. Popkomm is more informal than MIDEM. According to Reiner Schloemer:

> Popkomm's power [lies in] communication and [musical] content meeting with a strong emphasis on the presentation of artists in lots of concerts . . . But the business aspect gets more important every year as we have more and more exhibitors and participants. The fact that Germany is the third biggest record market in the world makes it very important for Europeans to attend Popkomm.

Application forms are available on Popkomm's website: www.popkomm.de. Tony Brummel (Victory Records) says:

> Foreign sales is about 25 percent of our business. Over the years, I've gone to Popkomm and MIDEM. It's very worthwhile if you get your packages to people and follow up with faxes and e-mails. Secure the meetings. It boils down to relationships. I know that I've done deals with people over the year because I've hit it off with them personally. And they believed in what my company was doing. That good will on their end turned into a lot of business for them as well. To an extent, this is still a people business and there are a lot of people out there who will do business with you because they believe in music and will believe in your vision if you have a vision that's worth investing in. All of our artists tour internationally.

There are also other events going on in different countries, such as U.K. Music Week. The festival circuit in many European markets is a great way of getting exposure for your music, if it fits. Networking and the Internet can help put you in touch with them.

MARKETING AND PROMOTING OUTSIDE THE BOX

This chapter discusses creative, alternative ways to brand your music through grassroots promotion and marketing, and discusses finding outlets that pay to use music. I've talked to labels about their survival in this supposedly tough market. Many found ways to beat the traditional system by breaking rules and being creative. Grassroots marketing is a foreign concept at the majors, but indies live by it. Below are suggestions to get you started.

FINDING ALTERNATIVE MARKETS

Alternative marketing means finding places to sell your product beyond traditional record stores. Study your market. Selling outside the box can increase sales. Depending on the music, some indies target non-traditional outlets to sell product, such as clothing stores, health stores, and gift shops. Bookstores work for some genres. Dan Zanes (Festival Five Records) found a great market for his children's CD in kid-related stores that sold clothing, books, toys, even kid's furniture. Zanes explored any venue aimed at kids. He explains:

> My CD looks different, more handmade, so it fits into places. I put on a clean shirt and went from store to store. Word of mouth got the CD outside of town. I'd get e-mails from other parts of the country. I believe in playing live to spread the word. I've done a lot of performing since this came out. In the beginning, if I knew someone at a school, I offered to do it for free if we could sell CDs. That was the starting point. I performed for families at fundraisers on weekends. The school kept the door. We'd sell CDs.

Zanes' market keeps expanding. His unique packaging makes his CD a special gift item for any store with kids' products. His passion for what he did pushed him and now his record label grows steadily. Trout Fishing in America also does some children's music. Manager Dick Renco says:

> We do a lot of work with libraries. [Trout Fishing in America] did a workshop for 150 school librarians, showing the librarians how they write poems. Part of our mission is to make art accessible. These guys prove that art comes from everyday lives. Libraries called them. They did a public service spot advertising libraries and reading programs. They do workshops with kids.

Keep your eyes open. Be creative by thinking outside the box about what kinds of stores and other outlets could be tapped to sell your CDs. Pay attention to your packaging from the get-go. That could make your CD stand out as special. In the next chapters, pros emphasize how great packaging can achieve more than great music. If people don't open your package, the music won't be heard. Zanes said some stores bought his CD without listening to it. That is marketing! Would you buy cereal in a plain white box with generic black lettering? We're attracted to products with nice packaging. If you think about yours from a marketing standpoint, the results might increase your chance of success.

Mail orders can generate grassroots, word-of-mouth interest in the music. Fans may play your record for friends, who may then buy it, too. If you do a mailing before the release, include incentives for pre-orders to get some cash. It's hard to break an artist with mail orders. Sales figures won't go through SoundScan. Include instructions for ordering by mail on everything you give out and on your website. Prepare fliers or postcards to give out at gigs. You may not sell many CDs, but a sale is a sale. Prepare for mail orders before a record is released. Don't wait until you're busy once the product is in. Advertise autographed copies or free swag if people order in advance. Upfront cash is nice.

ALTERNATIVE VENUES

Find alternative venues that offer opportunities to perform, get paid, and sell CDs. Once again, get into the habit of thinking outside the box. Watch for places to cultivate gigs that aren't clubs and concert halls. Rich Hardesty created an empire in the college market. Besides targeting traditional clubs and frat parties, he finds ways to create new fans, sell CDs, and make good money. Since so many college kids are underage and can't go to bars, Hardesty goes to them. Sometimes he plays private parties for excellent money. He explains:

I tell them to charge 10 or 15 dollars a head. I can make anywhere from 800 to 3,000 dollars. They have it in private houses at college campuses. I always sell CDs. And you entertain a market of underage kids who will support you as they turn 21. The kids sign your mailing list, want your autograph, and you're creating a fan for life. I think underage kids are an untapped market. I hear from them all the time that they want to see me but can't come to a bar.

When David M. Bailey resumed songwriting and performing, he looked for places to perform and expose people to his music. He says:

It sounds cliché, but you just gotta get out there. I played at our local church; at our campus support group; at a pottery shop. I scouted places to play and dropped off press kits with a recording. It's hard to create a draw. I looked for opportunities to play where people were gathered for another reason.

Bailey discovered that conferences offer opportunities to perform in front of large audiences, sell CDs, and get paid. Hunting them out is a matter of being alert. He reminded me that there's a whole industry of people who manufacture things that have annual conferences. Bailey says, "Everyone knows somebody that goes to these. Get a business card, a decent recording, a photo, and a bio." Bailey has something to say that people like. In many cases, he pitches himself as an inspirational speaker with a guitar. He began with church conferences because he had contacts, and worked his way out. He says:

You do one concert for a group of 1000 people and they actually represent 49 different churches. Over the next six months, invitations from all these places trickle in. This worked for me well in the church arena, but I think it's true in any sector—one really good concert in front of a group of people from all over creates not just word of mouth but actual invitations to their own places.

Organizations hire entertainment for conferences, usually pay well, and attract interesting fans. Some artists support their label by working fairs and festivals. With appropriate music, you can make good money, sell

CDs, and increase your mailing list. Stay vigilant for opportunities. Schools, churches, organizations for kids, and a gazillion other places can give you exposure if you ask. Don't be afraid to ask somebody if they need live music for an event if you think yours would fit.

BUSKING

Composer/electric violinist Lorenzo LaRoc found an unusual avenue for promoting his CDs—the New York City subways. He plays the new five-string plexiglass electric violin, his signature trademark. LaRoc works for a program called Music Under New York (through Arts for Transit), funded by the New York City Transit Authority. They give him a license to perform his original music in high-tourist subway stations, in designated areas at specific times. Each performance stimulates huge CD sales. LaRoc says he's moved over 40,000 CDs from exposure in the subway. It's different than performing with his seven-piece band, Masterpiece, but worthwhile:

> When I heard about the program, I thought as an independent artist trying to promote his new band, let me go down there without my band to lure people into the clubs with flyers and business cards. My CDs are selling like crazy through word of mouth. It never slows down. I can never saturate this market because there are millions of people who take the train. At any given point there are tens of thousands of tourists. It's a new audience at every gig. I'm a happy camper. On my new CD I have top musicians. Here I am in the subways, a street musician selling one of the top jazz albums out.

Playing underground is lucrative on many levels. LaRoc has a table with business cards and gets hired by people who discover him there. He gets bookings for high-end gigs, private corporate work, playing at the U.S. Open, and for New York City mayors. Playing underground also attracts great PR opportunities. He's appeared on several TV shows. A concert at Avery Fisher Hall for Music Under New York went national with Charles Kuralt. He had 1,000 mail orders from that appearance. LaRoc says:

> I'm an entrepreneur who happens to play a mean violin. As an independent artist, I've worked for some of the world's best musicians. I knew that until a label signed me, I'd have to finance

it myself. This program is the perfect conduit. I put everything I earn into me. I have a very loyal following in New York. My desire is to get on the radar as a composer, writer, and bandleader.

LaRoc was in the *New York Times* seven times in five months and was interviewed by other publications. He says auditions for Music Under New York are held once a year but warns that this isn't easy. He does his own booking, advertising, and promotion, as well as rehearsing with his band. He also gets hired for events with New York City & Company—the city hall's tourist organization. He makes $250,000 a year with all his revenue streams. I asked LaRoc what it's like to be an underground performer:

There's a big underground trip around the world. We're like troubadours of the seventeenth century, traveling from kingdom to kingdom. What's beautiful about what I do is it's live. It's one thing when people love my CD—another to see me live. It is the greatest feeling on earth. You get an instant response and can look into people's faces. They see me sweat. I'm a very visual, movable violinist. I get applause and people come to my shows and buy CDs.

RECORD RELEASE PARTIES

If you have record release parties, choose a venue with a good sound system. Try to cut a deal with the club. If they think you'll bring a large crowd, you may get more perks that you don't have to pay for. Record release parties are usually scheduled to last for two hours. It's easier to get a club's cooperation if you hold the party early in the evening. Sometimes the artist performs for the public later. Some labels have an open bar for an hour, but that is costly. If the artist has a large following, you may be able to cut a deal for him or her to do a free public performance at the venue in exchange for an open bar during the party. Some labels have a champagne toast, or something special and a cash bar for other drinks. Some clubs allow you to bring food, others provide some. It's a party, so you need something. The artist usually performs.

Send special invitations to the media, radio people, agents, managers, retailers, and anybody in the music industry that might help your artist. Invite loyal fans and players who helped get the record out. Don't plan a release party if you aren't sure you'll have a crowd. It'll do more harm than good if a few industry pros hang out in an empty room. To avoid that, be prepared to call everyone you invite to confirm that they're attending.

FREE? MUSIC

I was against giving music away for free—until I interviewed people in the industry for this book. Now I advocate doing it. Brian Sirgutz (Elementree Records) emphasizes, "You're not selling your music— you're selling yourself, the name recognition, your brand. The music is a vital part but it's not the whole package." He says that by giving away your music, you may lose one sale, but you'll gain two. People assume Napster was detrimental to record sales. Not true says Derek Sivers, founder of CDBaby:

> Obscurity is a far greater threat to musicians than piracy. That's the real enemy. If you get so scared that people will steal, people will never hear [your music]. When Napster was at their peak, CD sales were at their peak. One out of 20 orders at CDBaby mentioned that was how they heard about the artist. Napster was becoming THE place to discover music—the ultimate word-of-mouth tool. They used it to find out about artists their friends told them about. As soon as the majors shut it down, CD sales dropped. Anti-piracy people assume that if people can't download for free that they'll rush to buy it. But it's not true. A majority of the free downloading was mild curiosity. It wasn't replacing sales.

Remember, don't just try to sell records. That's how you get one-hit wonders. When you create fans instead, your records always have fans to buy them. Fans will join your street team and support your artist by coming to their gigs. Dan Zanes says, "I gave them away as fast as I could at the beginning. I had total faith in what I had. My idea was to get it into as many people's hands as possible and trust it would create momentum." When you brand your label by letting potential fans hear your music, they buy other releases in the future. Rich Hardesty has gotten far by giving away lots of music. He explains:

> I have about 38 live CDs, recorded at shows. I mostly give them away for free because it's a fan that will keep coming to shows. Fans pass them around. They end up on the Internet. It's live,

and I'm not worried about it being passed around because it creates new fans. That's the bottom line.

Michael Hausman (United Musicians) says they streamed Aimee Mann's entire record from her website, believing that if fans like it, they'll buy it. Major labels know there may be only one or two great songs on an album. Hausman says, "That's why many full records aren't streamed. But if you have a good record, and we think we do, we do it." Fans look for indies with integrity that are known for having a full album of good songs. When fans know you do, they appreciate it and buy CDs. Dave Roberge (Everfine Records) agrees:

> I think people have been duped. They'll hear a song on the radio, buy the record, go home and play it, and it's nothing like the song they heard on the radio. After the second and third time they're spending 16 to 20 dollars to get duped. So they're going to the Internet, getting their one song, and the band is relevant for that one song. As an independent, I believe we need to go back to making great records that people want to buy.

When you make great records, fans support you by buying them. People are sick of being disappointed because they bought a record based on a great single and the rest of the songs stink. If you give them a taste, they'll want the whole thing. Rich Hardesty heard from a high school girl in Portland, Oregon. He sent her free music and now her whole school are fans. Giving away samples creates demand in places you've never been. Hardesty adds:

> Who else would turn a high school in Portland on to my music? A marketing team for a record label has all that money but I did it for free. Now she's doing artwork for me and created a bunch of fans. I do that with many high schools. If I get a fan letter, I ask if they'd like free CDs. It costs one dollar to send media rate. I send a live show, hoping they'll copy it and give it to everyone they know.

Why would fans buy a CD if they get music free? Hardesty gives away live shows and sells the studio CD. Dave Roberge says fans want CDs with nice packaging. "We've focused on delivering innovative packaging, delivering the product in a way that somebody has to go out and own it. You've got to spend money on the packaging." He also supports taping at shows. Skeptics assume that allowing shows to be taped, copied, and passed out, hurts sales. O.A.R. has an open taping policy to create a community where fans have a sense of ownership of the band. They interact by trading songs and live performances. O.A.R. were questioned about this when they had a live record to sell. Roberge says it helps:

> Can a band with an open taping policy sell a live record? We've proven you can. Fans buy it because there's something special there. We focused on the packaging and put something together that they had to have. And here we are at 64,000 units for a double, live CD with an open taping policy. I certainly challenge anybody who says that's detrimental to record sales. By allowing fans into your world and giving them as much access or inner activity as possible, the more they're going to give you. They know you're not deceiving them. They want to work with you.

Free CD samplers are one of the best ways to hook new fans. Use street teams (see below) to distribute them. The Internet is another place where free music can be promoted. Consider putting some songs on MP3 files and send them to potential fans. If you believe in your music and give people a taste, you can create fans who will buy many of your CDs down the road.

STREET MARKETING

Street marketing is a great marketing alternative. Indie labels are known for their ability to create awareness through grassroots efforts. Major labels' big machines can't maneuver the streets easily. Hip-hop artist K. Banger (The Dirt Department) uses a tool available to everyone to reach an audience. He explains:

> Independent artists must never underestimate the marketing power of **word of mouth!** It can be very frustrating to talented artists when they do not have capital to invest in the necessary components to be heard and seen on a broad scale. But once we understand that marketing stirs up word of mouth, we can rely on our creative side to market ourselves at low cost. Word of mouth attracts people to assist in expanding your business venture from a

financial point of view. When my prospects saw the streets were talking, they knew The Dirt Department was worth getting into.

Look how fast rumors can spread! Once again, awareness begins with great music. When you get people talking, awareness begins. K. Banger's word-of-mouth campaign began with family and friends. He explains:

> They let their people know about my CD. One friend told an acquaintance with a slot on a Rutgers, New Jersey station. The radio-show host played it. Although the station doesn't have strong signals, it was a turning point in my local market. The host warmed listeners to me, buzzing the website URL. I did promo rhymes to promote their show and sponsored it since they were giving me so much burn. Next thing you know, all the hip-hop programs on the station are blazing my tracks. I didn't pay for advertisement. No payola or marketing stuff. It spilled over to a Rutgers station with a stronger signal. The urban director got e-mails from major labels asking about me. I sold CDs with ease, off and on-line. People said they heard me on radio, and my name was everywhere. For someone with few resources, that was a great start! I didn't expect word to spread so much from this little station in the middle of nowhere. But it had a huge effect, especially in my hometown market.

K. Banger works it wherever he goes. I met him when he hit me up to buy his CD after I'd spoken at an industry event. I thought that took balls and paid attention. He's someone who speaks to everyone and spreads the word about his music, all for the price of opening his mouth!

STREET TEAMS

Indies are turning to street teams to spread the word about an album to potential fans. Street teams can effectively generate an early buzz on a release before its street date. If you have the budget, you can hire street marketing companies to put street teams together in any market across the country. If you can't afford it, create one from fans. Tony Brummel (Victory Records) says:

> They do anything from various promotions on the Internet; going to retail and setting up displays; securing in-store play; filling out

stock checklists for us; giving us reports on what programs they see other labels' product in; compliance for listening stations that we pay for, especially at the chain level. The big thing is going to concerts and passing out posters, stickers or samplers and doing everything in their community to promote our records.

Ryan Kuper (Redemption Records) says street teams are great for niche oriented labels. Bands with loyal fans work well for labels to spread the word. They pump that first week of sales up as much as possible. Jay Woods (New West Records) is a big believer in having people talking up your record in stores:

We don't have the luxury of a big staff or having RED at our beck and call. So we constantly try to recruit people to be [our] eyes and ears for us in the stores. There's only so much you can do over the phone. Part of it is an imaging campaign and letting people know. There are 30,000 new records out this year. We did ten. How do you think those stand out in 30,000 new pieces? That's our challenge. You've got to let people know they're out there.

Show great appreciation for your street teams. Continually encourage people to sign up to join at gigs and on your website. Create a separate newsletter for street team members. Let them know news first. Make it personal. Thank individual members in it for specific things. Give them free tickets to gigs, advance copies of new releases, a song no one else has, and any perks you think of. When fans feel like a part of something special, they'll work hard. Create a community as GrooveLily did when they began their Petal Pushers (PP) program. Valerie Vigoda says they create a sense of community to make the fans feel special, because they are. They work together to spread the word. Vigoda explains:

The Petal Pushers turned into their own vibrant, growing community of friends. They have gatherings and parties. There is an active on-line discussion group, and we make "exclusives" available to the PPs as often as we can. We put one very avid Petal Pusher in charge of the program. He's the point person— asks each PP how they'd like to be involved, and encourages them to do what they're comfortable with: postering, flyering, contacting media, giving sampler CDs out, helping at the merch table at gigs, and in some cases, promoting shows. A small group of PPs funded our bumper stickers, which say "Petal Pusher Powered!" People enjoy being part of a community, helping to spread the word about music they like . . . all we do is show appreciation as much as we can, and try to channel their incredible energies!

Jesse Fergusson uses marketing companies to organize Def Jux's street promotion. But it works best when the street teams love the music. He advises:

There are marketing companies around the country that you can pay to get stickers into the hands of kids who buy records. Print 15,000 and pay companies to get them distributed. Street promotion is important on a grassroots awareness level. If you give posters to those teens in your city markets, they go to retail and support the record by talking to buyers and securing display space. Nothing works if the people you're paying don't believe in the record. What might be better for a touring band is generating your own relationships in those markets with smaller groups of people who may be more dedicated because they see a future with the artist, and they're fans who love the music. You can buy all the promotion you want. But if it isn't good enough for somebody to really get behind it, it won't work.

ALTERNATIVE RETAIL PROMOTION

Send street teams to any place that a potential fan might go. Give them T-shirts to wear at music events that fans of your genre attend. They can give out samplers, stickers, or any swag with your name and website on it. They can also talk up your music with the enthusiasm that only a passionate fan can generate to fans of similar artists. Onno Lakeman (Red to Violet) says:

We have given people T-shirts and flyers for U.K. festivals and it works. In the U.S., we did the same during events so that thousands of music lovers visiting the festival see someone wearing the shirt and handing out flyers.

Street teams create awareness. Where might potential fans shop? Fans can bring promotional material to retail stores that music lovers may go into. These stores don't have to sell the CDs. But they might give out swag to support the music, if enthusiastic fans approach them. Tony Brummel (Victory Records) agrees:

> That's a big alternative marketing area for a label like us—a lot of alternative type accounts that might be interested in our artists will do things for us, outside regular music retail. For example, we continually supply skateboard shops, surfboard shops, places like that, with free music, T-shirts, and giveaway items. In turn, they'll give out our samplers, put up posters, and play the CDs in their store. They don't sell the CDs. We still want sales to be in music retail.

LICENSING MUSIC

There is a strong market for licensing indie music in a variety of areas. Getting music into film and television generates a good income. Why would music supervisors want indie music? Because you can act much faster than larger companies, and you will take less money. As Jay Woods says:

> There [are] two ways to make money in the record business: One is selling CDs. The other is to license material. That's a viable part of what we do. We have had little leverage, and now we have a little more. The more we have, the more serious music supervisors take us. It's taken some time. Part of the reason Cameron stayed in L.A. was to be in the middle of that stuff. We have gone to music supervisor soirees and service those people. Most of the stuff we've had licensed for films or TV comes from meeting people over time.

Many indies say licensing music helps them stay independent. Valerie Vigoda says, "We've been featured on daytime TV shows recently." Jonatha Brooke wrote a song for a Disney movie and has songs on *Dawson's Creek, Providence,* and many more. Both made the contacts through friends and networking. And of course, great music helps! Some labels actively pursue music supervisors. Others try for publishing deals. Often visibility can attract people who want to use your songs. Jeff Epstein (Cropduster Records) says:

A lot of our artists have gotten into independent films and TV. People have solicited us. We didn't go out of our way. A lot of the press was very helpful. When you're in *Billboard* magazine, for example, people take notice.

Music supervisors cruise music websites such as CDBaby. There are websites that offer opportunities to post music, and people looking to license can peruse it. There are several non-exclusive ones that organize the categories of music by field. Mark Carpentieri (MC Records) warns, "As a label, it depends on how much you own of the masters and the songwriting. If you're a self-produced artist, you own everything. It becomes more difficult for the person trying to license music if they have to split things up."

There are also broadcast houses like Broadcast Programmers and MUSAK that make compilations for places like elevators and building lobbies. I spoke to Leanne Flask at DMX Music in L.A. They accept music for satellite radio but also consider licensing music for other avenues, such as providing in-flight music for airlines. If you think your music might be appropriate, call and she can point you to an appropriate programmer for your music. Then submit a CD.

JUST DARN CREATIVE

There are other income opportunities and promotional approaches for your label. People love music. Find ways to tie yours into things outside the box. For example, Jeff Epstein says, "One of our artists, Julia Greenberg, was able to do a show for *Self* magazine. She did an invite-only live show with 300 people and everybody got a Julia Greenberg CD." Onno Lakeman and EL have their own independent production company to supplement their income producing music for others. They provide background music, promotional business videos, and lots more. He says, "We create, and creation gives us income."

Find creative ways to promote your music to attract fans. Jeff Epstein says that one year, they arranged to do a Cropduster showcase at SXSW as a label. Three of their artists put on airline jumpsuits and went around giving out their planes, asking people to come. Mark Carpentieri says putting bounce-back cards in his CDs increases his mailing list:

We feel it's important to directly connect with our customers. As the retail landscape gets worse for niche music, when we release a new CD, we want to connect with people. We've used bounce back cards since our first record. It gives us a better reach of our customers: who they are, where they bought our CDs, and maybe get them to buy more through us directly.

Since he has a huge fan base in the college market, Rich Hardesty has taken his act to Jamaica for spring break for many years. He got spring break companies to pay for him and provide free trips to raffle off. He invites his mailing list to join him in Jamaica. Many do! Hardesty says:

> When I played my first gig in Jamaica, there were kids from all over the country. So I stacked my suitcase full of CDs and bumper stickers. I had a marketing plan to get as many CDs out with the website on it to all these [diverse] kids from different parts of the country. I hired Jamaicans to promote and give them out. A big spring break company put me at the most popular bar. There were about 3,000 people. It was so successful that they sponsor me every year. I've taken my band or done solo acoustic shows.

Hardesty's mailing list expands with each trip. He loves Jamaica and created an opportunity to have a free vacation and great promotion. It also increases his mailing list with new fans from all over the country. When it comes to music, creativity brings opportunities. Get into the habit of thinking outside and under and over the box. Where can I pitch my music so that people who might like it will hear it? Be vigilant. Great opportunities can spring from anywhere you put your energy. IF you have great music, find a home for it, and vacation homes for yourself as well!

GETTING PUBLICITY FOR YOUR PRODUCT

Many labels point at publicity as the best tool for fueling an artist's career. According to Derek Sivers, founder of CDBaby:

> Press is the single biggest factor—the difference between musicians who are selling thousands and those selling none is the ability and the persistence of the musician to go out to the media with an interesting angle and an interesting twist and get stories done about them. Anybody can get the world's attention if they can find the unique angle in what they do.

Jesse Fergusson says, "Here at Def Jux, publicity has been very effective. It's free advertising." When people read about your artist, they're more likely to buy the record or attend a live show. David M. Bailey agrees. "When I go to a town, if there's a good article written with a photo, that's tangible proof I was there. I can extract quotes." A good record review generates sales. Dan Zanes (Festival 5 Records) says, "There's an article in the *New York Times Magazine* that I think put me on the map. Everything changed."

Publicist Karen Leipziger, KL Productions, says, "People need to be made aware. Publicity can make the right people aware in the right way." It lets potential fans know the record exists. Getting PR requires knowledge about the media, a good plan and press kit, perseverance, and most importantly—music worth promoting. Hiring a publicist or having one on staff is always advantageous, or, attempt it yourself. Mark Carpentieri (MC Records) says:

> My background is PR. It's so important to get attention to an artist's music. You're trying to get your artist exposed to people

who wouldn't know that artist and go buy the record—discover them. That may be the biggest challenge a label has.

HIRING A MUSIC PUBLICIST

A good publicist knows editors at publications and producers of TV and radio shows, and knows which are best for publicizing a client's product. Publicists give you a professional introduction to the media. Only hire one that specializes in music/entertainment and has relationships with appropriate writers, etc. Their job is to maximize your artist's chances of getting covered by the media. Jonatha Brooke says, "The benefit is hopefully you're seen enough. You hope it's worth it because it's really expensive to pay a publicist every month. We committed to it." Jeff Epstein says that hiring a publicist elevated Cropduster Records:

> Everyone contributed to finding a publicist that would work for slave wages but believed in what we were doing and who had a track record with other larger labels. Once we got some decent articles about us—we were on the cover of *Gig* magazine, *Billboard* did a couple of pieces, and we were getting lots of local press—people searched us out.

Should you hire a publicist or have one on staff? If you believe that good exposure for your artist would substantially increase sales, it can be worth it. If your artist's contract allows, the cost of an independent publicist for a specific artist may be recoupable from their royalties. If you hire one, start before your street date. Karen Leipziger agrees:

> The more lead time someone has, the better chance they have for someone to pay attention to them. A lot of publications have long lead times. They should ideally get a publicist three months before the record comes out. If you start contacting people the day an album comes out, it's way too late.

How do you find a good publicist? Word of mouth is best. Ask other indies for recommendations. Watch for artists getting great exposure. Call their label—ask for the publicist's name. Get friendly with journalists—ask whom they like working with. Hire someone who's experienced with your genre. I once hired a publicist to work a hip-hop act. Although she was confident, she didn't know jack about hip hop. She tried hard but wasn't familiar enough with those who wrote about it. If you consider hiring a publicist, ask for references.

PUTTING TOGETHER AN EFFECTIVE PRESS KIT

If you can't afford to hire a publicist, prepare to work hard and be patient. It takes time, but you CAN reach the media. Create an eye-catching press kit. Media folks get tons of material. Be creative about making yours stand out. Make the recipients happy by keeping your material as short and to the point as possible. Quality is always better than quantity. The less you send, the faster they can go through it. Aaron Burgess, managing editor of the internationally distributed music and youth culture monthly, *Alternative Press Magazine,* says:

> Simplicity is good. I'm very pressed for time and prefer bullet points over bios. I rarely read full bios or press clippings, especially the more extensive they are. I want the relevant facts immediately. I prefer contact information and release dates for the artist to be prominent on the one-sheet or press kit. I do file business cards. I like at least two options for reaching the press contact—preferably phone and e-mail addresses.

A basic press kit contains a bio, photo, and cover letter. Include the music, even if you burn a CD-R. Jesse Fergusson says, "My recommendation for a press mailing is four months prior to the street date. Give print media plenty of time to listen to the record and argue about it with their editors." Timing can mean the difference between getting press and anonymity. Brian Stillman, managing editor of *Revolver Magazine* and contributor to *Guitar World* advises:

> Getting us advances of the CD is key. Lately we've noticed that a lot of record labels, because they're worried about piracy or other things, are getting us the CD two weeks before it hits the stands. That's impossible to make work. Even when we go to press there's another three weeks before it hits the stands. We don't want to be late on a record review, for instance. If you want something reviewed, which is really your most likely entry into any magazine, get advances out at least a month in advance, even if you have to burn them yourself. Make sure they have all the

information—song titles, who produced it, who's on the record, if your artwork's not finalized. If some really good indie label gets me an album a month in advance, and I'm still thinking about what's going in our review section, and I've got nothing else, I'm gonna review their stuff, if it's good. I've got to put something in there. I do my best to get recognition for bands that deserve it.

Getting material to the press in advance is key for publicity! If you want to make money, take your music seriously and give publications what they want. Meanwhile, create a buzz in every corner you can. Anything you do in advance of the release helps when it comes out. Karen Leipziger explains:

> Start letting people know way ahead of time what's in the works so there's interest in the project before it comes out. There is so much music being put out but much of it isn't very good. All these people are fighting for the same limited space. A label and publicist not only [try] to get to the right person but [try] to get that person to pay attention to it. If you want to get it into the "to be listened to as soon as possible" pile, generate interest ahead of time so when somebody sees it, they'll open the package and listen to it.

WRITTEN MATERIAL

Imagine what it would be like to read through a large assortment of press kits every day—tedious. After a while, artists can start to seem alike. So when journalists get a kit that jumps out at them, with written material that makes them laugh or want to know more, it stands out.

Create a biography (bio) that tells the story of the artist, no more than two pages, doublespaced. A bio should be interesting, presenting a clear picture of the artist in a way that makes a journalist want to read it. If it sounds like a résumé, it may not get attention. A bio is written to entice people in the media to write about that artist. Dig for interesting facts about your artist and include them, even if they don't relate to music. Brian Stillman says:

> A good press kit has a solid bio with a history of the band. I want to know if they've been around. What have they done? Who have they toured with? That gives me an idea that people are into

them. I want something that says why they're not just another metal band—things that are outside the music. If they're a good band and have a singer who's a fire breather, we're going to be interested in talking to him because there's a twist. If your band has anything even remotely interesting, include it in the bio. That could be the hook to entice an editor. Music magazines want interesting people. We can't play the music for people, so we need something to talk about. Everyone has interesting music, but what makes you entertaining besides that?

Keep it fresh! Dick Renco (Trout Records) says, "We keep the bio updated with what is happening." Karen Leipziger recommends, "Include an interesting description of the music, not just saying it's great—something that makes it sound unique and specific to get people interested." Make journalists want to know the act! I once used a funny play on words with the band's name in the opening paragraph of their bio. We got write-ups because I made journalists laugh. The rest of that bio was facts about the band. Journalists loved reading that bio after all the bland ones and thanked me by writing about them. If you feel you can't write a stand-out bio yourself, hire someone.

Include press clippings about the act. Brian Stillman says, "Clips let me know that there's a buzz on the band, and writers often find a cool angle that the band didn't think to push." Mount them on paper, with the publication's masthead. Enlarge or shrink their size, depending on what looks better. If you get a bunch of short reviews, consolidate them onto one sheet, or include them on a quote sheet. Short blurbs that appeared in a publication can also be included. If the artist is doing a lot of live performances, a gig sheet can let the media know about them. Paul Hartman, editor of *Dirty Linen,* emphasizes, "Please don't send two pounds of paper [including] every single newspaper calendar listing, etc."

A cover letter should accompany the press kit. This introduces your label or the artist. A cover letter is a sales pitch, and should be written to convince the media to write a story or a review. If you can catch their attention with the cover letter, they're more likely to look at the rest of the kit. Organize your written material. Michael Mollura, associate editor of *Music Connection,* a magazine that caters to indie music, advises, "Everything should be easy for an editor to sift through. If I have to go through pages and pages of material just to get contact information, it's a problem." Publicist Ellyn Harris of Buzz Publicity emphasizes, "Make your press kit look clean and have contact information on EVERY-THING. Make it easy for someone to contact you if they want to." Paul Hartman adds, "You would be surprised how many people don't put their address anywhere on the CD." Without contact info, no one can send you a tearsheet of the article or let readers know where to buy the CD.

PHOTOS

When people open a press kit, a photo gets attention faster than words. Photos should capture the artist's personality. Michael Mollura says "Head-shots don't really work. Have photos that are clear, with an intention that fits into the category of music they're playing. When there's a contradiction between how a band appears and how they sound, it's distracting, and does-n't help their cause." An interesting photo with energy impacts more. Karen Leipziger says, "I've seen newspapers and magazines run photos of artists because the photo was interesting. They didn't care what the music sounded like if it was a cool and interesting picture." Send an 8 x 10 black-and-white glossy, with a note that color photos are available. Include contact info on photos. Put a sticker on the back. Brian Stillman adds:

> I like photos that let me see what the band looks like. If they're totally insane looking, that makes for good magazine coverage. If you include a photo, ID it. We run into many problems trying to find out who's who in a band. If you send me a photo of your band, that clearly shows who each dude is, and underneath each picture put their names, I am a happy camper. Then I figure out who you are without having to track down the publicist. That's a tiny little detail that I wish more than anything bands would do.

When looking for a photographer, check out several portfolios. Don't settle for just anyone. Some photographers are more artsy than others. Some emphasize movement. Some take flat photos. Get good photos the first time by being careful about who shoots them. Network to find a good photographer you can afford.

Have a variety of images. Put photos on your website so people can download them. Brian Stillman says, "An awesome thing for a record label to have is high resolution photos on their website—300 dpi. Have large ones that a magazine can use right off the site." It's cheaper for you—no copies or postage! Aaron Burgess says he uses them, especially for smaller front-of-book pieces, if they're not doing a photo shoot. He adds, "If somebody has a good 300 dpi, high quality image that I can grab from their website, it makes things easier for both of us."

PRESS KIT PRESENTATION

Folders that open up to show a pocket on each side hold the components of your press kit easily. Spruce them up with stickers or paste-on labels with the artist's name. If you have a nice logo, print it onto stickers that can be placed on the covers. Be creative in putting your kit together to make it attractive. A nice press kit catches attention more quickly than the music inside. And no matter what format you use, include a business card. Most folders have a slotted space for one inside.

PRESS RELEASES

Send regular press releases. A press release is an announcement of something newsworthy, such as the release of a record, a new band member, a showcase, etc. Include a catchy headline at the top. If it announces a specific event, include all pertinent details (date, time, place, cost, etc.) in the first paragraph. Don't use adjectives to describe too much. A press release is an announcement of news and should read like that. Keep it short, preferably on one sheet. The less you write, the greater the chance it'll get read. Build up excitement about the artist. Whenever he or she has an event or something special, send a press release. If the artist has a special gig, note how to get on the guest list.

When I'm working an artist, I send a postcard for all gigs, and a press release whenever possible. It enables journalists to become familiar with the artist's name. I've had instances where I met journalists who were familiar with my artist but didn't know why. It was because all the press releases made the name stick. Nowadays, people sometimes fax press releases instead of mailing them. Another alternative is an e-mail release (see Chapter 19 for more details).

COMPILING A GOOD MEDIA LIST

In order to work the media effectively, study it. Read publications. Learn names of editors, writers, and reviewers. Get familiar with their formats. Gather media resources early. Find as many publications as possible. Pick up free local papers and scan all magazines to see if there's a place for your artist. Do they review CDs or gigs? Be creative about formulating reasons why the media should want to cover your artist.

I begin by going to as many magazine shops and bookstores as possible. Look through each magazine and note which do reviews, which use photos with captions, and which have columns covering your genres (as well as who writes them). I discreetly write down names, addresses, and phone numbers of possible writers or editors to approach at magazines I don't want to buy. You may find a whole bunch of publications you never knew existed when you research.

Be diverse. Besides straight-out music magazines, there are many that specialize in related aspects of music. If your artist is a good keyboard player, think about approaching *Keyboard Magazine*. There are loads of guitar magazines too. If he or she is also an engineer or does technical work, check magazines that cater to audio engineering. There might be an angle for a story or some kind of mention. Getting even a mention can lead to sales, and enhance your press kit. As in everything else, be creative about reaching the press.

The Musician's Atlas (www.musiciansatlas.com) has a city-by-city list of local publications—newspapers and other publications that support the local music scene. Use them when your artist plays in a specific city. Talk to folks wherever you go and get names of more publications to add to your list. Check local TV shows to see if there's a place for your artist.

Always get the names of specific folks to send your press kit to. Don't just mark it "Editor" or "Producer." Call each publication or radio and TV station. Ask who's the best person to send a press kit to about a music act (be as specific as you can). Publications list their writers and editors on their mastheads, and television shows usually list producers in the credits for each show. See who handles the stories or reviews about music in your genre, or who does great stories in general. Always check the correct spellings of names, and make sure they still work for the publications or stations before sending anything.

OPPORTUNITIES FOR MEDIA COVERAGE

Be aware of your options when planning publicity strategies. Some publications are easier to get into than others. Ellyn Harris advises, "Start with local and regional press—weeklies, dailies, wherever they are. If the artist is from that region, they're much more likely to be interested in talking about them." Begin with the most local and work your way up. Each clip enhances the artist's story. The more you get, the more opportunities there are. Be realistic. Make sure you pitch the right magazine.

Don't waste time with inappropriate ones. Lydia Hutchinson, editor and publisher of *Performing Songwriter* magazine says,

> One thing that I tell artists who are trying to get exposure for their independent CD is to gain an understanding of the sheer number of CDs that are out there vying for the same, limited editorial space. And as hard as it is to stomach, the odds of just getting a review are going to be tough (here at Performing Songwriter we get over 3,000 indie submissions a year, with space for 96 DIY reviews at this point). But once there's some understanding of that, hopefully the publicity effort can be approached as sheer business. Understand the fact that each page actually has a certain cost to a publication, and that editorial choices might be made based on other coverage that is in that issue. And before you send anything in, educate yourself on the publication: Who is the target market? What are the number of pages allotted for reviews? To whose attention do you send your release? What are the check-back procedures for that publication? The bottom line is once your product is finished, the sacred, creative part is over. Now it's time to approach getting it heard as a business.

COLLEGE NEWSPAPERS

If you have trouble getting your first clips, try college newspapers. Visit nearby schools and pick up their papers. See which writers do stories or reviews about artists similar to yours. Call the paper and ask who'd be good to contact and how to best reach them. Or, someone may know of a journalism student looking to get his or her feet wet reviewing a CD.

Invite a local college paper to send someone to your artist's gigs. Treat them well! They could give you your first clip. Send the appropriate writer a CD and ask him or her to review it. Remember, students write for those papers. Most aren't jaded and might like an opportunity to write about your artist. Make them feel important. It might seem trivial to get reviewed in a college paper, but a clip is a clip and adds value to your press kit. Being in a college paper can stir interest in the CD, since students buy lots of music.

NEWSPAPERS

Newspapers, which reach a broad audience, are a great avenue for getting your artist's name in print. Start with local and free ones. Depending on your angle, you might interest them in an event going on in their city or a human interest story about local residents. They might review a gig. Newspapers have different sections. Figure out which editor to send material to. Sections focusing on a more localized news format are easier to get into. Have a variety of photos. You can get press just from a very cool photo. Dick Renco explains:

> We make sure we have good-looking photos and don't send the same one over and over. These guys (Trout Fishing in America) are visually intriguing. Newspapers don't really care about music. They care how their paper looks. Send an intriguing photo with a great line and you'll do better than if you had 500 words with no picture. We're always surprised and delighted when we move into a market and compete on the same night with a major artist on tour, but end up getting the ink in the paper, or the interview.

Some newspapers have large entertainment or listings sections to announce gigs, another place for a good photo. Since newspapers deal with current events, timing is critical. Also, they deal more with events and topics than personal profiles so may not be interested in your artists. Approach the editor of a special section and have an angle that may interest that person. Mark Carpentieri says:

> One of the nicest ways of getting PR is working locally. Any time a local band has a new CD, that's usually worth a photo and mention of the date, and things like that, by people who champion local music, whether it's the weekly entertainment papers, or the daily paper with a once a week section. Any time you have anything like that, I think people want to root for you.

Another possibility for exposure in newspapers is news services, such as Associated Press (AP) and Reuters. Their stories and reviews are made available to members across the country—most newspapers. Anyone receiving them may choose to run them in their local newspaper or other media outlet. Getting a news-service story gives you potential access to newspapers across the country. A reporter might interview a band that's doing something special or touring. You must, like with any publication, give them a reason to write about you.

Human interest stories are good to pitch to a news service. There has to be an angle for a writer to do a story on your label or artist. People want to read about something interesting, not that an artist they've never heard of has a new CD. Create a fresh idea and find someone to write about it. If your artist hasn't done something interesting enough outside his or her music, try for a review that could be published in a variety of newspapers. Send a CD to a music editor and give a good description of the music at the top of your press release.

There are offices in many large cities. Check the Internet for locales of AP and others. Call the one nearest you and ask who'd be most likely to write about what you're offering. Pitch them. At large AP offices, people assign writers to stories. When you read local papers, pay attention to which articles give credit to a service. Track down those writers. You may have to approach several until you find one in sync with your needs. When you do, cultivate a relationship.

MAGAZINES

I asked Michael Ellis, managing editor of *Billboard* magazine, about the difference between consumer and trade magazines. He explains:

> A consumer magazine is designed for fans of music. A trade magazine has a much smaller circulation. It is only designed for the people that work in the music business. A trade magazine is edited for people who work in the music industry, either full or part time. It is not edited for the general fans of music. It's much more of an insider's publication. It's not so much about the artist and what's new in their careers or lives, but is much more about the issues that are of concern to people working in the business.

Consumer magazines sell records, because their readers buy music. Trades get you more industry attention. Everyone strives to get into *Billboard*. While there are opportunities, you need to understand them. Ellis says their goal is to be the authority for information each week. They report all aspects of the music business—everything important that's happening worldwide. You can get a good education by reading *Billboard*. They have charts and articles about every type of music and an international section too. Is there room for you? Ellis says:

> We cover the independent sector, just as much as any other part of the business. We look for stories; for things that are happening. What is unique or special about an independent label? We would

look at something unusual or different about an independent label that makes them stand out in the field of literally thousands of independent record labels, ranging in size from moderately large to infinitesimally small. Is there an unusual business model for an independent? Do they specialize in one type of music that nobody else is covering or that's underserved? We look for special, interesting angles that we tend to cover in all of our stories. An independent should first go to Chris Morris. He writes the Declarations of Independents column, which is devoted just to the independent sector. They should pitch him first.

Ellis says there's not just *one* person to pitch. Chris Morris covers indies on a day-in, day-out basis. Ellis advises you to look in the masthead. It lists all the editors for all the sections. Look at the different departments and figure out which one your story fits into. Then find the editor and contact him or her. *Billboard* comes out weekly and covers industry news, so it's more timely.

I've emphasized that for most consumer magazines, stories are written well ahead of publication. Timely ideas won't work without a long-term angle. Study potential ones carefully before sending material. Magazines offer opportunities for feature stories, reviews, blurbs in a column, and interesting photos as fillers. Be realistic and work your way up from small to large magazines too. Karen Leipziger advises, "Don't expect to get the cover of *Rolling Stone*. Contact places that make the most sense for them to cover." Jesse Fergusson offers hope:

> A lot of smaller music magazines aren't as big an organization as they'd like you to think they are. Send something to the attention of the music editor. It can help. As long as you have some credibility as a label, they'll pay attention. It might take a few times but they will. Follow up as much as possible.

What are consumer magazines looking for? They want something that would be of interest to their readers. Spell out the story—what would their readers find interesting about your artist? The first paragraph of a cover letter or press release should grab them. Aaron Burgess says:

> Any number of factors can influence our decisions to choose one artist over another. We poll readers a lot and an artist can factor

prominently into our regular reader polls. The artist can be doing something newsworthy. There can be an industry buzz around the artist or big SoundScan numbers at press time. For a lot of the smaller labels, it's more based around the story. What is the artist doing at that time that is newsworthy, interesting or makes for good gossip. We have a section in the magazine set aside for smaller labels.

If you're going to a national magazine, you'd better have the record available nationally. Magazines don't like hearing from readers who read about it but can't find it anywhere. National magazines prefer to write about nationally known artists, or those buzzing loud on the way up. Brian Stillman says:

> The first thing I check is what label they're on. We're a national magazine and in a position where we have limited real estate. We usually limit ourselves to bands other people have heard of. We get a lot of good indie stuff. We want to publish stuff that other people are going to want to read about. If they've never heard about it, they don't want to read about it. It's the sad reality. But we will cover smaller indie stuff if we feel there's a buzz out there.

There are magazines that have reviews for niche markets, such as *Dirty Linen*. Paul Hartman describes it as "the bi-monthly magazine of folk and world music, which includes Cajun, Celtic, blues, bluegrass, singer/song-writer—a whole spectrum of music not covered by mainstream media." He likes a CD with a one-page bio and one page about the songs if no booklet with details accompanies the CD. Photos are optional. The Internet offers many PR opportunities too (see Chapter 19). According to Ryan Kuper:

> I would say that 30 percent of what my publicist sends out is to websites. Oftentimes, these sites accompany a hard copy magazine, but some are exclusively on the web and hold a strong presence in the market. AgoutiMusic.com, GeekAmerica.com, Epitonic.com, and Pitchforkmedia.com are some of the ones I go after. Reviews in these sites, especially prime opening-page placement, can be extremely valuable.

Kuper says that many sites review a lot of new music. The ones he suggested focus on alt/indie rock but there are many that are wide open, such as *Rolling Stone* online. Searching, networking, and *The Indie Bible* will help you find them.

TELEVISION AND RADIO

There are opportunities for free publicity on television and radio: interviews, news features, video exposure, talk shows, and segments of a specific show that spotlights interesting or different stories. These forms of media are hard to reach in the beginning, though it's not impossible to do so. News shows need timely stories, such as a specific event which is happening at a given time. An unknown can get a break if not much news happens on the day of his/her event, and the producer needs to fill a time slot. Luck can play an important role in getting on TV or radio. Smaller cable or public access shows are the easiest to get onto. Radio shows, especially specialty programs, those on noncommercial stations, and those in smaller markets, do interviews with artists.

FANZINES

A fanzine is a publication that's usually devoted to a very specific genre of music or one artist. The scope of music fanzines has broadened, often including a specific flavor within a broader genre, such as metal or punk. Some are more organized than others. Depending on your music, fanzines offer the potential to increase your sales and create a huge buzz around your artist.

Look for coverage in one that caters to fans who love your genre, or a band in your genre. If you get a publication hot on your artist, its readership may jump on the bandwagon for his or her music. Since every fanzine is different, the potential for increasing your artist's fan base from exposure in them varies. According to Jim Testa, owner of *Jersey Beat Fanzine,* "Lower end fanzines are usually sold in record stores, directly to fans at shows, or at any cool store (a clothing store that caters to skatepunks, for instance, might have a fanzine rack). Bigger fanzines use distributors which go to book stores, record stores, etc." Don't write fanzines off because they aren't as professional as commercial magazines. Testa says you can benefit from using a fanzine because:

They are affordable. My fanzine may only reach two or three thousand readers, but those are people who are already interested in a certain kind of music. Dollar for dollar, it's at least as good an investment as advertising in a mainstream magazine with astronomically higher ad rates, where only a small percentage of readers may be interested in the music you are marketing. When dealing with smaller or newer zines, record labels can often trade product for advertising, which benefits both parties. Fanzines help you find your target audience. You directly reach the audience you want.

Music publicist Nicole Blackman, of Nicole Blackman public relations, adds:

Most of the bands I work with could not live without their fanzine fan base. I go to them [the fanzines] first. I will go to a fanzine before I go to *Alternative Press*. If I go to AP or *Rolling Stone* and then try to go backward to the fanzines, they won't have it. 'You either come to us first or you don't come at all,' is the message. I respect that, because these are people who live and die for those bands.

One fanzine that gives exposure to lots of new music is *Muddle*, the outgrowth of a fanzine started by Dave Brown when he was in high school. He and Ron Richards teamed up in college and changed the name to *Muddle*. They began just reviewing music, and the publication grew from there. According to Brown:

We sent it to record labels we liked and all of a sudden things started happening . . . Twenty issues and seven years later, *Muddle* continues to exist where advertising pays for production of the magazine. Our circulation is 7000 and distributed world-wide. The whole philosophy behind *Muddle* is to have fun. We spread information, dealing not just with music but with lifestyle pop culture. We assign features to the things that interest us most in life. Be it music, comics, social awareness, fiction, photography, illustration, design, TV/film, humor, etc., *Muddle* covers it all.

Muddle (www.muddle.com) has grown to include all genres of music. Brown says, "We're interested in promoting independent bands and artists that normally wouldn't get attention in [major magazines] . . . Our philosophy is if it sounds good we'll review it and try to help promote it." Many indies advertise in *Muddle* and get a strong mail order response.

APPROACHING THE MEDIA

Ideally, write-ups should appear as records hit stores. Send a CD with a cover letter to all magazines that review music, preferably addressed to a specific reviewer or editor in charge of assigning reviews. The letter should provide relevant info about the release date, price of the record, and address or telephone number for ordering, as well as something about the music and artist. It should include a photo of the artist, and indicate that more info and photos are available. Include any stickers, T-shirts, key chains, or other merch you have in the package. Gregg Latterman (Aware Records) says:

> If an artist is touring, I won't wait for a publication to request the music or photos. I'll contact someone and let them know I'm sending the materials. It's much more effective than sending a press release telling them to let you know if they need anything. In a lot of cases, when they see good materials, they may decide to do something if the material is strong. Ultimately it's about the music. If the music isn't there, none of the other stuff is important.

Before pitching the media, identify goals, and possible angles for a story. The greatest CD can be ignored if it doesn't grab attention. Journalists are bombarded by material. Come up with something fresh. What makes your artist different? Why should someone want to write about him or her? What will intrigue a writer about the artist? Focus on a hobby or sideline. Emphasize what would be of interest to readers. Put it together in a package that shows you take your label seriously. Michael Mollura says:

> They can send packages. I look at every package that comes in. At our magazine, major label artists go through a different system than an indie artist. A label that an editor doesn't know should contact him first to establish who they are so he knows them when he gets the package. Indie labels send me e-mails to let me know what they're developing.

E-mail or fax journalists to tell them you're sending material so they can watch for it. Make the message short and friendly. Say something that will make them want to open your package. Capturing their interest can mean the difference between their listening to your music, or tossing it aside.

FOLLOWING UP

Don't send out a great press kit and wait for reviews and features to come in. You need to follow up on everything. Develop a system for keeping track of whom you sent press kits to and make follow-up calls. It can be tedious and confusing when you speak to many people in one day. Maintain accurate records to keep things sorted. An efficient system makes the process smoother. Approach journalists with a personal touch. Build those relationships! Ellyn Harris says:

> The tricky part about doing your own PR is being able to sell yourself. If you have a really good, salesman-type of personality and can sell your artist with enthusiasm and sincerity, then you can do it. That's what PR is—selling with enthusiasm. It is time consuming.

GETTING A GOOD SYSTEM IN ORDER

Keep track of the media with a comprehensive list that includes the names, addresses, and phone numbers of all the writers and editors you need to contact. Find your own system. Some of you may be comfortable with an informal one. Others might prefer a very detailed format for recording info. If you intend to keep your label going, develop good habits. Your system should be one that can be passed to employees as they take over various projects. Ellyn Harris advises:

> Set up your own campaign. Make a list with all contact information—address, phone, fax, email—of the publication. You can put them on a call sheet. When you make each call, each mailing, each contact, [note] that and make a plan to follow up.

Index cards are a great way to sort info. For Revenge Records, I wrote the name of each publication/media outlet on a card, with contact info. Then I recorded all pertinent info about that publication, including the names of journalists/editors; music genres it covered; its schedule; whether it did reviews, features, short news stories, or other types of columns; whether it ran photos with blurbs. I recorded all details when approaching or following up with a publication, such as best times to call and any quirks about it I learned in my interactions with them.

I recorded my progress on the back of the cards, listing dates when I called and their responses. I noted when a publication said to call back. I kept a file box with Monday through Friday sections. If I had to call back within a week, I'd put the card in the appropriate day. You can also use press call sheets to record information like Harris recommended. When designing those sheets, leave enough room to make notes. Keep a master list on your computer so it can be easily updated. I've used a date book for notations about when to call individuals back.

MAKING THE CALLS

Start building good relationships with your first media contacts. This can mean exercising patience when a person doesn't return calls or follow through on promises. Be persistent but don't come across as a pest. A friendly, polite follow-up phone call won't offend anyone. Polite persistence pays off. Brian Stillman advises, "Be tenacious without being annoying. There's a very fine line between the two—the difference between getting aggressive and getting on my nerves."

Media people are busy. Speak to an editor's assistant, if there is one, to see if your package arrived, and if the editor listened to the music. If the package can't be found, offer to send another. Before you call, be prepared to say exactly why you're calling. Ellyn Harris says:

[The first time you speak to someone] ask how they like to be followed up [with]. E-mail or phone? I call first because I like person-to-person contact. I'm good on the phone. You'll probably get a machine. Be prepared to leave a message. Have a script to use for their voicemail so it's quick, to the point, and well-said. Tell them what they'll be receiving and why they'll be interested in receiving it. Visualize their office with piles of CDs and press kits. Make yours stand out and let them know it's arriving. Otherwise, it may get stashed in the corner. The more personal attention you can give your package, the better it is. They're busy and not dying to talk to new people. Be polite.

Send material in a distinguishable envelope. When you call someone who hasn't seen your package, being able to describe it—for example, "the package with artist stickers," or " in a hot-pink envelope," or "addressed in big purple letters"—makes it an easier target to locate. Asking someone to look for a standard mailing bag makes it harder. If you send an attractive package, they'll more likely notice it. According to Israel Vasquetelle, publisher of *Insomniac Magazine,* known as the world's only hip-hop publication that's both consumer and trade:

> Packaging is everything from the envelope you send your music in, to the included literature about your band, cover art, and jewel case. Think of packaging as dressing for success. If you were going for an interview to try to land a big corporate position, you would definitely dress your best. So why do so many artists send out poorly packaged music? Some artists don't even think about packaging. They figure the music is good enough, but it's the packaging that may grab enough attention to get them to pop it into the player. The question is: "Is it appropriate and professional?" If you ask yourself that simple question when deciding on packaging, you will make better decisions.

Journalists are busy. Show respect for their time. If you get who you want, ask if it's a good time to talk. And don't call too much! Aaron Burgess advises:

> If you want to build any kind of positive, long-term business relationship with the magazine through me, don't be a pest, don't call me every other day, don't tell me that you're advertising and that I should write about you because you're advertising. When I hear it from someone, it's an instant turn-off. Be genuine. Be professional. Be diligent in your follow through, but don't be a pest—one to two follow-ups after sending me a release. I will get back to you. I'm busy and don't always answer my phone or e-mail right away. But I will get back to you. If it's just a general pitch to ask if I'm writing about a band, I prefer e-mail. If it's a more detailed pitch or something newsworthy, phone is great. I respond to both. You've got to have a good hook for me to really grab it. We get a lot of noise here all day. A lot of calls.

Don't give journalists an argument when they've said they can't do something. It's counterproductive. Continuing with a hard sell adversely affects relationships with them in the future. If they can't do a story, thank them for their time. You may have another artist down the road. If you don't leave a bad vibe the first time, you might get what you want later. Brian Stillman encourages:

> I don't mind getting calls but won't commit to something over the phone. Don't keep calling. After that send e-mail. Don't sweat it if I don't respond right away. If I'm interested, I'll respond. If I don't, maybe I'm not interested or maybe I'm taking my time for a million reasons. I don't mind follow-ups every month or so. If you have something new, tell us. If you have an advance release schedule, awesome. Our lead times are considerable and to be told about a release two weeks before we go to press does no one good.

Getting obnoxious or angry is never productive, even if it's justified. Smile to yourself before calling to get in a good mood. Always be polite. No matter how pissed off they make you, sound friendly and appreciative. Don't complain about how many times you called. Thank him or her for making time to speak with you. Some things are just in the nature of this biz and must be tolerated with good grace. If you need media coverage, prepare to bend and flex and accept what you don't like. Get over any attitude about media people being difficult. They get inundated with requests and can't respond to everyone as they might like to. If you get their attention at all, be grateful. Michael Mollura advises:

> E-mail is the best way to follow up. I do 98 percent of my communicating through e-mail. Find out the style of each editor or reviewer and how they like to be approached. Different editors have different styles. It's more comfortable to find out first via e-mail. If somebody sends me an e-mail asking if I got their package, I'll go see if I got the package. An e-mail gets into the line of fire.

Karen Leipziger advises, "Be consistent and have repeated contact. Some people prefer e-mail. But some hate it. Part of this is getting to know people and what they prefer as a way to reach them." Working hard and being persistent enables you to successfully work the media. Valerie Vigoda (GrooveLily) says:

> Try to give people a good story. Sometimes the media will take a press release or bio and use it word for word. We make sure our

photos are exciting and eye-catching. We're lucky right now to have a Petal Pusher-turned-publicist: a terrific young woman with lots of charm and enthusiasm. We find enthusiasm gets results just like experience, sometimes even more (as long as you're also organized and follow through). Attitude is everything.

Don't be discouraged. Even if someone turns you down, be patient. Come up with fresh ideas periodically. Be polite and friendly. Persistence helps you eventually get what you want. Ellyn Harris, who was instrumental in getting the Grammys to add two categories for dance music, encourages:

> Be brave! Think outside the box. Contact everyone you've ever met in the entertainment business. Tell them what you're doing. Everything that's been the most fun for me are things that everyone said, "You can't do that." It's the mentality I used to get a category for dance music at the Grammy Awards. People had been trying for ten years. I followed through with my passion for the music and didn't let the ball drop. We got two awards categories. Don't be afraid. If you think things through creatively, just try it. Don't say "no" to yourself before someone says it to you.

ADVERTISING

There are loads of places to advertise your product, if you have extra cash. This route needs careful thought. What are your objectives? Don't incorrectly assume that advertising will result in a write-up or airplay. If that's your main reason for taking out an ad, think twice, unless money isn't an issue. But there are benefits to advertising, as long as you keep your goals realistic.

You can advertise the release of your record or a special gig. If your act is youth oriented *and* you have a photo showing the artist(s) looking hot/stylish or other traits that attract kids who buy records, stimulate interest by including one in your ad. If a publication covers your genre specifically and its ad rates are realistic, advertising might help the most in reaching your target audience. Some publications have rates for many levels of ads, from business card size on up, and reach audiences who buy very specific kinds of music. Include your website in any ad. Have samples of your music on your site so they'll want to buy the CD. Ryan Kuper (Redemption Records) says:

There are certain magazines that I feel are more suited for our material. Their demographics are what we are trying to hit. I definitely believe in print advertising. I have found that the monthly half-page, full-color ads I have placed in magazines like *Alternative Press* have been very effective. These ads usually feature one act or two acts and possibly some tour dates, and information about what is coming out. I think they help sell records as well as generate general interest in the bands and the label. Sometimes buyers see the ads and think, "This label's got it together. This ad coincides with reviews and I've seen in other magazines and I'm hearing it on the radio. This is a cohesive push." For the same reasons, I place banner ads on a lot of websites as well.

Ramona De'Breaux, music director of Hot 1079 in Atlanta, believes that radio ads are a good way to get your music on radio. She advises considering one, with your music playing clearly. If your act is playing a decent venue, advertise it. Radio ads can be pricey, so make sure the station reaches your audience. Certain hours are much cheaper than others—like those in the middle of the night. Lots of folks listen to radio at those times, so it may be worthwhile. De'Breaux adds:

> How can you compete with all the money that majors put into their promotions? Instead of spending your money unwisely, buy a commercial, and play your record on the commercial, so people hear it over and over. For the money you waste on people who say they have the hook-up for you, go and get more exposure buying a commercial and marketing your songs.

Advertising helps develop a relationship with a publication or radio station. People in sales generate profits made by those media outlets, so they often have good relationships with those you want to reach. When negotiating an ad, it can't hurt to ask if he or she can introduce you to someone who might review the record or write a story, or to the music director of a radio station. The salesperson may or may not accommodate you. He or she may string you along until receiving your money. Politeness combined with persistence pays off, but recognize when someone has no intention of anything beyond running your ad.

GETTING RADIO PLAY

Radio play offers an opportunity to reach listeners who might buy what they hear. It's probably the best vehicle for selling records, but can be the hardest to ride. There are different levels of radio play and indies usually work their way up. Getting radio play is difficult at best, but can be achieved with a combination of hard work and great music.

COMMERCIAL RADIO

I don't want to discourage you, but I must be honest. Commercial radio is tough to crack. Majors put lots of money into radio promotion, and get much more priority. People at commercial radio stations say they add an average of three to ten songs per week. That's it! Competition is heavy. But it's not hopeless. Indies DO get commercial radio play. Incredibly hard work may be necessary.

UNDERSTANDING COMMERCIAL RADIO

There are different levels of commercial radio markets. Those in larger cities are considered primary ones, while others are considered secondary or tertiary. Most commercial stations play one format. The most common formats are CHR (Top 40), Adult Album Alternative (AAA), Album-Oriented Rock (AOR), Hot Adult Contemporary (AC), Country, Modern Rock, Urban, and R&B.

The main players at a radio station are the programming director (PD), who programs shows, and music director (MD), who listens to music and makes recommendations. At smaller stations, one person may do both jobs. Commercial stations are businesses making money from selling airtime to advertisers. Advertisers want to be on stations playing the most popular music. To please them, playlists are often limited to music by artists with high visibility. Beth Krakower, president of

CineMedia Promotions, works with titles considered "special projects" or "classical crossover" (movie soundtracks, Broadway cast albums, reissued titles, and an eclectic range, fitting into non-commercial radio formats like classical, cabaret, jazz, and classical crossover) and advises, "Remember that commercial radio's purpose is to make money by selling advertising. Because the stakes are so high, commercial radio stations are not in the business to break bands."

DJs often don't have freedom of choice. On most commercial stations, the PD chooses a pool of records. Unless they host a specialty show with more latitude, most DJs can't play what they love without approval. Commercial stations add songs each week to be played in rotation—they'll be played at regular intervals. Heavy rotation refers to songs that haunt you because they're on so frequently. Light rotation is regular play but at longer intervals. The bigger the story on an artist, the heavier the rotation. Songs grow on people when they hear them over and over. Hearing them occasionally has much less impact.

Commercial stations prefer CDs with a story; they want artists that tour regularly, sell records, attract media, and get airplay on other stations, and charts. They don't want an artist no one's heard of. Develop a story before approaching them. Competing with the clout of what a major label's money buys is tough. We "just" have great music, and are up against the perks majors give. They have gigantic marketing/advertising budgets. They throw parties and offer all sorts of freebies. Don't worry about payola. I've heard stories of exorbitant legal gifts.

Major labels spring for promotions, freebies for stations to give away, and send artists to events the station sponsors. But don't despair! Many indies do get commercial airplay. Lisa Worden, Music Director of KROQ, a top commercial alternative rock station in L.A., says, "It doesn't matter if it's an independent label. We look for the best new music to expose our listeners to and try to pick stuff that we think they'll really like." Many commercial stations play at least some indie music. Ramona De'Breaux, MD of Hot 1079, a top commercial urban station in Atlanta, says they play about 10 to 15 percent indie music. Why?

We found a niche playing hip-hop artists that weren't getting exposure on the other formats here. We were the first station in Atlanta to say, "We're the hip-hop station." Ten years ago, it was difficult to fit a hip-hop song in the format. Now it's hard to fit R&B

in because it slows it down. Hip-hop sells quickly and is new all the time. What mainly matters is if it's a good song.

Sometimes an indie with fantastic music can create its own little machine and cut through the crap. With lots of hard work, perseverance, creativity, very radio-friendly music, and luck, an indie label can get commercial radio play. Lisa Worden says with *many* stations, it's about the music. She adds:

> It depends on the station. I think other stations get bad raps. Advertisers do not determine what is played on a radio station. I think that's a false impression that's out there. [What determines it is] hits for the radio station—what the listeners want to hear.

PREPARING TO WORK COMMERCIAL RADIO

Give yourself the best shot of getting on radio by not approaching stations in ignorance. Make them take you seriously with a professional pitch. Select a single you're promoting on the album. Stations like short ones. If necessary, do a radio mix. Radio prefers a CD single. If you have an album or EP, indicate the song you're pushing. To get on radio charts, all the stations must play the same song. Don't tell them to choose what they want to play—they probably won't.

Commercial radio stations see what records are selling and playing on other stations. Broadcast Data Systems (BDS) tracks radio play with computerized technology, so stations learn what's being played and how often. Many stations hire radio consulting firms that help choose the records played. Call the stations for their names. Get them excited about your music. If you persist, you may find a station to support your music. Dave Roberge (Everfine Records) did:

> We have had some radio play at a commercial station in Chicago, 94.7—the Zone. They embraced a couple of independent artists. I have the highest regard for a station like that, competing against the bigger stations out there but is still taking chances because they know what people want to hear. They don't want the manufactured pieces of crap anymore—they want a sense of discovery. That station is providing it. But, they're few and far between. [O.A.R. is] drawing between 2,000 to 5,000 people in every market. The kids are going crazy for them. Any radio

programmer that doesn't see that as a legitimate thing would have to be crazy, but that's how it works. It's about coming up with promotional dollars and getting onto radio that way.

Tell commercial stations the artist's story, with press clippings, a tour schedule, radio play in other markets, record sales, chart positions, etc. A full press kit isn't necessary, but a one-sheet is. Like the one for retail stores, it must include a short bio, marketing and promotional work, and whatever might convince a PD to play your record. A well-presented sheet can make a difference. Send as little as it takes to tell it—make each detail count. Also, make sure your record is in stores in markets you're after. Radio stations get pissed if they play your record and then receive calls from listeners complaining it's not available.

What catches radio's attention? Ramona De'Breaux says attractive packages are opened quicker. Packaging is the first impression. If it doesn't show you take your music seriously enough to dress it nicely, it might not get heard. De'Breaux says she knows it's not right, but packaging influences whether an intern puts a record into the definitely "listen to" pile or an ignored stack. She adds, "If your package looks good, then they'll read the one-sheet. If it looks like crap, no one cares."

Ultimately, it's the music that matters. But it won't matter if they don't hear it. MDs say packaging can set one artist apart from others. The goal is to get heard. Get them to listen to it by making sure your packaging is competitive. Then your music can convince them. De'Breaux warns:

> You must remember that you're competing with majors who have great packages that are appealing to the eye. That gets people to listen. The main thing is to get them to listen to it. 75 new CDs come in a day. No one has time to listen to everything. Look at your CD and compare it to others in retail stores. Then get real!

CONTACTING COMMERCIAL RADIO STATIONS

Radio stations often have specific hours each week when the MD meets with label reps and promoters. Call for the day and hours. Many stations require an appointment. CDs can also be mailed to stations, followed by a phone call. Ask at what hours the MD takes calls. Be persistent. When speaking to MDs, thank them for their time. Ramona De'Breaux says at

Hot 1079 they have Independent Music Day, where music department staffers listen to projects from indie labels. During a two-hour period, indies can just come in. The staff gives them feedback.

If you can afford it and have a great record with promotion on it, a radio promoter may help. Promoters have relationships with people at stations. But with so much competition, they often give greater priority to records they're paid more to promote. It's hard to find a good one. Talk to other indie labels. Be very explicit about your agreement. Watch the semantics in the agreement. Promoters might be seeking a bonus for "getting the record played." That could be interpreted as a single play. Specify that it must be played in regular rotation.

Begin in what's referred to as softer markets first. Those are smaller ones, tertiary ones, that may not be tapped as much by the majors. There are many, usually further away from large cities. Use *The Musician's Atlas*. It lists stations in most cities that play at least some indie music, and includes the format, and type of music. You can also find stations listed with their websites in *The Indie Bible*. There are also lists of stations on music websites. Be persistent about developing relationships in the markets you're after. Getting airplay in smaller markets is the first step to larger ones.

After you send a CD, follow up. Lisa Worden says, "There's a fine line between being persistent and bugging. I always tell people, follow up with a couple of phone calls or e-mails, and if you don't hear back, there's a reason." They'll contact you if there's something good to say. Be polite when you leave messages. NEVER sound impatient! Ramona De'Breaux says:

> Know how to follow up. Some people call and are annoying. There's obnoxious annoying and functional annoying. Functional is okay. A guy called and sounded very professional. Gave his name and asked if I could give him a call back and let him know what I think of his project. An approach like that is cool.

Even if commercial stations don't play your record right away, start developing relationships. Be realistic. Don't expect airplay before there's at least a small story about your artist. Report progress as your story builds. E-mail is probably best for that. Persevere but be patient. MDs are swamped and can't speak to everyone. Reaching them takes time. When you finally do reach the MD or an assistant, be polite. Show respect for everyone's time. A relationship based on respect and good feelings may get you airplay or a return phone call later on.

If your music fits the format of a specialty show, contact the DJ who programs it. If you're putting out dance music, get friendly with DJs from mix shows. If a record does well on one, it pumps up the artist's story and the PD may consider it for light rotation. What promotion can you offer a station? Would they like your artist to give a live interview or station ID? Can you do a ticket give-away for a gig? Can your artist get involved with events promoted by the station? Watch for things you can offer. Beth Krakower says:

> With movie soundtracks, I approach commercial radio more from the on-air promotions angle. Since the film studios arrange screening partners (stations in key markets to "present" a free screening of the film a few days before its official release), I approach these stations more to tie-in the soundtrack with the film, i.e., win a copy of the CD and a free pass to see the film.

Commercial radio play is definitely possible if your music is great and you work the system slowly. Danny Goldberg (Artemis Records) offers hope that radio play is possible for the right record:

> If the record is strong enough, it can get on the radio. You see certain artists on indie labels with such a strong grassroots following that some radio stations want to play them. But a higher threshold of intensity is required if you don't have a good promotion department and expertise. You need a so-called magic record. A great magic record trumps everything. It can come out of a company with a small staff and limited funding. But most records don't have those magic things. Most artists develop painstakingly over a period of years. I think that 90 percent of artists that do become successful have a staff that works phone call by phone call, station by station, spin by spin, store by store, article by article, and try to chip away at the exposure mechanisms.

NONCOMMERCIAL RADIO

College and public access radio stations are indie-label-friendly. Noncommercial stations don't depend on advertising. Their listeners are

are often passionate fans of music. While major labels covet airplay too, most non-commercials are more concerned with the music. Their listeners are often music lovers wanting to hear new and creative music instead of the same songs repeated. They pay attention to music, unlike those who just listen passively to the music played by commercial stations. Beth Krakower says:

> With consolidation of ownership of commercial radio, there are fewer and fewer opportunities at commercial radio for these projects. Most titles that I promote find their own on public, community, and college radio stations.

THE POWER OF COLLEGE RADIO AND PUBLIC ACCESS STATIONS

Noncommercial stations like breaking new music. Rita Houston, MD for WFUV, a powerful public radio station in New York City, says she listens to almost every record received, noting, "We want to be the place that discovers a gem." She recommends patience for any indie label wanting airplay and advises:

> There are things labels can do to help a radio station along . . . I like getting a package that has a little bit of information about the artist along with the CD. I don't need [a full press kit], but when you're listening to something, you need to have a little perspective on it. That [perspective] could be what the artist is about, or who produced the record, or what inspired the album.

Houston says a bio helps her see where a CD fits into her station's format. WFUV is artist-driven, so Houston's not as interested in singles. Noncommercial stations like albums and choose their own songs. In terms of follow-up, Houston says, "Persistence is the prize in life . . . I'm impossible to get on the phone because there's only so many people I can talk to every day." She does take calls from those who have developed good working relationships with her.

Noncommercial stations are more likely to give airplay. How do you find them? There are loads in the *Musician's Atlas*. Beth Krakower advises visiting the websites of national networks of the main public radio outlets, www.npr.org, www.pri.org, and www.pacifica.org. Most DJs choose what's played on their shows. Although noncommercial airplay isn't as powerful as commercial radio, it can start a buzz to build your foundation. Krakower agrees. "Particularly for certain demographics, public and non-commercial radio is a great first step to begin creating a story for your project before approaching commercial radio." Dick Renco (Trout Records) agrees:

> It takes three to four years to break a market if you don't have immediate radio support. If you have radio support, it's almost immediate. We found stations through research. The guys were working in Arkansas, Louisiana, and Texas. Part of our plan was to find out independent public radio stations that had either specialty programs or at least programming.

Can an artist break with noncommercial radio? Absolutely! Rita Houston says, "In our format, which is AAA, it's mostly public stations that are leading the way and breaking new artists . . . Look at Joan Osborne, Paula Cole, Fiona Apple. They all started on public radio." Onno Lakeman got on radio from Holland:

> I simply started to contact American radio stations and most of them liked the music and played the CD. I have found out that American radio has a great approach towards music, especially the smaller and college stations. If they like it, they'll play it. This way music is only being judged on the music.

WORKING COLLEGE RADIO

The DJs at college stations are more concerned with the quality of music than its popularity. Since they're volunteers, they try to be true to their reputation for playing the newest, most cutting edge music available. Fortunately for us, they look to indie labels for that music. Rudy Chavarria of Rude College Promotions says, "The bottom line for college radio is the music. If it's brilliant, they'll love it. You just have to get them to listen."

Dealing with college radio folks can be exasperating. They're hard to reach because they're students, with classes or commitments. Many have scheduled hours at the station, but are not always there when you call. It's harder to develop lasting relationships because staff changes as they graduate or quit. Rudy Chavarria says most music can work on the college level but alternative, hip-hop, world music, reggae, and techno get the most play. Stations may play a different genre every two hours. It depends on the DJs.

Is college airplay worth coveting? Indies I spoke to were mixed about its value. Jesse Fergusson (Definitive Jux Records) says, "We work it—I don't know how helpful it is but it's the only radio promotion we can do." The general consensus I got was that college radio is a good vehicle for developing visibility for an artist. It keeps their name out. But no one was sure that it sold records. Robb Nansel (Saddle Creek Records) says:

> I think college radio is necessary. Just because a record is doing well on college radio charts, I don't think there necessarily is a direct correlation to record sales. But you have to get the record out there to those people.

Ryan Kuper (Redemption Records) adds:

> The jury is still out on college radio. It definitely raises the level of consciousness for bands but I don't know if it drives much sales. AAA is the same way. A band can be number one on the AAA and college charts and still only sell 6,000 units. Others can sell 30 to 60,000 copies.

To work college radio, compile a list of stations in the region you're starting in, especially stations that chart. *CMJ* (see below) is the best place to start. There are also listings on-line. Rudy Chavarria recommends you first fax teases:

> We'll fax quotes about the record to all of the radio stations that are reluctant to add the record and a list of the people that are giving us a lot of love. Then they see the record is onto something and will open the package and give it attention. E-mail has taken the place of what faxes used to be. Less people send faxes. People like seeing one because it's something they can hold.

Send a CD to the MD, who'll put it into a bin that all DJs can use. I asked Chavarria about sending an electronic file of music first. He agreed. "They'd probably love an MP3 file. They can e-mail you if they want a CD. It's faster." And saves money! When stations play it, call nearby retail stores, let them know and send a copy. Covet street teams in colleges. Get students who are passionate about your music to promote it. Chavarria says, "Students can flyer retail stores, student unions, fraternity and sorority houses. Use postcards with the album cover on the front. If someone gets it at a party, they can fold it, put it in their pocket and have it." Dave Roberge says:

> We've tried to make a conscious effort to not do what we call a full-out radio promotion campaign for a particular single. We've done an awareness campaign, where we want to just make people aware of the band. So we focus on the CMJ top 200 stations. We send information about the band. If the band is in their area, we invite them to the show. We try to set up remote radio opportunities to give away tickets and create loyalty at the stations. We send music but don't ask them to spin a certain track and we'll give ten tickets to the show. It's about creating champions of the band right now.

Target individual DJs. Send a CD and get to know them. A nice element of college radio is the relationships you can develop. Students are friendlier. You can cultivate support. Get to know key DJs. If they like your artist, they'll spread the word. Send postcards with the CDs so they have your website and other info handy if someone inquires about it. Ask for support when your artist plays nearby. Offer an artist interview. Developing relationships with college stations can get you lots of love! Jay Ziskrout, chief operating officer of CMJ (see below), works with the college market and advises:

> These kids are all volunteers and love what they do. Have some distance. Don't be so close to it that perhaps you pressure someone too much at a college radio station. I would use them for feedback, as much as trying to use them for airplay. You can get valuable feedback. Find out how they prefer to receive music. Just sending a CD may not be enough if certain programmers prefer to get a file digitally. Try to accommodate. A lot of times the music director will decide whether it at least meets the minimum criterion for being on the station. Then it's up to the DJ to play the record. When it's added, it's made available to be played. Take the extra time to work the different DJs. You need to create fans at the radio station. Give away tickets. Make them feel [like a] part of your career. One of the driving factors for many in the

business is the feeling of being part of an artist's career. If an independent can create that sense of involvement/participation, even in a small way at university stations in their hometown, use that as a base to reach retail. Give them free tickets. Don't just put them on a list. Make them feel like they got something special.

SATELLITE RADIO

New technology may change the face of traditional radio. Since things change so fast, I won't go into broad details. But satellite radio seems to be growing fast. There are more opportunities to get airplay with satellite radio. According to Lee Abrams, chief programming officer of XM Satellite Radio (www.xmradio.com):

> Airplay on XM is like obtaining airplay on most radio stations. Each station/channel has a program director. Service the PD with CD's and use your best salesmanship to get added. Labels need to think out of the traditional radio/records relationship envelope. XM will do many things that terrestrial radio is incapable of or traditionally rejects.

XM Satellite Radio offers over 100 channels. People subscribe to get it. Abrams thinks 2005 may be the pivotal year, with steady growth until then. He adds, "XM isn't an audio service, but a collection of 101 living breathing radio stations, each with a staff of hand picked . . . radio and music creative experts." Keep an eye on the satellite radio companies. If you get in on the ground floor, you can cement relationships for the future.

RADIO PUBLICATIONS

There are trade publications for radio. Just as there are different levels of radio stations, different trades cater to them. *College Music Journal (CMJ)* (www.cmj.com) is for college stations. *Friday Morning Quarterback (FMQB)* (www.fmqb.com) and *The Network* (www.thenetworkmag.com) are the next rung. *Billboard* (www.billboard.com), *R&R* (www.radioandrecords.com), and *Hits* (www.hitsmagazine.com) are trades for major commercial radio. Each has reviews, charts, and other features. Sending a press kit with a CD can get your record a review. According to Rita Houston, "What the trades allow you to do is build a story on a national level. . . Most programmers, myself included, read the trades cover to cover every week. That's another source of information for me." The UK has *The Radio Magazine* (www.theradiomagazine.co.uk).

CMJ provides resources at the college level. Jay Ziskrout says they started with what's now known as the *CMJ New Music Report*—a weekly industry trade magazine. He adds:

> It features tracking what about 800 college radio stations play every week, and what a couple of thousand retail stores sell every week. There are other spotlights and informative articles about happenings in the music industry. It has several ancillary products . . . including in-store play CDs, radio samplers, mailings, information services for the music industry to use.

CMJ has individual college playlists. Charting in CMJ doesn't carry nearly the same weight of other charts. But, as you appear on more station's charts, it increases your artist's visibility and other stations may request a CD. Ziskrout says labels can advertise using their packages designed for smaller labels with lower budgets. Their *Certain Damage* CD comes out every six weeks and offers an economical way to reach stations with your music. He explains, "For the very small budget (you don't have to hire staff), you can spend a little money and get your music into the hands of people who make decisions regarding playing and selling artists." It goes to all subscribers of *New Music Report* plus others, including retail. CMJ also has CMJ *New Music Monthly*—a consumer magazine. Every issue contains a free compilation CD—a way to reach music consumers.

I spotlighted CMJ because it's the most accessible at the beginning. Other trades offer some of their services. Some have services to send your CD to radio stations that report to them. Getting onto a CD sampler that goes to radio stations allows many to hear your music. College radio is the most likely to play something they like on a sampler.

Just as you would with other magazines, try to develop relationships with trade magazines and push to get your records reviewed. Radio trades advise advertising in them. Many indie labels feel that unless you have a particular situation that would make your record more likely to get radio play, consumer magazines are where your budget should focus. Talk to other labels to see what worked for them. Try to get free reviews.

CREATING A PLAN OF ATTACK

If you want radio play, design a realistic strategy. Start by building a foundation of smaller stations. Work up from noncommercial stations to smaller commercial markets, and from there to larger ones. Keep building your story. Your artist should be known before approaching primary stations. His or her story must be impressive to crack that level.

Unless you have a big buzz, start with public and college radio stations. As you work colleges, coordinate performances at or near those giving you airplay. When there's a gig, ask the station to interview the artist. Get the college paper to cover it. Work this foundation so your story attracts more stations. Mark Carpentieri (MC Records) puts a bounce back card, without stamps, in each CD to see what people think. Stations return them or respond by e-mail. He adds:

> I ask who's filling out the card, as there are lots of changes. We ask what radio charts they report to, what cuts they like, their e-mail address, is it appropriate for another show, how many hours a week do they play this kind of music? For blues music, a lot of the people who host shows may come in for two hours for their show. They're not as easily reached as trying to track the programming director at stations where you call at certain hours.

I spoke of how record labels work as co-ops. The Acoustic Rainbow CD (www.AcousticRainbow.com), released by Poetman Records, is a cooperative CD for AAA radio artists. Michael Jonathon, who is also a singer/songwriter, originally found 800 stations that played grassroots music and decided if a group of artists pooled resources, a CD could be sent to them. He charges a sizeable fee to be included, to cover the cost of making and sending it around the world. DJ's get a two-sentence blurb about each artist. Jonathon screens songs to find those with the best chance of airplay. There are no more than 14 tracks on each CD.

Jonathon has no interest in spitting them out like a factory. It's a quality, not quantity driven project. He's doing this to get great music heard. DJs know that music on Acoustic Rainbow is great quality. Jonathon says, "Unless the music is heard, nothing matters. Reaching the audience is the issue. The only way for the biggest audience to hear your music is radio." He collectively pools everyone's resources to do the most for the least amount. He now services 1,677 DJs in 28 nations. David M. Bailey has been happy with the results:

I've gotten radio airplay in Australia and Japan. I got my first ASCAP royalty check for it playing in Japan. They send you who played it with contact information to follow up. It's a lot of money, but I think it's worth it. I cannot say that I sell one CD from it. My own opinion is it doesn't happen like that. You've got to spend money to create real or perceived visibility.

This kind of airplay gives you material for your press kit. However you get your music to stations, follow-up must be done. Keep accurate records each time you call, similar to how I recommended keeping track of publicity. Use a sheet listing stations, with contact info and space for notes. Index cards work, too. I made notes of what each MD said and the date. Always thank the MDs or DJs for their time. Jeff Epstein (Cropduster Records) says:

> Whether you're using a company to solicit for you or not, you've got to be consistent and get on the phone and constantly call and send packages that look interesting. Send something a little special, not the same thing that everyone else is sending. Send them a piece of swag—whatever is going to differentiate you that can possibly make the program director play it.

If phone calls get time-consuming, find an enthusiastic intern/fan to do radio promotion. As you get more airplay, inform stations that aren't playing your record yet. Tell your distributor. Be patient. Rita Houston says, "If you have fans and are out there working your butt off, building a story, then radio's going to have to follow you. Get to work!"

GETTING RETAIL AND CLUB PROMOTION

If you want your records to sell, get off your butt. Active promotion builds your label. If you can't hire independent promoters, work the record yourself. You have to. Nurture those all-important relationships. When club DJs and people who work in retail know and like you, your foundation gets stronger.

WORKING RETAIL STORES

Once you have product in stores, create a system to keep in touch with them. Take notes when making calls, about what they think and when to follow up. I'd also note personal stuff they share. Bringing it up during later calls creates a personal connection and builds the relationship.

Be persistent, but don't be a pest. I called at less busy times, once a week to see how the record was doing. It reminds them to stay aware of your record. It also shows stores you're serious about marketing your product—you're not an indie that leaves product and disappears. Always thank people for their help. Even if they're indifferent, say their support is appreciated. And even with distribution, stay on top of stores. When they sell out, nudge them to order more. Let your distributor know a store needs more. They should keep track, but don't count on it. They'll take you more seriously when they see your efforts.

Let stores know your artist is available for in-store appearances. Ask people you deal with in stores if they'd like an autographed photo of your act. Have the artist(s) sign a bunch. I liked: "Thanks for your support." Ask if the person wants the autograph made out to him or her personally. Sometimes a clerk is more likely to hang a picture that's autographed to him or her. Photos are easier to find space for. Some folks check out a record if they like a photo. Determine what retail promotional materials are best for your music.

GETTING VISIBILITY IN STORES

You can get in-store visibility with placement on display racks or in listening booths. Andy Allen (ADA) says, "Make sure that when somebody walks into a store, they find the music there. The easiest way to do that is to have it in front where people can see it." People may not intend to buy your record, but if it's in their face, they might. If people hear a song on radio, seeing it on a rack reminds them. Folks use listening booths to hear CDs they're not familiar with. A review might pique interest, but people still want to hear it. Jonatha Brooke says:

> We know where our markets are really strong. The distributor helps us figure out when positioning in stores and record booths will be cost effective. If you're willing to spend the money up-front, they're valuable tools, especially at the beginning of a record cycle and when you're touring.

These promotions are the most cost effective when you have other promotions going in the market and there's already an awareness created on the artist. They aren't free. Labels pay stores to position their product on racks and get into listening booths. CDs don't end up on displays by accident. That space is bought, like ads in a magazine. It can be expensive, but indies say it can get good results. Most store promotions are bought through a distributor. Yours will generally put up the money and recoup it from sales of your record. You don't have to lay money out up front. Some stores pressure labels to use their programs. Robb Nansel (Saddle Creek Records) explains:

> There are stores that won't take your stuff unless you get into their program. A lot of stores have automated ordering systems. If they take one CD and it sells, all its computer knows is we had one and will order another one. It can take weeks for that one re-order to get in. So they never really have stock. The only way to get a big buy-in is to buy into a listening post. Then they'll take 15 and when they sell, the computer may order 20 more. The computer is smart enough to do that, but not smart enough to know that if we sold one in a day, they should get more than that.

Labels can get onto racks and into listening booths without going broke. Some stores are cheaper. Start with smaller markets. Develop relationships with people in smaller stores. Sometimes a friendly, personal approach makes a difference. Managers of a mom-and-pop store can sometimes support you if they choose, with lower rates or more. I've finessed my way onto displays for free when a space wasn't bought anyway. That's where good relationships help. Personal thank-yous were very effective in getting stores to go the distance for my label. Practice smiling! Research by talking to stores and other indies. Mark Carpentieri (MC Records) says listening posts can work well for a good record:

> Are they worth it? It depends on the program. Some are worth it. Some are really expensive listening post programs. Some stores do better jobs than others. I like listening posts in general. If you have an artist that's very visible, you can do the pricing positioning and it works. If your artist is not as visible, you want the curious person in the record store to hear the record because they don't know the artist and may not want to spend 15 bucks to find out.

I spoke earlier of the benefits of giving away CD samplers. Richard Ellis (Aron's Records) says in his store they can be more effective than purchasing space in a listening booth. He advises, "Put your money into printing a couple of thousand two- to four-track CDs. People may listen in listening booths, but when they take it home, they digest it more thoroughly. I see people who picked up a sampler come back and buy the record." He sees a lot of business from value-added stuff.

Points of purchase (POPs) are displays set up near cash registers to entice shoppers to buy other products as they pay for items they've already decided on. Richard Ellis says, "A lot of indies don't have any POP, such as posters, to promote the record. I prefer a 24 x 36 flat of the LP cover— anything that's easy to use for a small, quick display for new releases." Many labels say they make up small posters to distribute to stores.

Some labels do co-op advertising with a retail store. The store agrees to order a specific amount of product and arranges an ad specifically for it in a local publication. The ad includes info about the product, the label and store. John T. Kunz (Waterloo Records) says, "The ad is co-opted with the store. Quite a few artists do well with our advertising." Richard Ellis says, "Some people put in their ad that they can go to Aron's and get a free CD sampler or other added value items, such as CD openers with their logos, contact info and website." Mark Carpentieri says:

We do tons of co-op advertising, a lot based regionally. I like to combine touring with the ad—get the most bang for the buck. If the artist is playing [a specific city], do an ad in the weekly and maybe tag in Borders, so you're helping your artist and yourself. It's a win/win situation compared to just doing a straight ad announcing that the new CD is available. Co-op advertising is the most expensive for the least buy because when you're talking about a buy-in, it's usually about a hand-ful of stores for a lot of money. That's why we combine it with tour dates to get more out of it.

Richard Ellis adds:

Co-op advertising works beautifully for me. I place the ad for the label. The label sends me a bill for the ad, and I send them a bill back and then they credit me off of my next month's purchases. Unless it's a big release, I don't think the titles in the ad matter as much as the fact that you're getting your name and address all over the place.

Decide what kind of marketing and promotion works for your music and budget. What's available depends on the regions and types of stores you work. Large retailers like Best Buy are less likely to have the kind of leeway a smaller store might. Find your strongest markets and work them first. As sales increase, you may have more latitude to buy into bigger programs.

MERCHANDISING

Labels and artists can make good money marketing merchandise to fans. If your label signs artists, get some rights for merchandising in your artist agreement. Merch is a staple for many artists. It can support them on the road. T-shirts, buttons, wristbands, caps, headbands, koozies (can hold-ers), posters, stickers, etc., are sold at gigs, in record stores, and by mail order. Valerie Vigoda (GrooveLily) says:

A large portion of our income comes from merch. We've found that giving people an incentive—free sampler CD or bumper sticker with purchase, for example—makes a difference, as does having *other* people besides ourselves hawking the merchandise at gigs. Fans make the best salespeople.

Merch can be a great promotional tool. You may give away as much as you sell. Folks in stores like free stuff. Some will wear a T-shirt if they like the artist. Onno Lakeman (Red to Violet) says they designed T-shirts that people like to wear. Instead of it having a typical promotion, it says, "Here I Am " (the name of their single) in big letters. Their name and website is on it, too. He says:

> I like that the person wearing the shirt gets attention and our band's name and site is also promoted. Sometimes buyers of the CD get a free shirt. We also send out giveaways for radio, to stores who ordered our CD's, reviewers, people who entered our contest on the site, and TV-giveaways. It's a nice way to offer something extra which is promotional too. It works. We get great feedback from people who have won the shirt.

Depending on the genre, merch sells well at gigs once a core of enthusiastic fans develops. Have everything available by mail order and advertise it in your mailings. If you have a website, plug your merch there. Once it sells, it's a double benefit—you make money and the artist gets free promotion. Rich Hardesty incorporates merch into his business:

> At shows, I get good-looking girls and guys that want to sit there and get a free CD of the show and a T-shirt. Sometimes I pay people. We have a marketing table. I have a big long shotgun case with my CDs lined up on the inside of it when it's open. On the tray part of it there's swag—stickers, picks, autographed pictures, and the free Jagermeister stuff.

DANCE CLUBS

When I worked dance music, I'd find out the best DJs for my record and their hours. Arriving early, before a club gets crowded, makes it easier to get in free. I'd introduce myself with a friendly smile, saying I was just going to drop a record with the DJ. The DJs were great. If they liked a record, sometimes they played it. I'd get their phone numbers and the best times to call. Often I'd get an answering machine, leave a short, friendly message, and try again the following week. Never sound annoyed, no matter how many unreturned messages you leave. Getting angry won't get a DJ to play your record. Persistence might.

Another way to reach DJs is through record pools—groups of DJs who pay to get free records. The person running one solicits free product from labels and promises that members will play them in clubs and at parties. Most record pools have charts of the records their members play. Servicing a pool gives you a good chance of ending up on that chart, but I don't think it sells records. I serviced many with my first few dance tracks and got little. Other labels like them. I found DJs are more likely to play a record they buy.

Should you service record pools? It depends on the individual one. To be fair, servicing pools can get more club play. I found record pools useful when they supported my label in other ways. When one called for records, I'd make an offer: Get my product into retail stores in their city and I'd service them. If they agreed, I'd send two copies for them to test. I developed long-term relationships with stores in an assortment of cities that ordered many of my dance records. If you give pools free records, get your money's worth!

LIVE PERFORMANCES

Live venues offer exposure and a place to sell product. Depending on the venue, your artist can be exposed to potential new fans. Music lovers get passionate about an artist who grabs them during a live show. When artists interact with fans, it stimulates sales. Artists who keep in touch with them have a greater chance for longevity. Loyal fans will buy each album that's released. According to Cliff Chenfeld (Razor & Tie Music):

> From a marketing perspective, we have an artist, Dar Williams, who's sold a lot more records than many high-profile major label acts. We've been conscious of having her stay true to her base— the folk community—even though her music has evolved a great deal . . . She maintains a very active database and Internet presence. She does concerts in places that somebody at her level probably wouldn't need to do for career development. She does that to maintain contact, she's very interactive with them [her fans]. She's not done dramatic changes from one album to another in an attempt to break a radio song. As such, we know that when she puts a record out, we're gonna get at least 80,000 to 100,000 people to come out for her, we've developed a hard-core, passionate group of people who love her . . . If you take

advantage of these things and not just spend zillions of dollars, trying to jam a song down everybody's throat, then I think [a label] has a shot at it.

GETTING THE ACT LIVE EXPOSURE

There are many ways to get live exposure. My book *The Real Deal* goes into details on building a following and finding venues. Read everything you can. *The Musician's Atlas* is a great resource for touring. It has a city-by-city listing of clubs, radio stations, local press, and many others, to help plan and promote a tour effectively. According to Mike Levine, editor of *Onstage* and author of *How to Be a Working Musician* (Billboard Books):

> Whether your tour is being booked by an agent or by [you], it's very important that it's routed in an intelligent way. This means that you want to keep the distances you have to travel between your shows as short as possible. Some long jaunts are inevitable, but hopefully there will be enough time built into your schedule so that you don't have to drive all night and day after a show in order to get to the next one . . . mental and physical burnout are major occupational hazards for touring bands, and pulling a lot of all night, marathon drives will bring them on a lot faster.

That's why it's better to begin regionally and work out in a circle. Then you're not jumping all over the place. Once your artist starts touring, provide whatever tour support you can. Jesse Fergusson says:

> I send promotional materials four weeks ahead of time to the venues—posters, stickers, CDs, photographs, bios—so that they can publicize the event with ammunition from the label. We don't make money when an artist tours. But if there's press about the event, we might sell more records. I set up retail support on tours, as much as possible, and in-stores in some towns.

Do PR for them. Tap into street teams—give them posters and flyers to distribute. Study the markets. Work it—radio, retail, and press—for each city they play in. Touring builds the foundation for sales. Saturate the markets as well as you can. Valerie Vigoda advises:

Even if you're playing at a festival or other soft-ticket event where your income isn't based on the number of tickets sold, don't rely on the presenter to do publicity. If you ask them for a list of media leads and follow up on those, you'll be way ahead of the game. The presenter will be happy you're taking the initiative to bring a crowd to your show.

Tony Brummel (Victory Records) adds:

It's always in a label's best interest, especially if it's underground-based music, to support your artist in the form of tour support. If you're trying to save money or don't have money, there are other areas to take those savings. It can be anything from buying a van, to giving money, to buying plane tickets, to making sure the band can pay their bills at home so they can stay on tour. That's how we sell records. Press doesn't want to interview a band if they're not touring; video won't play a band. Retail doesn't want to put a band into an expensive, higher-tiered program if they're not on the road. For us, it's about keeping our bands on the road all the time, as much as possible.

Touring isn't easy. Robb Nansel says, "Going on tour for any band is hard. It takes persistence. All our bands started by doing house shows, with maybe ten people. Those ten people eventually turn into twenty, then you're playing in a small club." When the record gets a buzz, there's greater potential for gigs. Get friendly with people who work in clubs. You never know how much influence a bartender has. Good relationships can get your artist in. Keith Grimwood (Trout Fishing in America) says:

We put a lot of miles down. We'd talk to other bands we'd meet and asked where they like to play. Ezra was very bold. He'd call up the Chamber of Commerce and just talk to someone in an area he liked on the map. We branched out. We'd look at other band's calendars. We chose bands that were similar and called the venues they played in. We began playing folk festivals in Canada and branched out to other states, a little further each time. When Dick joined us, he connected the dots.

Talk to managers of clubs featuring artists with a name or large following. Offer to have your artist open for free. Some clubs will try a newer act if it costs nothing and they like their music. If you play with a roster of acts, ask to go on after one with a large following so you can potentially play to some of their fans and increase your mailing list. If there are clubs with open mics, encourage your artists to perform, or at least hang there, to meet other musicians and expose people to the music. Hip-hop artist EL-P (Definitive Jux Records) says:

> After Company Flow started to dissolve, I continued going on tour, bringing other artists. I still had the idea that I was doing artist development. I liked that I could bring someone in under my name, no matter how small a level it is, and grease the wheels a bit so these guys get heard on stage. When they have a record, they're not just coming out blindly. With a small label, if you're coming out completely blind and haven't laid any groundwork or created a buzz, you can't afford the big explosives.

EL-P says he markets all the acts on Definitive Jux through touring. Do what you can to get exposure. Damon Dash (Roc-A-Fella Records) did whatever he could to get Jay-Z out when he first started. He says, "We were performing a lot up and down the region. We saturated the Chitlin Circuit, which is the region from Boston to the Carolinas. People were talking about us." Dash says Jay-Z ran on stage at a party at the Palladium during a performance: "Everyone went crazy for Jay. That started the attention and got radio play . . . We came with a buzz. We performed and were battling people. We generated a great degree of energy so people were attracted to us." The record went gold. Dash says doing what it took to get attention was a lot of work, which created a successful label. He reflects:

> You have to be able to put the work in. I don't think I could do that again, being on the Chitlin Circuit, performing every time we had the chance. We used to have to run on stage to start it out. It took a lot of energy creating it, but if you're hungry— yeah! If you want to go through all the underground outlets, we would go anywhere there was a mic and just perform. We'd battle anyone who wanted to battle.

Rich Hardesty's niche is college kids, and students at the Indiana schools he started in are from all over the U.S. He says when they go home on breaks, they play his CD for friends. When they graduate, they move elsewhere. So his core of Indiana fans ends up all over the country. This allows him to play cities he's never been to and have a crowd. He explains:

> For example, I did a show in L.A. for the Rosebowl. Some alumni from Purdue suggested I come there and play in a bar because Purdue was playing. Alumni remembered me. Because of networking on the Internet—I sent out an e-mail and posted it on my website—we packed the bar silly with my alumni following—people coming for the Rosebowl. The bar owner said he'd never seen anything like it. It was cool how the alumni support kicked in. They remembered their college days and wanted to relive it again.

Hardesty attributes at least part of his success to his interaction with fans. "I have always been a people person, taking time to talk to the fans instead of ducking into the break room." He learned what worked best in his market. Since he tapes his shows, he used interaction with fans as another marketing tool. He explains:

> I'd say people's names into the mic throughout the show. They'd have their name on the live recording and think that was a big deal. People made copies for friends. They asked if they could. Live shows [are] what helped sell me. My live music is way different than a recorded CD.

Protect yourself or your artists while touring. Valerie Vigoda advises getting everything in writing and advance all the gigs well ahead of time. She says GrooveLily tries to book venues that are more likely to have a built-in audience and budget. Try whatever works for the artist, but get them on the road if you want to sell more records!

GETTING COLLEGE GIGS

College gigs can be very lucrative if you have the patience to go after them. It's a tremendous amount of work, but it can be worth the effort if your artist gets on a college tour. Colleges usually pay real money, which keeps your artist (or you as the artist) happy. If you ask for it, often they pay expenses. There's potential for exposure in their publications and radio stations, where gigs can be promoted.

To work colleges, start with directories or referrals. Pick an area, preferably one that's NOT near a major city. There's often less competition and more demand for entertainment. An artist can join National Association of Campus Activities (NACA) (www.naca.org), considered the nation's largest organization for campus activities with nearly 1,200 member colleges and more than 600 associate member talent agencies, performers, and other firms in the college market. Joining gives you access to their directory. They have conferences, and for a fee, artists can showcase, performing for people who book entertainment in colleges. It's expensive, but if your music fits the market, I'm told the money for gigs makes it worth the investment.

Start at local bars near your targeted colleges. Invite people from Student Activities to come see you. When your crowd increases, let them know. Or, just contact Student Activities departments cold. Don't send music until you see if they might be interested in booking you. Describe your music, play some over the phone, or send an MP3 file. Only send a package if you sense real interest. Some colleges want videos. Get letters of reference when you perform in a college for your college press kit.

If you want to do a real tour, organize it so it makes sense. Pick a city and book many months ahead of time (which colleges usually do). Work from city to city. Call all colleges in the region until you get at least one that can get you from the last college to their city. Do that around a region or around the country. Create a system like those I've mentioned to keep in touch with those you speak with. Be persistent and enthusiastic. Be prepared to describe your music well or even play a sample on the phone. Don't just send packages randomly, unless you're rich. Make sure each person is really interested before you send one.

USING THE INTERNET TO PROMOTE
AND MARKET YOUR PRODUCT

Since writing the last edition of this book, I've seen the big expectations about opportunities on the Internet deflate. Ask five indie labels whether the Internet has helped and you'll get five different answers. Some swear by it, while more are disappointed. Jay Woods (New West Records) says:

> The Internet opens up a lot of doors, but in some ways it's been a smoke screen. Years ago, people were saying the Internet was going to be this great vehicle for selling music. It's become that to some degree. But it's only a supplement and more of a marketing tool. Now we're proceeding cautiously.

Danny Goldberg, (Artemis Records) adds:

> I don't think the Internet has lived up to the hype about it a few years ago as far as replacing touring, radio, retail, the other ways of developing a following. But it's a tremendous tool to communicate with fans, help focus and develop a fan base, and sell T-shirts and other collectibles to fans.

If you haven't gotten on-line yet, I highly recommend you do. It's a fantastic tool for branding your label. Find ways to develop your on-line presence—another option for exposure. Internet veteran Suzanne Glass, founder of Indie-Music.com has seen it all and says:

> The Internet, as it relates to musicians, has changed considerably over the few short years of its existence. It used to be there were far too many websites trying to "help" musicians. While the "gold rush" period was heady, it also led many people, musicians

included, to assume simply being "on the Internet" was enough to make money. Now that this concept has been disproven, some people feel there is no value in being on-line. Neither extreme is true. The Internet has always been just another tool in the quest for success.

Tools make things work, so use it! Just don't expect too much. You may be pleasantly surprised if you take advantage of the promotional opportunities the Internet offers.

INTERNET REALITY

The Internet isn't the panacea folks forecasted. Five years ago, predictions for the Internet were over-rated. Everyone expected it to turn the industry upside-down. It didn't. People haven't rushed to buy technology to download music. CD sales are still the most popular way to purchase music. Jonatha Brooke says:

> Most sales come through retail. There's a big surge when you first release a record on the Internet. And then it kind of peters out. It's not the huge, huge source everyone thought it would be. It's still retail.

The Internet is still VERY valuable. I believe we now underestimate how much it impacts how we do business, since we're so used to having it. Communicating by e-mail is as common as using phones. The anticipated impact on sales didn't happen but the Internet provides access to the world. Suzanne Glass explains:

> The Internet allows musicians to reach their fans and industry contacts, with greater ease and less cost. It allows musicians to expand from their hometown base through research and on-line networking. It also offers many opportunities for reviews/airplay/sales of artists' music. It's a tool, which allows us to do more, with less money and energy.

The Internet still opens doors for many independents. I believe it is what you do with it. Many musicians swear by it. Many are disappointed. Ryan Kuper (Redemption Records) says, "I don't think it's everything it was cracked up to be. You can get decent sales from the web, especially if the band is really touring, but it really just subsidizes retail." But it's not just about sales. Danny Goldberg says, "In terms of getting music to people, you can e-mail a song cheaper than you can mail it. There's some savings in terms of being able to disseminate music thought the Internet." It's an inexpensive marketing tool.

E-mail is a cheaper way to communicate. I see the Internet as a big library of information and incredible access to people. Suzanne Glass suggests, "Use the Internet for research . . . you can locate contacts on-line, which would have been nearly impossible to find off-line. You can also e-mail people who you would never get through to with a telephone call or regular mail." There's a wealth of resources at your fingertips. When I wanted info about trademarks, I went to the government's website.

The Internet offers marketing opportunities. You can promote your product, and sell records. You can listen to music, see what other labels put out, and allow people to hear your music. There are a zillion resources for learning about the music industry. While records aren't selling on-line in anticipated numbers, they are selling. Just don't overestimate what the Internet can do for your label. Your success is contingent on many strategies. Suzanne Glass says:

> The bottom line is, think of the Internet like you would your telephone or the Post Office [or library]. It has become an item most everyone has and relies on, but it is not a be-all, end-all method to success. The same old rules of "work hard" and "get lucky" still apply.

Some genres benefit more than others do. It takes tons of time to work it to the max, and you may not want to invest that time. But I highly recommend that if you're not on-line—get there! Throughout this chapter I'll show you why. You need many tools to launch your label. The Internet can provide extra visibility.

GETTING YOUR OWN WEBSITE

In the first edition of this book, I said having a website was optional. Not anymore. Why? A website is the hub of your efforts to brand your label and artists. It's where folks can get info about your artists and hear their music. When people want to check me out, I send them to my website.

The Internet allows you to create awareness. Tony Brummel (Victory Records) says, "Your website and Internet presence are definitely part of your overall branding." As more people find your site, more will become familiar with your label. When you get reviews and radio play, potential fans have a place to go for more info and to hear the music. As your artists' names get around, people check out your website to read about them, get photos, check their tour schedule, and lots more. David M. Bailey says:

> My website has been a monster in terms of keeping the whole thing afloat. For an independent performing songwriter, there is no better tool than a website. My site is a command center for people who want to know what's going on day to day. My newsletters are posted on there. I have my treatment history for folks interested in where I've been medically, all the albums and how to order them. I make sure new photos are posted.

Some folks don't pay for their site, if they can be on someone else's for free. That's why some sites have long e-mail addresses with names separated by slashes. In this case, register a domain name (see below) for your label and have that address forwarded to the longer name. For your own dotcom, one option is HostBaby (www.HostBaby.com). Created by Derek Sivers, founder of the popular on-line music store, CDBaby (www.CDBaby.com), HostBaby is geared to musicians. Sivers created this to fill a need. He explains:

> I strongly believe that musicians are tired of depending on another company's services. I think they'd rather keep everything on their own website, when possible: MP3s, concert calendar, e-mail list, CD and merchandise sales. HostBaby is a great place for musicians to put their own dotcom websites, run by somebody who knows what musicians really need. They can plug in the info.

GETTING A DOMAIN NAME

If you intend to develop a serious on-line presence for your company, register a domain name. Someone may already own the name you want. With the Internet becoming so popular, many names are taken. The faster you register, the more chance of getting one at least close to that of your company.

Many on-line companies will register your name, such as www.register.com. Before choosing a domain name, search to make sure the one you want is available. You can do that on Register.com. If you're on someone else's site, register with a company that has a forwarding service and they'll forward your registered name to the free site. It's free if you don't mind advertising accompanying it, or pay to have it forwarded without ads. As your company grows, move the name to a site that's all yours.

CREATING YOUR OWN WEBSITE

How do you find a website designer? Word of mouth referrals are best. Get in touch with several designers. Compare price, quality of work, etc. If your budget is limited, query art schools for someone who wants experience and a reference. What can you offer? Will your site get many visitors who'll see their work? Can you recommend the designer to others? Let fans know you need help.

A website should have many dimensions. Since a page on a computer screen is flat, its content should give it depth and make it interesting to visit. The home page lets visitors know who you are and what you offer. The content should be clearly laid out as a road map to the rest of your site. Study how other people present information. Decide what folks might find interesting about your label.

Be careful about using too many photos, spinning logos, or elaborate graphics that take time to download. When visitors have to wait, they may move on. My computer isn't high speed and, when a page very slowly unravels, I lose patience. A good website gets the info across in a creative style that's simple and clean. The info is most important. Mark Carpentieri (MC Records) says, "You need to have information on your website that people want to see—tour dates, pictures, news—so that if they want to know where one of our artists is playing, they can go to the website."

Look at a bunch of sites for similar musicians or labels to get an idea of what to include. People visit music sites to hear music or learn about the artists. The information is most important. Make your site reflect the music you release. What are you trying to convey to visitors? Choose specific goals before investing in a website. As it's being designed, look at it objectively and see if you'd enjoy visiting it if it weren't yours. Make it interesting and creative.

What should yours have? A "News" section has updated info about your artists and/or your label. If you have more than one artist, give each a separate section with a bio, press clippings, and photos. Post tour dates. Many music sites have an "About the Label" section. Have a way for people to contact you and info for ordering your products. Don't forget a link to sign up for your street team. Valerie Vigoda's (GrooveLily) website has been beneficial:

> It makes our mailings to our fans free of charge (we used to spend way too much money on postage!), enables us to have our own on-line store, allows us to foster a growing community of listeners through our discussion board and our Petal Pushers program . . . it's invaluable.

Audio clips are important. The best way to attract new fans is to let them hear your music. Have samples of songs, a whole one, or the whole album available. Your call. Ultimately, it's about the music, so let visitors hear some! Have MP3 files of songs handy in case an opportunity comes your way.

It's crucial to maintain your website so it's current. Fans don't come to stale sites. Update release dates, tour dates, reviews, photos, etc. I can't emphasize enough that you must do this regularly! Fans stop returning to the same stuff. If you don't know how to update, find some-one to do it. It's worth it! Let fans of your artists know what's needed. You might find someone to do it free to support you. Or learn how to update it yourself. Onno Lakeman (Red to Violet) says:

> We update the site every week, with features such as a fresh "lyric line of the week," "news headlines," my personal "indie talk column" (I describe my week as an indie artist and label), latest reviews. There's always a CD-single or T-shirt giveaway going on. It has cool music links. There's a video to see us and free audio clips, including a full version of "Here I Am." From the counters I see that audio and video are the most popular features. So it's still about music!

Some websites have general industry news or new tips about marketing or recording so folks want to return. Put up fun photos of your artists— of their most recent performance or playing in their downtime. Change them frequently. Make each individual artist's page personal. They can write letters to fans or tell stories from the road or recording sessions.

This also needs to change often. Dick Renco (Trout Records) says, "As soon as we list a date on our website, ticket sales start happening and record sales pick up in that market." Some sites have contests and give aways. When you get real traffic, consider having a chat room or bulletin board for fans to communicate with each other.

Links to interesting websites may appeal to visitors—other music or to music industry organizations and conferences. Gather resources such as news affecting musicians. It takes work to do this, but it encourages people to visit you, which is the goal. There are huge numbers of music-related websites that provide interesting information. By having them on your site, you give visitors a lot in one place.

MARKETING YOUR WEBSITE

Your website won't mean jack if only you and your friends see it. Why should someone visit? How will anyone know it exists? Market your site by getting its address onto everything you give out. Have it on your CDs, press releases or bios, business cards, stationery, and mailings for gigs. Suzanne Glass says:

> The most important part of increasing website traffic is *offline*. Make sure your URL and email address are on everything you print. When you write your mailing address, your URL should always be right next to it. Put the URL on your bio, press kit, mailing labels, CD covers, and everything else.

It's critical to have your web address on everything. Make up cards with the URL to give out at gigs, inviting fans to visit. Leave them in stores. Tell fans how to find your artists on-line. Recording artist Jane Siberry (Sheeba Records) says, "[Our] site has grown unbelievably because of feedback, which I constantly ask for. People write in with suggestions for Sheeba from all over the world." Passionate fans become more passionate when you cater to their needs. Fans may create their own website tributes to your artists. Those sites can be the most creative, most dedicated you have, as well as great promotion.

Some people work hard to try to get their site listed on search engines. I never did, and my site still comes up on most searches. There's only so much you can do at first. Put your energy where it counts the most. Suzanne Glass advises:

Bands should not worry much about search engine rankings. It is unlikely someone will find you searching for "country music" or similar terms. Bands should make sure their website can be found when a search is performed using their exact name. Labels will have more luck with search engines, as they will be found under searches such as "independent alternative music."

Find websites for artists and indie labels with similar music. Contact each to see if you can link to its page and it can link to yours. It costs nothing except time. Your website would then be listed in hypertext on those sites and theirs would be on yours. Getting on sites with traffic may bring some to yours. This form of promotion benefits both sites. Explore music-related websites. Get listed on as many as you can. The resources are limitless. Suzanne Glass adds:

> Get listed on sites like MP3.com, IUMA, Indie-Music.com, etc. While each site will only bring you a few visitors, it does add up. Make sure you include a signature with each e-mail you send, with a clickable link to your website.

CREATING AWARENESS ON THE INTERNET

The Internet gives indie labels more opportunities than ever to compete with larger ones on a more equal ground. We all have the same shelf space on the Internet! Tony Brummel says:

> The Internet has always helped from an awareness standpoint. We've been selling since '95. It's another promotional portal. That's why it's so important to have your URL on everything. From a promo sticker, to a sampler CD that your street team might be handing out, to every ad in every magazine. Our label has such an artist following. Our roster is diverse but a lot of the people that buy records on Victory buy everything. Some of the bands are so different yet they do.

Developing an on-line presence is a cost-effective way to market music, although it requires research and work. Some people say that banner ads or just getting your name onto as many sites as possible doesn't help. I disagree. The more often your artist's name is seen, the more aware-ness that's created. It may take time to make an impact, but, as people become more familiar with the names they see, they pay more attention, and get more curious.

NETWORKING ON-LINE

Communicating via e-mail is a quick and easy way to show instant appreciation. When someone gets you a gig, e-mail your appreciation. If a fan does something to spread the word, e-mail your thanks. Robb Nansel (Saddle Creek Records) says, "Our website is very active. We rely on the Internet for communication. We're constantly interacting with people. E-mail is free. When we started, we were booking our own tours on-line."

Suzanne Glass says, "Networking (with fans, other bands, labels, radio, etc.) is the single most important thing you can do on the Internet." E-mail can be used to announce what's going on at your label. As you gather e-mail addresses of fans, build a list to keep folks informed about what's happening at your label. Use e-mail to notify fans about an artist's gig. Press releases can be e-mailed to publications. There are endless possibilities. One click and you reach those you want to on-line. According to Dan Zanes (Festival Five Records):

> I get e-mails every day telling me how the music fits into their lives, what they like about it. I feel like I'm really in contact. The Internet has been unbelievable for me. One of the biggest things I've done is to establish an e-mail list. I send out e-mails every week or two, letting people know where we're playing, when the new record is coming out, what's going on. I send links to things I think are interesting or important so they get to know me. The e-mail list has been incredible. We can go to a town where we've never played. If I send a couple of e-mails prior to the show, asking people if they know people in town to let them know about it, there will be a lot of people at the show. So much has to do with this e-mail list. People sign on the website or at our shows. I made sure that my website was listed on all the websites for kids. Someone did it for me. He used metatags.

NEWS GROUPS AND CHAT ROOMS

News and e-mail groups are popular ways to interact with others who might love the kind of music you release. They offer forums to post messages and read those posted by others. Participants respond to each other. When you join one, you'll see responses to previous messages. You can post your own. Each group is targeted to a specific topic. There are thousands of these groups for all genres and aspects of music. Suzanne Glass says:

> News and e-mail groups are great for networking and getting answers to questions. If you join a group of 500 musicians on a list, someone has probably been through whatever it is you're trying to do. It's super easy to shoot out a message asking for advice, and chances are, you'll get several qualified answers that will help solve your problem.

Explore the Internet to find the best music forums. Yahoo.com has some good ones. Ask others about groups they're familiar with. Look for those that relate to the music genre you're marketing. Try different groups before getting involved. See what folks are saying. What's the tone of messages? Some groups are more welcoming/interesting/informative than others are. Don't jump in and post before getting to know them. Get a feel for it as an observer before participating.

Once you're part of the group, invite people to visit your site. Let them know about what you're doing. Invite people in any group, with like-minded interests, to be on your mailing list. Explain what it's for. Suzanne Glass adds:

> Another great thing to do with groups is set up gig swaps with other bands, or collaborate to put on multi-performer shows. Also, groups are excellent for moral support, and for expanding your base of operations to many new towns. It's so easy to meet other musicians. Plus, it's easy to identify people you will work well with after reading their contributions to a User List.

Artists also increase their presence by going to chat rooms. Rather than posted messages, chats are live discussions, with people communicating directly back and forth. You can go to sites with chat rooms for artists similar to yours, and network. Questions are answered immediately— instant gratification! Learn the routines of chats and let like-minded music lovers know about your music.

DEVELOPING AN ON-LINE FAN BASE

Never before have fans had such an arena to express passion for their favorite artists or had this extent of power to take an unknown artist and develop a strong enough buzz to make him or her known around the world. Many artists develop an on-line community of fans. Some have message boards or chat rooms on their websites where fans communicate with each other. Robb Nansel says:

> We have a very active web board so people can talk with each other. It's a community. People keep coming back for that. We sell our stuff. We do pre-orders on our site and ship two weeks before street date.

Message boards or chat rooms build a community and allow fans to feel like part of something. They discuss anything from feelings about the music to finding someone to go to a gig with. Fans who meet on-line meet in person as they follow their favorite artist. Some labels host live chats so an artist can "speak" directly with fans, a safe way to interact with them. If you create a community feeling among fans, they'll support your artist and spread the word. Give them a way to communicate with each other. Dave Roberge (Everfine Records) adds:

> Right now we have a message board that is linked directly from the band's website as well as the label's website. It provides a general discussion area, notes from the road, where the band posts journal entries after every show and a ticket exchange program so that if somebody is looking for tickets, they can trade with other fans. We try to accommodate the fans' needs and use them as a focus group. [For example], if we're going to develop an official fan club, the first thing we do is go to the band's message board. We use this group of dedicated fans as our focus group and incorporate them into the planning process so they think we're thinking about them every step of the way. And we certainly are. Although they're a fragment of the band's fan base, they represent what the fan base is looking for in terms of the diehard fans. That could be different artist by artist. But we try to tap into the heart and pulse of these kids who are buying the tickets and CDs and find out, "What do *you* want to see from the band?" What better way to get what they're looking for but from the source?

The Internet brings folks together. Someone in Germany and someone in Ohio who love the same artist can connect through message boards and chat rooms. Loyal fans build fan sites, link to each other and create momentum. As they post messages, others want to know about the artist. All of a sudden people are talking about your artist around the world, and you've done nothing except cater to the early fans, who get the word out. Search for communities of fans who might like your music. Some artists create a community from the circles of fans of a popular group.

Be everywhere you can be! IF the artist is VERY GOOD, people who love one artist may gravitate to yours when they learn about them. E-mail discussions create more visibility. Labels say they're amazed by the orders they get from people around the world when their artist hasn't left the country. Fans check out music at on-line stores, buy what they like, and then go to the artist's site.

The Internet is quick. Once fans develop enthusiasm for your music, it can spread faster than you can pay for promotion. This is more common with artists that appeal to younger music lovers who use the Internet a lot. Some music may not generate on-line momentum if its audience isn't people who look for new music or spend time on the Internet. But try it. The Internet is unpredictable. Your efforts may not manifest much, or they could bring many pleasant surprises. Making your music available for free on-line can manifest more pleasant ones. Rich Hardesty has accumulated a huge fan base by sharing his music:

> I post a song on an MP3 file and share it. If you type my name into a search engine, thousands of things come up. All my songs are on temporary steal sites. DJs around the world are playing my songs. The songs get bootlegged live and end up on the Internet. If someone is going to an extreme to get a live copy, it's an honor to me. They're a true fan and will spread it.

The world becomes a teeny place when people connect on the Internet. Fans meet on-line and at gigs, exchange e-mail, and compare notes. The power of a loyal community of fans can be the best promotion you can buy—and it's free! If enough fans push with passion, a huge buzz can be created. Post your website and your artist's tour schedules to any sites that allow it. Many artists swear by being on MP3.com. David M. Bailey says, "I've put my stuff on mp3.com. It helps a lot." Be creative!

Cropduster Records wanted to get fans of all their artists involved, so they created Friends of Cropduster (FOC). Sean Seymour explains:

> We wanted to bring all our friends on board and started something called Friends of Cropduster. Get FOC-ed. We added that to our website, so friends could cross-pollinate, have their friends come to our website and vice versa. We were always willing to help everybody.

A great way to keep in touch with fans is to create a label or individual artist's newsletter. Let fans know what your artists are doing. Announce anything new. Include any info they might find interesting. David M. Bailey says:

> On my site, we have a sign-up for a newsletter. I send about one a month with all the songs, lyrics, and tour schedule. I put anybody who writes to me or orders on the e-mail list. I write them, not in a "newsy" way, but more like I'm writing a personal letter to a friend. I try to create a sense of togetherness. It's cool that we are all sort of in this together. I really feel that way about the people who have been supporting me.

Newsletters are a great marketing tool, depending on what you include. My newsletter, "Daylle's News & Resources," has tons of helpful information for people in the music industry and has increased my mailing list dramatically. You can sign up for a free subscription at www.daylle.com. I ask people to forward it to others and they do, because the info is valuable. If you do a newsletter, especially at first, try to include some helpful info that people will want to share. As your fan base grows, it can be more about you and your music. Onno Lakeman has found his newsletter to be a very successful tool for marketing from Holland:

> Our newsletter helps to keep the buzz going. Also, I have the headline news ready for the site every week, and I can send it out to someone who has interest in the band, or use it for updates on another music site. It's a great updated source I can use. Recently, with the anti-spam rules here in Europe, I cannot just send our mass e-mailings anymore. So I do target e-mails only. I visit sites and personally ask someone whether they'd be interested.

Tours are now booked and promoted on-line. Dick Renco says, "It's dramatically changed the way booking is done. The immediate exchange of information helps." Dave Roberge adds, "We are a big supporter of Music Today and fan ticketing services. Ten percent of tickets for every show go directly through our fan base—lower service fees than your typical TicketMaster." By interacting with other artists, tour resources can be shared. Many sites offer tour support, venue info, etc. I have a lot of such information on my site, www.daylle.com. Most sites focus on one genre of music, often a variety of rock. Pollstar (www.pollstar.com) is a weekly publication that lists tours and has other resources for touring, including directories listing a variety of tour-related information.

ONLINE EXPOSURE AND RESOURCES

Suzanne Glass advises, "Use search engines and links from favorite sites to locate sites which might review your music, or Internet radio stations which might play indie CDs." Many sites have links leading to others, which link to others, and so on. One resource that will save you tons of time and help you to target the most appropriate sites faster is the highly acclaimed directory, *The Indie Bible*. This is a directory of almost every useful site on the Internet. According to its publisher, David Wimble:

> The Internet offers thousands of places where today's recording artists can gain exposure for their music. There are hundreds of on-line vendors that will sell your CD, several thousand Internet radio programs that will play your music, and an endless number of on-line webzines that will review your music (and place that review online for others to see). Your music can now be available to the public 24 hours a day, 365 days a year!

The Indie Bible (www.indiebible.com) is a must-have for anyone looking to develop an on-line presence. It's the only comprehensive directory of Internet sites, and it's reasonably priced. Besides on-line only magazines and radio stations, it also has sites for many that aren't just on-line.

ELECTRONIC PR SUPPORT

Even if you don't expect much traffic at first, a website serves a tremendous promotional purpose if you're trying to attract the media. Whenever you send a mailing, press release, etc., include your website address. Have a hypertext link to your site on every e-mail you send. More and more PR people are using e-mail to reach the media. Instead of mailing press releases, they're sent electronically. According to Jason Consoli, publicist for TVT Records:

My favorite and most utilized part of the Internet is e-mail. I use e-mail religiously to keep in touch with writers, editors, and other publicists. Publicity requires a lot of phone work, and often I just want to get bits of information around to many different people without having to pester them with more calls than they need. I often get more replies to my electronic messages than to phone messages. I think my contacts appreciate that I leave the small stuff to e-mail, and they don't mind replying with the feedback I need. Of course the web itself is chock full of information to reference, which comes in handy when writing a press release or a band biography.

Create an electronic press kit on your site. Make it appealing to those who might write about your artists. Include a good bio, tour schedule, an assortment of color photos, quotes, links to press you've received and anything else you think of that would make someone want to write about your artist, play your music, or get involved in some way. Derek Sivers says:

The words you use to describe your music are crucial. If the words aren't interesting, nobody will listen to your music. Those words have to be so interesting that people will want to click to listen to you. In a magazine, people still have to like the words about you.

Your website is a great source for writers wanting more info about your artists. Let them know they can get it on your site. Often they don't want to talk to you when they want a photo or more info. It's easier if they can check out the artist first. As was said earlier, editors like being able to grab high-quality photos from a site. Make what they want available and increase your chances of getting press. A good press release lures editors to download stuff, without having to contact you. And it saves money on reproducing photos and mailing them.

Most major publications have websites. Publicist Nicole Blackman says that, when some publications cover a band, they insert a hypertext link, highlighted in color, where the artist's name is in the on-line versions of their magazines. Readers can click on that link and go directly to the artist's website. Links to the write-up can be placed on your site. Blackman uses links on the websites of bands she works with, so fans can follow the progress of those bands. She says:

> We like to have those links in the press area for bands. We don't copy the information and put it up on our own site. For each band we say, "Here are some past reviews, interviews, and other things on the band. Click here." [We offer] a whole directory on our bands—if *Billboard* magazine did a story on them or *Rolling Stone* reviewed them four years ago, we mention all that. It's a great archive source, especially for new fans of a band who aren't familiar with its past work, or someone just hearing about [the band] . . . It's a great way for fans to instantly be able to track a band's progress chronologically in the last couple of years.

ON-LINE MEDIA

Read on-line magazines before sending material for reviews. Brian Sirgutz (Elementree Records) emphasizes beginning at the smallest level and working up. He assures, "There are on-line webzines that are local and regional." When you get reviews, include links to them on your site and in your electronic press kit. A review is a review! Get what you can in the beginning. Derek Sivers says:

> Press can mean any kind of media coverage and mostly involves knowing how to niche yourself to create an interesting story and not be another girl on a guitar or guy on a piano. Have some angle to what you do to make it a kind of eyebrow raising, interesting story. On-line has a different set of rules. Capturing people's attention by being unique matters more than anything.

There are many powerful music websites that do reviews and articles that can increase sales and get people to your site. If a good music site or magazine wants a CD, send it. Search to find as many as you can. Use *The Indie Bible*. It provides info about each site so you know what it offers before you go to it. Send material to as many as seems appropriate.

If you can do it electronically, it costs nothing but time. If your time is limited, recruit people from your street team to search for you. Don't waste this promotional opportunity. According to Jason Consoli:

> The Internet is a great and powerful way to promote music. From a publicity standpoint, when a website reviews a record of yours, the reader often has access to sound clips from that record. It is often the combination of reading something on a piece of music and then hearing that music on the radio or in a club that makes someone want to buy it. With web reviews, both elements are achieved simultaneously.

There are also on-line-only radio shows. Visit some. Check the Yahoo! search engine's music section and *The Indie Bible* for Internet radio stations. Find out their submission procedures. Don't waste money sending random CDs to every station you see. Research to find those that are best for your needs.

SELLING MUSIC ON-LINE

The Internet is considered more of a marketing tool than an arena to sell records. This may change with time, which is why so many folks are trying to establish themselves now. While sales numbers may not be huge, you can still sell product on-line if you're creative, resourceful, and build up a fan base. Jesse Fergusson (Definitive Jux Records) says:

> There's such an Internet community for indie hip-hop. It's not yet to the point that people envisioned it, but we're selling large quantities of records off of a few key hip-hop sites: Sandboxautomatic.com; hiphopinfinity.com; hiphopsite.com. Some of these are selling 800 copies in the first week. Indie hip-hop starts in these urban centers. Suddenly it explodes, and the biggest fans are all over the country. There aren't enough indie retail stores around the country who get access to all the music. But if there's a store up on Thirtieth Street in Manhattan that any indie rapper in New York knows he can sell on consignment his new CD, mix tape, vinyl, anything. All that stuff gets fed into that market, and then everybody can access that through the Internet. The indie marketplace becomes worldwide at that point. There are kids in Copenhagen who are getting my mix tapes.

With space dwindling in stores, the Internet offers an opportunity to develop your own "shelf space" on-line. Keith Grimwood (Trout Fishing in America) says, "The Internet is a whole new shelf." It offers an alternative to just using a traditional distribution system, especially for indie labels. There's no competition for space as there is in retail stores. Mark Carpentieri says:

> The Internet levels the playing field in the sense that if you look for one of our artists on a [music website], our records will appear. That's a great thing. If you send music to a site it will be posted [unlike a store where the rep might not pick up the product or you can't reach them to make a pitch]. For some of our releases, those on the Internet are the most popular.

Many indie labels say that on-line mail order business isn't as strong as they'd like, but product sells. Include a P.O. box on your site where a check or money order can be mailed. Create an order form that can be downloaded. Many people prefer credit cards. You can accept them through companies like Paypal (www.paypal.com) or CCNow (www.ccnow.com). They allow customers to make secure on-line credit card payments and take a small percentage of sales as a fee. There's no charge to use them.

Some on-line stores offer indie labels links to their sites. They give your artist a page with a URL, which can be added to your website as a hypertext link. Any visitor wanting to order your CD with a credit card can click on the link and get the page for your CD at an on-line store. They accept credit card orders and mail product to purchasers. CDBaby is a favorite among indie labels. Derek Sivers brings his musician's mentality into its operation. He explains:

> CDBaby started because I was selling my own CDs and had a credit card merchant account. I told my friends that were selling their CDs by check or money order that I could process credit cards for them. I never meant it as a business. It was a hobby that became a living. I was a full-time musician. The last time I had a day job was in 1992. Now I get a thrill building something that helps 30,000 musicians make their music. We pay every Monday night for our sales that happened that week. We pay immediately after the sale.

CDBaby gives you your own web page with sound clips (just send the CD and they do the rest), a link to your own website, reviews, and all the text you want. You can send people there to buy your CD. You set a selling price and they keep $4 per CD sold. There's a one-time fee to set up a new CD on your page. And they tell you who bought your CDs. Most on-line stores are non-exclusive, so you can sell elsewhere too. If you have a bar code, many report sales to SoundScan. The more you're on the Internet, the bigger potential for sales. According to Jeff Epstein, (Cropduster Records):

> A large part of our sales is from the Internet. We've gotten sales everywhere—from Russia, UK, France. Some are searching for independent music; some is word of mouth. They find us on CDBaby, Amazon.com. We're everywhere, on every website. My philosophy is the more places you can be, the more chances you have to be discovered. We're Internet savvy so we're able to put up an interesting website.

Technology changes fast. Because of this, I won't go into the specific formats for getting music out on the Internet. It might be outdated before you read this. When I wrote the first edition of this book five years ago, experts predicted that by now we'd see a shift to digital sales. But it hasn't become the big vehicle for selling music that folks anticipated. If you check the major music industry sites, you'll find updates on the latest technologies. But don't count on downloading to replace CD sales for a long time. So what's in store? Suzanne Glass says:

> I personally think it will take a while to see significant change. For big changes in on-line sales of downloadable music, we will need a large increase in infrastructure, so most Internet users have access to broadband connections. This is happening very slowly, and current economic conditions have delayed it further. Until then, people will for sure continue to buy CDs. However, more and more of those CDs will be sold on-line, as people relax with e-commerce. I also see a trend towards larger companies growing larger. New companies coming on-line have already slowed significantly, and even large companies like AOL have not figured out how to make

a consistent profit with their websites. Expect fewer companies to control more of the on-line media, just as it has happened offline to radio stations and newspapers.

So how much do you invest in your Internet activities? As much *time* as you can afford. Money-wise, I'd wait and see how it goes. The Internet still has a lot of growing up to do. But don't underestimate it either. It's definitely a tool worth using, as long as you're realistic in your expectations. Danny Goldberg adds:

> I think that it's incrementally grown. It is a big help, and you have to be crazy not to use it every way you can. On a daily/weekly basis, new opportunities develop to use technology. But it's more of an evolution than a revolution.

SOME ADVICE FROM THE PROS

Danny Goldberg, CEO, Artemis Records

Put out few records. A mistake that a lot of people make is they put out too many records. It takes enormous focus to make a difference. It's more important to have one artist that makes a difference than to have ten artists that make less of an impact. Focus on a few things and make a real difference to a few things, rather than going buckshot and trying to do too many different things that are a mile high and an inch deep.

EL-P, co-founder/recording artist, Definitive Jux Records

Figure out why you want to start that label. Have an idea behind it. If you can't figure out within an hour why you want to start a record label, without the answer being "because I want to make money," don't start a record label. You're gonna fail because you're not gonna have what it takes unless you have a lot of money. There is a new generation of kids that came out of our little industry that isn't going to be so susceptible . . . There's a difference between fame and happiness and a modern-day trick of combining the two—the rare and elusive combination of being financially stable and being happy. It's a long-term plan and not many people are willing to stick around for the long-term plan. You need patience. I have the word tattooed on my arm. Somebody, somewhere, has to eventually not want the buy-out and actually do what they set out to do or were destined to do. It's hard. We're getting the offers for the buy-out. I spent my entire career being offered major label deals and I have not taken one. We put a record out ourselves that we made in our house; we did the artwork on our kitchen table . . . We were eating off of that record for two years. Once we realized that, the whole perspective changed for us. It became the license for me to actually follow this line of thinking.

Jay Woods, Senior Vice President and General Manager, New West Records

Be clear and realistic in your goals. It's an inside job. You have to ask yourself what are you really willing to do. You can't expect anybody to do it for you. You have to do it yourself. Dig deep and say, "What lengths am I willing to go to?" And expect the same from your artists, especially if they're developing artists.

Jonatha Brooke, Owner/Recording Artist, Bad Dog Records

Learn by the seat of your pants. You can only learn by putting your butt out there and taking big risks. I've learned if you don't take chances, you get nowhere. If you take chances, you're gonna lose your shirt but hopefully it will come back at some point. It's worth it.

Damon Dash, Founder, Roc-A-Fella Records

Learn the business—exactly what you're entitled to. You have to have your business correct. Be knowledgeable of it . . . know when you're getting jerked or when somebody's trying to pull something where it's not as lucrative for you as it is for them. Get with some talent that you're 100 percent confident in—where you love them and are willing to invest everything in it. If you feel this way then don't let anybody tell you anything different . . . I knew Jay-Z was the real deal. No one could tell us to change this or that. The reason we were so focused is because we were so confident.

Gregg Latterman, President, Aware Records

Sign music that you can be passionate about. If you're doing it to make money, don't do it. You have to do it because you love it or you'll never be successful. Try to find a niche in the business. Do things the way you want, not the way you think you're supposed to do them. Everyone should read all the how-to books because you need all that background information. Take all that and try to make it work. Be street smart. That's what this business is all about.

Dave Roberge, President, Everfine Records

You can't take the approach that things are going to start happening for you. In this day and age, you've got to make it happen for yourself. A lot of it is sitting back and watching how things work and trying to understand how the industry, and the different players, interacted with each other. The first thing you have to do is learn the business that you're trying to break into. If you don't try to educate yourself and go into it with the "I am a sponge" mentality, you're going to hurt yourself. I see a lot of people come in and think they know everything. That's very difficult—every day the industry is constantly evolving. You have to be adaptable to change and innovative, to be on the forefront of identifying when that change is going to come. A lot of times, by being there, you can turn it into a competitive advantage.

Jonathan Levy, CEO, Moonshine Music

Just because you think your record is the greatest thing in the world, it doesn't mean it's going to be a hit. It's easy to let your passion for the music cloud your business judgement, so set a reasonable sales goal and then set your limits on marketing and promotion accordingly. As an indie, we don't have the luxury of waiting for the third album to break even, so be sensible about your goals. If you're new to the business, remember that anyone with experience can sniff bullshit a mile off! Why? Because we've heard it all before and we've seen plenty of people come and go. Your actions and successes will speak louder than your words. Your distributor can be your best friend or your worst enemy. If you give them good product that sells through, you'll get paid. If your product doesn't sell through, don't cry when they won't take your phone calls. I can tell you that the one thing we never had a problem with was getting paid and you won't either if your music sells through. Probably the most important thing is not to jump in without experience. Working for a label is the best training ground. When you start your label, don't hire your friends, hire industry professionals and be prepared to eat shit for the first couple of years! Good luck.

Ryan Kuper, President, Redemption Records

Pick a niche and stick with it! Keep a general sonic focus until you can afford to make baby steps outward. Be careful to not spread yourself too thin by over-committing to bands. It will only hurt all those involved. Remember that these acts are in your hands . . . think of them as your children. Remember who helped you along the way and keep those relationships strong. Always stay alert of market changes and advances in technology that may affect your business. Establish a healthy relationship with your distributor and any third parties you hire to work for you. These people will work for money, but will work harder if they like you and feel your passion. Understand all aspects of your business and don't think you are above a conference, a book, or having a mentor. You never know what may be revealed to you.

Dedra Tate, President, Flavor Unit Entertainment

My advice for someone starting an independent label is: First find the artist you believe in. But instead of recording a whole album's worth of material and investing so much money on songs that you aren't sure are gonna hit, try to find a hit record, especially for the type of market that the artist is from. Take that hot single and just try to bang it as many ways as possible. It's a lot of legwork. You have to be in the streets and have the name building up and all that stuff. Press up a 12-inch, try to get it on the mix shows, and really flood that market so that you can build up a big demand and hence create a demand for your artist, which can help you get distribution if you want to go that route, or help you have a lot of gravy for putting that artist back in the studio and getting serious producers to work on the project to make it more credible.

Valerie Vigoda, Recording Artist, GrooveLily

Learn about auto repair. Seriously. And then make sure you work with people you really, really like—because you'll be spending an awful lot of time with them.

Jane Siberry, CEO/Recording Artist, Sheeba Records

Do it slowly and carefully. Build from the bottom up. Don't hire too many people too quickly. Keep everything as uncreative in the office as possible so you have a solid structure. Don't budge under the pressure of "this is how it should be done." And honor more than anything the people coming to you to buy what they want.

Michael Hausman, Managing Director, United Musicians/Manager for Aimee Mann

Start wherever you're at in your career. Don't worry about what everyone else is doing and how big they are. Start with your strengths. If you only are well-known in New York, Philadelphia and Boston, make sure you take advantage of everything you can in those markets and grow it from there. Get a gig where you live, then an hour from where you live, then three hours. Do it that way. You can waste a lot of time and money driving all over the country losing money trying to turn people on to your music. And if they're not getting turned on to it locally, they're probably not going to get turned on to it anywhere else.

Tony Brummel, President, Victory Records

Get ready to work 22 hours a day for a couple of years.

Mark Carpentieri, President and Owner, MC Records

Before you start a label, try to figure out: What are you presenting that no one has done before? If you do what everyone else is doing, it's not going to work. People have already done it and doing it well already by being established. You have to come up with a different kind of artist, different kind of music, something that is not being addressed. If you're addressing that, then you've got a chance.

patrick arn, president, gotham records

If you want to break in to the industry on your own terms, consider becoming a manager of a band or artist that you believe in. This is much cheaper and much less risky than starting a label from scratch. If you are set on starting your own record label, be aware of the competition, and decide what niche your label can fill. To start a label out of your bedroom with the intention of competing with the majors is unrealistic. To market your label as the home of your local area's growing heavy metal scene is much more reasonable. Understand that it takes a lot of money to start and run a record label. Be sure you are not undercapitalized. I wish I had not listened to everyone who told me to invest my own money. Other people's money can go a lot further, and carries much less weight on the heart. If you believe in yourself, allow potential investors to believe in you as well!

cliff chenfeld, co-president/co-founder, razor & tie music

Disregard all conventional modes of thinking. I think where independent labels can flourish in today's market is to find niches and alternative means of getting music out to people . . . finding niches for artists who might not fit the cookie cutter model that has been created to break the great majority of major label artists. There's a large number of artists who have the potential to sell anywhere from 50 to 500,000 records that major labels are not going to be interested in for a variety of reasons. It might be that they're not obviously commercial enough from the outset or that it takes four albums to get you there. Major labels may not have that patience. The thing to do when you're setting up your own label is to think about what openings the marketplace offers you. Don't think that because [a certain music] is the rage, if you can find the next band that sounds like them you'll be okay. The majors kind of copy and do that. The majors can repeat the success with four or five like-minded bands. But the radio stations are going to be inundated with stuff that sounds like that from major labels who they have to play ahead of you. If you're coming to them with the same kind of stuff that the major labels are giving them, you're by definition going to lose. You have to come to them with something different.

John Szuch, owner, Deep Elm Records

What's been key to my success is starting from absolute scratch, as opposed to working at another label and trying to start something based on what I learned there. It's wanting to do something, learning about it, and learning the hard way—doing some things right, doing some things wrong, understanding how publicity and college radio works and doing that myself. Really learning the nuts and bolts and trying to get a comprehensive understanding of the way the business works and what's out there. You can't do that overnight. It's helpful if you hire someone for college radio promotion to know what they should be doing. You have to be smart. You have to be careful. There's a lot of people who are not very trustworthy in the business and a lot of people who are. So you have to pick and choose your friends in this business very wisely. I think it's good to be honest with people about what you're doing. Honesty is the best policy when talking to an artist about what you think you can do or help them accomplish.

Edward Chmelewski, president, Blind Pig Records

Do your homework. Know your market. Music aside and the quality of music aside, you've got figure out who you're going to sell this too. What's the market for this? Who's going to buy it? How am I going to reach those people?

Brian Surgitz, president, Elementree Records

Don't be afraid to fail. Multiple failures equal success.

David M. Bailey, recording artist

You have to hand CDs out like water. It's a great way to say thank-you to anyone.

Ezra Idlet, recording artist, Trout Fishing in America/Trout Records

Do it! I think the technology is set up today for musicians to do this more than at any other time. Digital recording is available at an incredibly low price. Recording has gotten so much better and cheaper.

Bobbito Garcia, CEO, Fondle'em Records

Understand what your vision is. Do you want to make money or do you want to put out good music? Sometimes they don't mix. I know a lot of people who put out great music and get frustrated because they're not selling anything. If you accept it—like if you put out progressive music it may not sell—you won't ever be disappointed because you're not expecting to sell a half million records.

Christopher Appelgren, president, Lookout! Records

A record label is part art and part commerce. When it works, these two contradictory concepts will support each other. Good art—music—sells records; strong sales validate good art. But as important as working with great bands, and the most often overlooked aspect of running a label, is distribution and sales. Selling records is the culmination of all the other factors of a label: a great band, good recording, smart-looking artwork, and effective marketing and promotion. I don't think that selling records should be why someone starts a label, without proper distribution, you will fail, no matter how great your releases are, or how much attention you get.